Rethinking World War Two

Rethinking
World War Two
The Conflict and its Legacy

JEREMY BLACK

Bloomsbury Academic
An imprint of Bloomsbury Publishing Plc

B L O O M S B U R Y
LONDON • NEW DELHI • NEW YORK • SYDNEY

Bloomsbury Academic

An imprint of Bloomsbury Publishing Plc

50 Bedford Square	1385 Broadway
London	New York
WC1B 3DP	NY 10018
UK	USA

www.bloomsbury.com

BLOOMSBURY and the Diana logo are trademarks of Bloomsbury Publishing Plc

First published 2015

© Jeremy Black, 2015

British Library Cataloguing in Publication Data

A catalogue record for this book is available from the British Library.

ISBN: HB: 978-1-4725-8323-9
PB: 978-1-4725-8322-2
ePDF: 978-1-4725-8324-6
ePub: 978-1-4725-8325-3

Library of Congress Cataloging-in-Publication Data

Black, Jeremy, 1955-
Rethinking World War Two : the conflict and its legacy / Jeremy Black.
pages cm
Includes bibliographical references and index.
ISBN 978-1-4725-8323-9 (hardback)– ISBN 978-1-4725-8322-2 (pbk.)– ISBN 978-1-4725-8324-6 (epdf)– ISBN 978-1-4725-8325-3 (epub) 1. World War, 1939-1945. 2. World War, 1939-1945–Influence. I. Title.
D743.B489 2015
940.53–dc23
2014019625

Typeset by Fakenham Prepress Solutions, Fakenham, Norfolk NR21 8NN
Printed and bound in India

For Richard Overy

CONTENTS

ABBREVIATIONS

ADD.	Additional Manuscript
BL	London, British Library, Department of Manuscripts
CHURCHILL PAPERS	Churchill College, Cambridge, Churchill Papers
EEC	European Economic Community
EU	European Union
ILP	Independent Labour Party
KMT	Kuomintang Nationalists
LH	London, King's College, Liddell Hart Centre for Military History
MSI	Italian Social Movement
NA	London, National Archives
NAA	Canberra, National Archives of Australia
NATO	North Atlantic Treaty Organisation
NKVD	Soviet Secret Police
RAF	Royal Air Force
SS	Schutzstaffel or protection squads of the Nazi elite corps whcih controlled the police, concentration camps and part of the military

PREFACE

History is both the past and our accounts of the past; the two linked but also separate. The accounts are inherently contingent, and the processes of producing and contesting them give rise to controversy. This situation is far from uniform for there are particular hotspots for discussion and controversy. The most prominent, ever since it began, has been World War Two. This book discusses and assesses the leading controversies, both military and political, and links them to a central strand of the war that is generally underplayed due to the focus on the fighting, namely its political character. Moreover, the after-echoes of the war, both military and political, are considered in terms of the issues and controversies of the conflict itself, as well as those that arose subsequently.

The past often is with us more obviously than the present. This is the case for most, not with the immediate present around us as individuals, that which presses most powerfully upon us, but rather with what of the present-day is glimpsed indirectly and therefore generally does not press so powerfully. Thus, if television brings us the news of today, it can also bring us images of the past; and the latter can be more prominent. The images and stories of the past can also seem more newsworthy, for news is not simply a matter of the new moment. Television and book, film and newspaper, are certainly full of images and accounts of World War Two. This is not true of all countries, not the case, for example, with Mozambique or Peru; but, nevertheless, it is the case with many. The global nature of the conflict ensures that there is a widespread aftermath in terms of collective as well as individual memories.

Controversies are to the fore in debates about the war in many countries, as is blame. 'Should' is the key term as far as much of the discussion is concerned, because the point is to blame. Thus, exposition and explanation generally find fault. In doing so, the present refighting of the conflict focuses on trends that are readily apparent in modern culture. First, particularly in the West, but also for example in China, the focus is on blame in a culture in which admonition is to the fore and issues are simplified by presentation in a binary fashion, and notably so in public debate.

Secondly, as an aspect of an oppositional culture that has flourished since the 1960s, criticism and blame are directed from within Western states at previous generations. This process entails a variety of historical targets, for example Victorian imperialists or Field Marshal Haig in Britain. However, attention is also devoted to refighting World War Two, not least because it is closer in time and prominent in the frame of cultural reference, playing, as it does, a key role in the national account of a large number of states. This context is notably significant in the case of criticism of British strategic bombing and of Winston Churchill, Britain's warleader from 1940 to 1945.

Thirdly, as part of a process that often involves self-conscious revisionism, accounts of the war and its significance are contested by, and among, the defeated. Most prominent among the defeated are those that surrendered at the close of the war in 1945 – Germany (including Austria) and Japan. But there is also debate from those countries which were defeated and surrendered earlier in the conflict, notably France in 1940, Italy in 1943, and the states of Eastern Europe, both those defeated by the Germans (Poland, Yugoslavia, Greece), and those defeated by the Soviets (Romania, Bulgaria, Slovakia, Hungary). In part, this questioning is an attempt to come to terms with the past, especially with the French critique of the wartime collaborationist Vichy regime which was created from the ruins of the defeated Third Republic in 1940. However, in part, the issue is a refighting of the conflict that can involve troubling, if not dangerous, revisionist attitudes.

The continuing overhang of the politics of World War Two is a key theme of this book, which aims to look for relationships that throw light on the conflict, on the processes by which events are understood, and on public history. An appreciation of the political issues of the time is important to an assessment of the subsequent politicisation of the discussion of the conflict.

Far more than discussion was involved in this politicisation, as the war was directly linked to what came after. Thus, in many respects, the politics of subsequent decades represented a continuation of the war. This was so in the strength of the Soviet military-industrial complex and the Soviet presence in Eastern Europe, both of which, in turn, lessened the possibilities of Soviet reform. It was also so in the weakness of Nationalist China, which opened the way for Communist triumph there in 1949; in America's rise to a global pre-eminence, but one that was greatly limited on the Eurasian landmass; and in the decline both of the Western European colonial empires, and of Britain.

Each of these trends was apparent, at least to a degree,[1] prior to the outbreak of World War Two. However, the war secured and accelerated them, prevented alternative outcomes, and set the scene for the politics of the last 70 years. Most obviously, World War Two set the scene for the Cold War between the Communist and Western blocs that lasted until the collapse of the Soviet bloc in 1989–91. Whether victors, defeated or neutrals in that conflict, states found their subsequent history greatly affected by World War Two.

The war therefore is understood and presented here as part of a continuing political process. The domestic politics of the war led into the politics of the memory of the war, with controversies about the events of the war becoming controversies surrounding this memory. This process is most accurately considered in the light of historical information, methods and insights. That approach, as seen in this book and others, demonstrates that a combination of the appreciation of different views with an employment of scholarly methods does not have to lead to a relativism without judgment or conclusions.

A relativistic approach may seem particularly appropriate when dealing with a war in which there were many combatants, each with at least one point of view that can help shape the historical record and that demands attention. However, as with other historical episodes, some views are more accurate than others. For World War Two, there are many accurate views, numerous inaccurate ones, and a large number of problematic accounts. Thus, the 'we are all guilty' approach is one that makes a mockery of attempts to ascribe relative responsibility, and thereby to make judgments. Our necessary task of doing so is a theme in what follows. In part, this is a matter of trust between the generations (which, of course, is true of all the combatants), but there is also the issue of prudently learning the lessons of a past age. Many of the issues of the war require a near-continual process of discussion because they have such a significance. This is the case most obviously with the Holocaust, the genocidal German treatment of Europe's Jews, which was a key strand of the war as it related centrally to the goals, means and methods of German warmaking.

The influence of the ideas and images of, and about, the war was, and is, more potent than we generally appreciate. To offer a minor personal example, as a 17-year-old studying for Geography 'A' level in the early 1970s, I was taught at length about the central-place theory of Walter Christaller, a theory explaining the location of settlements on an isotropic (all-equal) surface, without being informed of its use by the planners seeking to create a Nazi new world in an East murderously emptied of its people by the German conquerors.

Moreover, the changing and problematic nature of the representation of the war can be illustrated from another personal instance, that of Exeter, the city where I live. The recent building of the Princesshay shopping centre, replacing that originally constructed on the site of wartime devastation, the destructive Exeter Blitz of May 1942, led to an information board that refers first to the British bombing of Lübeck and presents the devastation of Exeter as a reprisal. No attempt is made on this board to offer a wider context, notably that the large-scale bombing of European cities during the war was begun by the Germans with the air assault on Warsaw in 1939.

Readers will have their own views of these and other episodes. In aiming to stimulate debate, this book seeks to engage with the critical faculties of readers. World War Two is scarcely a subject over which agreement can be anticipated, which helps explain its importance as well as its interest.

For the opportunity to develop ideas, I am most grateful to students at Exeter who took my World War Two special subject, to invitations to lecture including on the deck of the USS *Missouri* in Pearl Harbor, at the Naval

War College in Newport, Rhode Island, to Trinity Hall, Cambridge History Society, and at the Edinburgh and Budleigh Salterton Literary Festivals. I have benefited from the opportunity to discuss current debates in East Asia with Yasuo Naito. I am very grateful to Mike Mosbacher for letting me use material previously published by the Social Affairs Unit, to Mark Brynes, Stan Carpenter, Bill Gibson, Tony Kelly, Nicholas Kyriazis, Karl de Leeuw, Stewart Lone, Michael Neiberg, John Olsen, Luisa Quartermaine, Barnett Singer, Roland Quinault, Matthias Reiss, Patrick Salmon, Richard Toye, George Yagi and Don Yerxa for advice, and to five anonymous readers who commented on an earlier version of this book. It is dedicated to Richard Overy who has done so much to advance our knowledge of the war, and marks his retirement from teaching in a Department where he has always proved an exemplary and popular colleague.

CHAPTER ONE

Causes

Debate over the causes of World War Two links contemporaries with those who come later. For contemporaries, such debate was largely political, an attempt to mobilise support, both domestic and international. For subsequent generations, in contrast, debate links the issue of war guilt for wartime opponents to more general questions of justification and vindication. As a result, this chapter cannot be readily separated from those on recollection, Chapters 5 and 6.

This chapter seeks to provide an account of the origins of the war down to it becoming global in December 1941. Then, Japan attacked the USA and Britain, while Germany declared war on the USA. Such an account is particularly necessary for the purposes of this book, because it demonstrates that the combatants, and their alignments, were far from inevitable and were certainly not seen in that light by contemporaries. Therefore, the discussion of how these alignments arose is a key issue in the politics involved in the war and its recollection.

This discussion also relates to postwar debates over responsibility, notably because of controversies over Appeasement: the policy followed in the run-up to war towards the expansionist powers that were to comprise the Axis, Japan, Germany and Italy.

Wartime alignments are also crucial to the process by which guilt or praise are apparently established by association. For example, Hungary appears 'bad' because it allied with Germany against the Soviet Union in 1941, whereas the Soviet Union is apparently vindicated for posterity because it was attacked by Germany that year. In practice, an understanding of the policies of these and other states requires a more subtle consideration of their situation, politics and options. For example, Eastern European powers had their own history and interests to consider. Hungary aligned with Germany in order to regain territories lost, in the Treaty of Trianon in 1920, as a consequence of being on the losing side in World War One. Constraints and/or opportunities, and their consequences, can be emphasised in the assessment of the Eastern European powers. It is certainly necessary to note that there was an element of choice. Thus, the politics of Romania can be criticised not simply because of alliance with Germany against the Soviet Union from 1941 to 1944, but also due to the policies it followed, notably genocidal anti-Semitism. Thus, tens of thousands of Jews were slaughtered when the invading Romanians captured the city of Odessa in 1941.

Debate over the causes of World War Two is a particularly difficult subject because of the number of different conflicts involved. This number is reflected in the widely contrasting titles, dates and periodisation offered for the war, as well as the danger of assuming clear causal links between these conflicts. Whereas the British date the war from 1939, the Chinese turn to 1937, and there are Spanish commentators who see the Spanish Civil War (1936–9) as the first stage of World War Two. The Soviet Union and the USA did not enter the war until 1941. Furthermore, the debate over the causes has a political dimension because of the continuing significance of issues of responsibility and guilt. As a result, the work of historians is located, at least for the public, within continuing controversies about blame for aspects of the war.

Appeasement

The most controversial aspect of the causes of war relates to the argument that the British and French were partly responsible because of a failure to adopt a robust stance towards Germany, Japan and Italy, the Axis powers, prewar. Voiced at the time, this argument was much employed by the Left during the Cold War that followed the war, in order to hold the West partly responsible for Axis policies and indeed World War Two. This approach shifted the blame to Britain and France, a rather curious response to the goals and actions of the Axis, and one, to a degree, matched by the argument that much of the responsibility lay with the global economic situation, with the Depression of the 1930s encouraging international competition and political support for extremists.

In practice, while systemic factors, such as the sustained global economic Depression that began in 1929, were highly significant in destabilising the international system, Hitler's responsibility for the war is a key element. He operated in response to a background that he did not create, as well as to international circumstances and developments. Nevertheless, Hitler also played a major role in shaping them and in encouraging a mistrust that made compromise appear a danger. The racial ideology and policy of the destruction of Jewry and the subjugation of the Slavs presented an agenda in which racial conflict was linked to an exultation of violence. Ironically, as it sought to direct popular anger the Nazi Press Office was subsequently to attribute the outbreak of the war to the Jews, which was a classic instance of blaming the innocent. Subsequently, the Jews were again to be (inaccurately) blamed for Allied bombing.

The focus on Appeasement continues to play a significant role in current controversies. Aside from this specific argument about the origins of World War Two, there was also the use of Appeasement outside this context, but as part of a call for action. Thus, in 2003 and 2013, opponents of international intervention in Iraq and Syria respectively were described with reference to the Appeasers, as part of a long process of castigating caution.[1]

These lessons have frequently been applied in a far-fetched fashion, which demonstrates their malleability and resonance. Aware of the near-universal usage across the West of the Munich Agreement of 1938 as the key episode of the Appeasement of Germany,[2] the spokesman of Vojislav Koštunica, the Serbian Prime Minister, rejected, in 2007, the proposal by the UN representative for independence for the former Serbian province of Kosovo, by arguing that this would be akin to the loss by Czechoslovakia of the Sudetenland, which Hitler acquired as a result of the Munich Agreement. In practice, the comparison was totally misplaced, not least because the Serbs had treated the majority Albanian population of Kosovo in a much harsher fashion than the Czechs did the majority Germans in the Sudetenland. However, such a comparative judgment was scarcely going to stop the polemical use of the historical parallel. Munich was also employed in 2013, by the Japanese when urging opposition to China's ambitions in the East China Sea, and by Israel when pressing for opposition to Iranian nuclear plans. In 2014, it was employed anew when discussing the response to the Russian occupation of Crimea.[3]

The scholarly dimension is very different, for Appeasement emerges as in large part a matter of circumstances, notably, in the case of Britain, the interaction between far-flung imperial commitments and strategy. There is a corresponding emphasis on the extent to which British policy options were constrained by the need to protect threatened interests across the world. The uncertainties affecting British policy related in part to this situation, but also to the extent to which it was by no means clear, prior to 1938, whether Nazi Germany or the Soviet Union was more of a threat. Furthermore, wherever the emphasis was placed, it was also unclear how best to confront these threats. The eventual outcome was far from predictable. In the case of the Soviet Union and Britain, there was hostility short of war in 1939 to 1941, then alliance against Germany until 1945, and then to opposition between the Soviet Union and Britain in the Cold War.

Some British and French commentators saw Germany as a potential ally against the Soviet Union. Moreover, Hitler initially hoped that Britain would join Germany in a war against Communism.[4] However, in Britain, Hitler's determination to overturn the (much criticised and misrepresented[5]) Versailles Peace Settlement, and to make Germany a great power anew, was correctly regarded as a growing challenge to Britain's interests. In the winter of 1933–4, Nazi Germany was identified as Britain's ultimate potential enemy by the Defence Requirements Sub-Committee. Germany was seen as a graver security threat than Japanese expansionism, even though the latter was already apparent in Manchuria, the northernmost province of China, a strategically-significant and economically crucial province which had been successfully invaded in 1931. Britain's unwillingness to accept Japanese expansionism in China helped lead the Japanese navy in 1934 to begin preparing for war with Britain.[6] This was a major step as the Japanese navy had developed on the pattern of the British navy, and with its assistance. Moreover, Britain and Japan had been allies from 1902, notably in World War One.

Focusing on Germany, Neville Chamberlain, Britain's Prime Minister from 1937 to 1940, made a major effort to maintain peace, and thus both domestic and international stability and the chance of economic recovery.[7] However, Chamberlain was weakened by his inability to accept other points of view or to learn from experience, and by his self-righteous and continuing optimism about his own assumptions. Indeed, these flaws helped vitiate the conduct of British foreign policy, ensuring that, however sensible in practice and/or as a short-term expedient, Appeasement was developed in a fashion that did not secure its purposes. Moreover, the implementation of Appeasement helps ensure that it is open to subsequent criticism.

Chamberlain feared that war would lead to the collapse of the British Empire and would also wreck the domestic policies of the Conservative-dominated National Government. He was indeed correct on both counts, although he was at error in seeing these outcomes as worse than the victory of Nazism. It was assumed that, if conflict broke out with Germany, then Japan might be encouraged to attack Britain's Asian Empire, which was rightly seen as militarily and politically vulnerable. This vulnerability encouraged the British government to search for compromise with rising nationalism in India, not least with the Government of India Act of 1935. A sense of vulnerability also led to the attempt to create a viable policy of naval support, based on the new base at Singapore (opened in February 1938), for the British Empire in the Far East: Hong Kong, Malaya, Singapore, north Borneo, British interests in China, and links to the Dominions of Australia and New Zealand.

An American alliance did not seem a welcome solution, as the Americans were regarded as posing a challenge to British imperial interests and, correctly, as unlikely to provide consistent support. This is a viewpoint that can be difficult to recover from the perspective of subsequent wartime and postwar co-operation with America, both of which were crucial to Britain. Nevertheless, it is a viewpoint that helps explain the importance of this later co-operation. British response to Japanese, Italian and German expansionism was affected by the nature of Anglo–American relations, and, in turn, the legacy of these years helped underline later calls for a strong alliance. Isolationist America, which, under President Franklin Delano Roosevelt, President from 1933 to 1945, had had cooler relations with Britain than those in 1929–31, and which passed Neutrality Acts from

1935, was regarded in the 1930s as self-interested. This, indeed, was a key element in American isolationism. Moreover, the two powers had failed in 1932 to co-operate against Japan during the crisis caused by Japan's invasion of Manchuria.[8]

Isolationist sentiment was strong in the USA, notably so from the reaction against President Woodrow Wilson and his role in the establishment of the League of Nations at the close of World War One. In 1937, this sentiment led Congress to consider the Ludlow Resolution which would have required a national referendum before Congress could declare war, unless in response to a direct attack. That October, Roosevelt's 'Quarantine' Speech, proposing that aggressor states be placed in quarantine, enjoyed only limited support in the USA in the face of isolationist views.[9]

Such views were linked to a conviction that the USA should focus only on the defence of the New World – hemispheric defence – and, despite signs, such as the 1938 trade agreement with Britain, this approach helped make the USA a problematic potential ally. The situation was exacerbated by limited expenditure on the American military in the 1930s. This was not as bad as was later suggested. The oft-repeated comment that the army was smaller than that of Portugal is unhelpful as Portugal had extensive colonies in Africa to protect (and from which to raise troops), notably Angola and Mozambique, while, conversely, the USA spent much more on the navy and air force. Portugal, for example, had no equivalent to the 35 B17 Flying Fortresses deployed by 1941 at Clark Field, America's leading air base in the Philippines. Introduced from 1937, this was the first effective American all-metal, four-engine monoplane bomber.

Nevertheless, the USA had a smaller military than it could afford as the world's leading economy and a major centre of population. Crucially, the USA, in the 1930s, did not press forward with rearmament as its wartime opponents did, as well as the Soviet Union, France and, indeed, Britain. In 1938, the American army could only put six divisions in the field, although it had one of the world's leading navies, an improving air force, and valuable developments in military planning.[10]

As far as Britain was concerned, Appeasement was designed to avoid both war and unwelcome alliances. Britain in the 1930s certainly lacked a powerful alliance system comparable to that in World War One. Although hopes for the French defence of Western Europe in the event of German attack were high, France had been greatly weakened by World War One. It increased its military from 1935 in response to the German remilitarisation of the Rhineland. However, France did not spend as much as a Germany solely focused on a military build-up, had a smaller population as a pool from which to recruit, as well as a smaller industrial base, had major colonial commitments, and also put strenuous efforts into developing its navy.[11]

Confidence in the ability of an Anglo–French alliance to prevent German expansionism in Eastern Europe was limited. Indeed, prior to the outbreak of a new war, Germany did well in the bitter competition for influence and markets in Eastern Europe that was a key aspect of the rivalry between the great powers.[12] In seeking co-operation there, the Germans benefited from the 'democratic deficit' across much of the region as well as opposition to the Soviet Union.

Moreover, unlike in 1914, neither Russia nor Japan was an ally of Britain. This absence was a key contrast, and even more so because both powers allied with Germany: the Soviet Union in 1939–41 and Japan throughout. However, despite significant economic assistance to Germany, the Soviet Union did not fight Britain, while Japan only did so from December 1941.

In the 1930s, the British government was unhappy about Britain's allies and potential allies. It was also unwilling to explore the path of confronting Hitler by making him uncertain about the prospects of collective action against Germany. Instead, the British government preferred to negotiate directly with the expansionist powers. This political response was matched by Chamberlain's focus on deterrence through a stronger navy and air force, each of which was to be based on Britain, rather than through an army that was to be sent to the Continent. This build-up was an aspect of what was an unprecedented international arms race as it involved airpower over both land and sea, as well as more conventional weaponry.[13]

The policy of negotiating with the Axis focused on Germany, because it was felt that Japan would be cautious if peace was maintained with Hitler. This was a reasonable view, at least in so far as Britain was concerned. It was certainly not so for China, which was the victim of Japanese aggression from 1931 and, even more, 1937, when a full-scale invasion was launched.

Italy, from 1922 under the bombastic and opportunistic Fascist dictator Benito Mussolini, was not treated as a serious threat, and, instead, was regarded by Britain as a possibly ally. Mussolini indeed long saw Hitler as a rival in Austria and the Balkans, although he shared both Hitler's contempt for the democracies and his opposition to Britain and France. These views became more important for him in the late 1930s.

On the part of Britain, a sense that compromise with Germany was possible, combined with a lack of interest in the areas threatened by German expansionism, encouraged a conciliatory search for a settlement; as did the extent that few were in other than denial about what Nazism was really like, in both domestic and international policy. In some respects, there was an attempt to re-integrate Germany into the international order that was comparable to the treatment of France after the Napoleonic Wars ended in 1815. Thus, Hitler was treated as another Napoleon III, the expansionist and bellicose ruler of France (first as President and then as Emperor) from 1848 to 1870. Yet, such an approach was mistaken. The search for compromise with Hitler was not only unsuccessful, other than as a series of concessions, but also, arguably, discouraged potential allies against Germany.

Nevertheless, a problem with the postwar and current emphasis on the follies and failure of Appeasement is that, at the popular level, this emphasis can make it seem that Britain and France were in some way culpable, if not as culpable as the aggressors; and that blame should be divided. This assumption, which was particularly strong among those concerned to extenuate the Soviet Union, is deeply flawed.

There is a parallel here with the treatment of the causes of World War One. Rather than treating all combatants as equally culpable, as was suggested or implied by some commentators in 2013–14, it is clear that, alongside systemic issues and tensions, particular responsibility attaches to the Austrian and German military élites.[14] In contrast, Britain, in 1914, acted against the unprovoked aggression and violation of international treaties represented by the German invasion of Belgium. The war was undertaken reluctantly by a people who quite genuinely believed in the value of peace, and were sustained by the high moral value of self-sacrifice, and not by a crazed jingoistic mob.[15] Indeed, for Britain and the USA, World War One was a just and justifiable war. Moreover, it did not end with a Carthaginian (harsh) peace, as, in contrast, the Germans were to claim.

The attempt to contain the Axis powers short of war failed in the 1930s. Nevertheless, however mishandled, the *realpolitik* involved in Appeasement was not inherently dishonourable, although it is not clear that such latitude should be extended to those in the British government and establishment who advocated a negotiated settlement with Germany after defeat in 1940. In the 1930s, a wish to seek a negotiated alternative to war was widespread across the political spectrum. Far from being a characteristic of reprehensible Conservatives, not to say fellow-travelling neo-Fascists, both the desire to avoid war and opposition to rearmament were also notably strong among liberal opinion and on the Left, and particularly so prior to the Czech Crisis of 1938. This point needs to be underlined because of the subsequent politicised placing of Appeasement, notably in Britain, as a means to criticise the Right.

As 'Britain' as a term stands for the British Empire, it is also necessary to discuss the response of the Dominions: Australia, New Zealand, Canada, South Africa and Eire (Ireland). Their attitude and effort had been crucial to the British effort in World War One,[16] not only in the fighting but also in the economic sphere. Yet, from the Chanak Crisis in Turkey in 1922 on, it had been clear that the Dominions were not only pursuing independent tracks, but also ones that could be at variance with those of Britain. In the Chanak Crisis, there was an unwillingness, apart from on the part of New Zealand and Newfoundland, to support Britain when Turkish nationalist forces under Kemal Atatürk approached the Dardanelles and Bosphorus, which were garrisoned by British forces in accordance with the postwar settlement imposed on Turkey. In the event, with most of the Cabinet unwilling to risk war, Britain backed down. There was no comparable difficulty in political relations with the Dominions until the late 1930s. However, at the time of Appeasement, and notably the Munich Crisis of 1938, the unwillingness of the Dominions to risk war was a key element, especially that of Canada, which had played a major role in World War One.

Moreover it is instructive to consider a figure from the political wilderness, not least because he reflected a strand of thought and had been a senior ministerial colleague of Winston Churchill, then also in the political wilderness. On his visit to Germany in the autumn of 1936, David Lloyd George, Prime Minister from 1916 to 1922, twice saw Hitler whom he was particularly keen to assess. Lloyd George's visit led to much criticism, as he was presented as being completely taken in by the dictator. The invitation originated with Hitler, who had praised Lloyd George's wartime leadership in his book *Mein Kampf* (*My Struggle*, 1925). The second meeting closed with Lloyd George urging Hitler, 'the greatest German of the age', to visit Britain, and providing the assurance that 'he would be welcomed by the British people'.

In practice, although Hitler wanted to enlist Britain against Communism, Lloyd George was not interested in taking good relations that far, and nor did he want them to compromise the Anglo–French alliance, which had played the central role in his wartime policy. Far from being a Fascist, Lloyd George can be located in the Liberal tradition, which was to seek good relations whatever the political complexion of the regime in question, as seen with the attitudes of Cobden and Gladstone towards Napoleon III of France. Of course, Liberals could also take a very different view, as, while in opposition, the hostile response to the Bulgarian Massacres in 1876 showed. Indeed, a week after his return from seeing Hitler in 1936, Lloyd George criticised Nazi political and religious repression: 'a terrible thing to an old Liberal like myself'.[17] Nevertheless, others were willing to overlook this repression in their enthusiasm for praising what was seen as a dynamic state that was apparently more promising than the capitalist democracies.

Despite his concern about Hitler's internal policies, Lloyd George was to be convinced that an understanding with Hitler could have been reached. However, the Munich Agreement of 1938 was just such an understanding, and, despite his ambition to ally with the British Empire, Hitler broke the agreement, as he would have broken other understandings that restricted him. He was interested not in a revision of the 1919 Versailles Peace Settlement in pursuit of a German nationalist agenda, but in a fundamental recasting of Europe. This goal meant war, for only in defeat could an agreement that left the Continent at Hitler's disposal be contemplated by Britain and France.

Moreover, Hitler was not a ruler with whom lasting compromise was possible, as Joseph Stalin, the Soviet dictator, discovered in 1941 when Hitler attacked his Soviet ally. Hitler's quest for a very extensive, eventually continent-sized, empire reflected his belief in the inherent competitiveness of international relations, his system of aggressive racist geopolitics,[18] and his conviction that widely-flung territorial power was necessary for effective competition with the other empires or imperial-strength powers: Britain, the Soviet Union and the USA. This was a conviction shared with Japan. Hitler wanted both to overthrow Versailles and, with increased urgency from late 1937, to redraw Eastern Europe, ideally on the lines, at least, of the victorious Treaty of Brest Litovsk negotiated with the Soviet Union in 1918 at a stage when Germany had done very well on the Eastern Front of World War One. In contrast, Hitler had less interest in Western Europe until 1940, and never showed the same commitment to territorial or ethnic changes there.

Violence was at the heart of Nazism, and it was a creed born of a violence that required the destruction of alleged enemies. All were linked: domestic dissidence, the Nazis claimed, had to be prevented in order to strengthen Germany for war. For example, the Third Reich's 'state bishops' recast the Bible and produced an 'official' version of the Sermon on the Mount which was a grotesque distortion. There were simple elements in the causes and nature of governmental support for Fascist or Fascist-style bellicosity and expansionism in Italy and Japan.[19]

Returning to the judgment of Appeasement and, more specifically, the Munich Agreement of 1938, the total failure of the Western powers to protect Czechoslovakia against a Soviet-organised Communist takeover in 1948 provided an opportunity to rethink more sympathetically the weakness of the Western position in 1938. Nevertheless, the opportunity for such a rethinking was not really taken, because the positioning of Nazi Germany and the Soviet Union (a wartime ally) in Western public opinion in 1948 was very different. In contrast, more positive academic re-considerations of Appeasement gathered pace in the 1980s, in part as a result of a better understanding of the multiple problems facing Britain in the 1930s, but, in some cases, as a key aspect of a revisionist case that the war itself had dealt Britain and its Empire a near-fatal blow, and thus that efforts to avoid it were commendable.

The latter argument came from certain conservative historians, such as John Charmley, but their thesis enjoyed only very limited political and public support. In large part, this lack of support was a product of the understandable widespread reluctance to abandon the standard account and to argue for the attempt to reach an understanding with Hitler. However, in part, the particular contours of the Right in the 1980s were the key issue, notably the successful call by Margaret Thatcher, Prime Minister from 1979 to 1990, for a robust opposition to the Communist bloc. Subsequently, it was argued that this opposition helped provoke the fall of the Soviet Union, and, by extension, that robust opposition to dictatorships was the appropriate course.

Thus, positive scholarly re-evaluation of Stanley Baldwin and Neville Chamberlain, the Conservative leaders and Prime Ministers who preceded Winston Churchill, and of the strand of Conservatism that was displaced by him, was not linked to Thatcherism in foreign policy. Indeed, her effort to increase ideological commitments, and to push the bounds of possibility, markedly contrasted with the 1930s' politics of prudence, and the resulting policies, notably Appeasement. The cult of Churchill, to whom Thatcher frequently referred as 'Winston', was also important. For example, in the aftermath of the Falklands War, in a major speech given at Cheltenham on 3 July 1982, Thatcher quoted Churchill when arguing that Britain could be great again. Addressing the Czechoslovak Federal Assembly in 1990, she referred to the shame she felt as a result of the Munich Agreement.

This cult continued into the 2000s and 2010s. In 2001, Tony Blair, the Labour Prime Minister, presented President George W. Bush with an Epstein bust of Churchill which he kept in the Oval Office; a bust removed by President Obama. In 2007, Gordon Brown, Blair's successor, at his first press conference with Bush, spoke of 'a partnership founded and driven forward by our shared values, what Winston Churchill, who was the first British Prime Minister to visit Camp David, called "the joint inheritance of liberty"'.

War in Europe

Appeasement was a key issue in 1931–8, in the response to Japanese, German and Italian expansionism. The situation changed on 15 March 1939 when Germany seized Bohemia and Moravia: the modern Czech Republic, bar the Sudetenland which had been gained already by Germany as a result of the Munich Agreement, a loss which gravely weakened the Czechs' capacity to defend themselves. By this seizure, Hitler destroyed the Munich Agreement, the most public product of Appeasement, exposing its failure.[20] This leaves to one side the argument that Appeasement 'bought' time for rearmament, especially a marked strengthening of the British Royal Air Force (RAF). It was now clear that Hitler's ambitions were not restricted to bringing all Germans under one state, which was the case argued when his acquisition of Austria (1938) and the Sudetenland (1938) were discussed, and, indeed, also the German excuse when, on 23 March 1939, an ultimatum demanding the immediate return of the Memel (Klapeida) region was successfully issued to Lithuania.

In response to the destruction of the Munich Agreement, an attempt was made to create a collective-security alliance system that would contain Hitler through deterrence. This system, however, was weakened by the failure to include the Soviet Union. Again, as with Appeasement, and in some respects linked to it, there has been considerable debate over responsibility for this failure. Critics have argued that Anglo–French anti-Communism bore much of the responsibility. While that attitude was, indeed, significant, far more was involved.

First, Stalin was hostile to the West, indeed as hostile as he was to Germany, whereas Hitler was hostile to both the Soviet Union and the West, but more so to the former. Stalin's hostility to the West owed much to an opposition to democracy and bourgeois liberalism, as well to a legacy of hostility from the Russian Civil War: Britain, France, the USA and Japan had all then intervened against the Communists. The Soviet Union was far more hostile to liberal democracies than Romanov Russia, Britain's ally in World War One, had been. There was also an incompatibility in long-term goals between Britain and the Soviet Union, one that provided a key context for diplomatic relations, as had been the case with the failure of Anglo–Soviet naval armaments diplomacy in 1935–9.[21] As the world's leading imperial power, Britain opposed Soviet views in a number of areas.

A shared interest in revisionism and opposition to democracy provided a basis for agreement between Hitler and Stalin.[22] Indeed, in the summer of 1938, Stalin had planned to approach Hitler for an alliance, in August 1939 they were to ally, notably against Poland,[23] and, in early 1940, there was to be pressure in Britain and France to send military assistance to Finland, a neutral power which had been attacked by the Soviet Union.

Secondly, serious differences between Poland and the Soviet Union played a key role in 1939. Negotiations for a triple alliance of Britain, France and the Soviet Union, an alliance that might have deterred Hitler from acting in 1939, collapsed largely because Britain and France could not satisfy the Soviets on the issue of Polish and Romanian consent to the passage of Soviet forces in the event of war with Germany. Romania was suspicious about Soviet intentions about Bessarabia, a region Russian from 1812 that Romania had acquired after World War One. Events were to vindicate this suspicion. Romania was also fearful of the German reaction if it agreed to the British approach.[24] Earlier, the idea of a four-power declaration by Britain, France, Poland and the Soviet Union had fallen foul of Polish opposition. There are major archival problems in studying Soviet policy, with limitations on access to sources and concerns about their reliability,[25] but benign accounts of Stalin's intentions are deeply suspect.

In light of the Soviet invasion of Poland in 1920, as well as what was to happen in 1939–41 and 1944–5, with the Soviets brutally occupying much and all of Poland respectively,[26] Polish concerns are understandable. However, the Poles were also naïve in imagining that Germany could be restrained without active Soviet assistance. Stalin was totally untrustworthy, but the Poles had no viable alternative. There were parallels between the Polish response and the divisions between the Baltic States in their response to the serious threats from Germany and the Soviet Union. Whereas the latter was the prime enemy for Estonia, the former was for Lithuania, while Latvia saw both as enemies. Similarly, Estonia and Latvia viewed Poland as an ally, while Lithuania had a bitter territorial dispute with Poland over the city of Vilnius and the surrounding area. This was a region that symbolised the complex and rival strands of identity frequently seen in Eastern Europe, strands that were substance as well as shadow. Polish forces had taken Vilnius from Lithuania in 1919.[27]

The German–Soviet Pact of 23 August 1939, named after their manipulative foreign ministers Ribbentrop and Molotov, who negotiated the agreement, was crucial in encouraging Hitler to invade Poland, given the unexpected (and implausible in the light of policy in 1936–8) determination of Britain and France to fulfil their guarantee of Polish independence, and the failure of his major ally, Italy, to act in Hitler's support. Hitler persisted against Poland despite the guarantee. He believed that Britain and France would not fight, especially as a result of his pact with Stalin. This freed Germany from a two-front war,[28] the disastrous situation that had faced Germany for most of World War One. However, the Pact greatly alienated Germany's ally Japan, notably because Japanese and Soviet forces were involved in a major clash in August 1939. Thereafter, Japanese policy-makers did not feel that they could trust Hitler.

In 1939, the British Chiefs of Staff advised that it would not be possible to offer Poland any direct assistance. This was to be borne out by the course of the war in both 1939 and 1944, and was also true of Britain's military posture towards Czechoslovakia in 1938 and 1948. Britain itself was left reliant in 1939 on the French, who were to be revealed, when Germany attacked in 1940, as a flawed ally, both militarily and politically. Already, in 1939, France, despite its large army, was unable and unwilling to attack Germany's western frontier. Such an attack could only have been an indirect help to Poland (important as that would have been); whereas, with a long common frontier, the Soviet Union could readily have sent forces to Poland's assistance. Co-operation between Germany and the Soviet Union was initially directed against Poland, and was also linked to an anti-Western turn in German policy. Indeed, the war in the West was an ideological struggle like that for *Lebensraum* (living space) in the East.[29]

Although crucial to the diplomacy and warfare of 1939–41, the German–Soviet Pact became an aspect of history written out of the Soviet account and, indeed, of that of Communist parties and leaders who praised it at the time, such as Mao Zedong. The Pact had led to great suspicion of Communists at the time. The French government clamped down on the Communists. In so far as it was discussed subsequently, the Pact was presented as an opportunity to gain time and space to resist German attack, not least by moving Soviet defences forward. Nevertheless, the Pact, which divided Eastern Europe into German and Soviet spheres of influence and expansion, was subsequently frequently referred to by external and internal opponents of the Soviet system. For example, the 40th anniversary of the Pact in 1989 was marked by opponents in the Baltic Republics, as an aspect of the discrediting of the Soviet Union.

The outbreak of war on 1 September 1939 was not the only conflict in Europe that has to be explained as part of World War Two. However, far from seeing a process of inevitable expansion of the conflict, it is important to underline the extent to which the expansion of the war was hesitant. Moreover, this hesitancy provided opportunities for the Axis powers. Crucially, Hitler's successive attacks from 1939 to the spring of 1941 found the Soviet Union neutral (or an active participant against Poland from

17 September), and the USA unwilling to come to the aid of fellow neutrals. Thus, as in the Wars of German Unification (1864–71), Hitler was able to fight single-front conflicts. Film provided historical endorsement for Hitler's diplomatic policy, with *Bismarck* (1940) showing the firm and iconic Chancellor, the maker of German unification and a model of leadership on the Right,[30] favouring a Russian alliance to protect Prussia's rear.

Moreover, when Hitler invaded in 1939, Romania did not aid Poland, while Norway and Sweden provided only limited assistance to Finland when it was attacked by the Soviet Union in the Winter War of 1939–40.[31] In Norway, the government proclaimed neutrality and forbade all officers and conscripts from taking part on the Finnish side, although it did send weapons to Finland. There were also several aid campaigns in Norway where food and clothes were collected and sent to Finland. Some men volunteered to fight on the Finnish side, including some who were on the Far Right, seeing this as a double opportunity to fight for a neighbour and against Communism.

In Sweden, the support for Finland in the Winter War was stronger. The Swedish government declared neutrality, but allowed its troops to volunteer to fight for the Finns, while there was also considerable support beyond the military. However, if there was significant sympathy for the Finns, *realpolitik* prevailed at the governmental level. Crucially, Norway and Sweden refused to allow transit for any Anglo–French relief force, a major factor discouraging an intervention that was planned but that would probably, anyway, have been unsuccessful.

Similarly, Japan was able to attack China from 1931 without the intervention of the other powers (including the neighbouring Soviet Union), despite the fact that they were not otherwise engaged in warfare. Japan was also able to fight limited border wars with the Soviet Union (1938 and, more seriously, 1939) that did not escalate,[32] and to attack Britain and the USA in 1941 without fear of Soviet entry into the war. When Roosevelt, Churchill and Chiang Kai-shek met in Cairo in November 1943, Stalin was not present as he did not wish to attend a conference of the powers at war with Japan. As a result, he was not a party to the Cairo Declaration of 1 December, by which Roosevelt and Churchill agreed to support the return to China of Taiwan (lost to Japan in 1895) and Manchuria (lost in 1931–2). In contrast, Stalin was willing to meet Roosevelt and Churchill at Teheran in December 1943; Chiang Kai-shek was not present.

Yet, despite the reluctance of most of the powers to fight, Hitler's inability to consider limits on his ambition, or to understand the flaws in German economic and military capability,[33] acted as an inexorable factor encouraging the expansion of the war. A correct sense that Hitler could not be trusted also meant that the rapid defeat of Poland did not lead to negotiations for peace. In the *Reichstag* (Parliament), on 6 October 1939, Hitler called for peace with Britain and France, but no real attempt was made to compromise with them, let alone with conquered Poland. Moreover, Britain and France were determined to fight on to prevent German hegemony in Europe, and planned for success through a long war involving naval and economic blockade and the active pursuit of alliances. The strength of the British war machine and global range of the British economy were significant to this planning.[34]

New combatants in 1940

While the German invasion of the Netherlands and Belgium on 10 May 1940 was an aspect of the plan for the conquest of France launched the same day, there was no such need for the German invasion of Norway on 9 April 1940, an invasion which, in turn, required that of Denmark the same day. A determination, however, to break the British naval blockade and to give the German navy operational flexibility and strategic possibilities played a major role in German policy in this instance.[35]

In the event, the conquest of Norway brought relatively little benefit to German warmaking, in part because serious weaknesses in the German surface navy made Norwegian bases less valuable than might otherwise have been the case, while the German conquest of France swiftly provided submarine bases closer to Atlantic trade routes. Brittany indeed was so positioned as if designed to threaten British maritime links. Furthermore, concern about the possibility of British attack ensured that the Germans tied up a large force in garrisoning Norway, a force that, in the event, had no strategic value, as there was no comparable risk of it being used to invade Britain. This force was not needed to coerce neighbouring Sweden, which was very willing to trade with Germany. Similarly, the German conquest of Yugoslavia in 1941 led to an even larger garrison obligation because of the problems posed by guerrilla opposition there.

The neutrality of the Netherlands and, more particularly, Belgium and their failure to create a joint defence,[36] gravely weakened the Anglo–French response to German attack in 1940. The failure to allow the prior deployment of British and French forces in these countries meant that these forces had to advance and to expose themselves to the German attack without the benefit of holding defensive positions. The rapid and total success of this attack was a striking contrast to the situation in World War One; and the 1940 campaign, culminating in the Fall of France in June, was important to the politics of the war, both those at the time and those subsequently.

The fall of France

Myths about the effectiveness of the *Blitzkrieg* served German objectives at the time, yet also contributed to the postwar assumption that the Germans were the most effective military but had eventually lost because of greater Allied resources. This was an argument frequently employed to provide a misleading ennoblement to the German cause. In fact, it is fairly well-established that the effectiveness of the *Blitzkrieg* has been exaggerated by commentators who remain excessively under the spell cast by the sheer shock and drama of the German offensives, and have therefore overrated the impact on war of military methods which, in practice, represented more of an improvisation than the fruition of a coherent doctrine. The Germans had assumed that a long war would be likely. The potential of weaponry and logistics based on the internal combustion engine was less fully grasped than talk of *Blitzkrieg* might suggest, not least because much of the German army was unmechanised, and indeed walked into battle. Horses also played a role in German logistics, and notably so against the Soviet Union. German achievements in 1940 owed more to fighting quality than simply to mechanisation which was a characteristic shared by Germany's opponents. In addition, the Germans encountered serious problems in fighting their way across the River Meuse against French resistance.[37]

Moreover, the success of the risky German strategy owed much to its flawed French counterpart which sent the French armoured reserve to the wrong place in an attempt to shore up Belgium and the Netherlands.[38] Deployed on the far-left of the French line, this reserve was unable to provide defence in depth against the German breakthrough in the centre, let alone to mount a counter-attack.

Nevertheless, however specific its causes, Allied failure in 1940 invites consideration of whether the entire military and political culture of the Western Allies was weak and defective, a charge that was of great significance at the time, and that has been important subsequently. This argument has been advanced most frequently for France. However, the speed of the Belgian collapse and the willingness, unlike in 1914, when most of the country was rapidly conquered by the Germans, to surrender, are also noteworthy; as is the even speedier collapse of the Dutch.

That this argument about cultural weakness was employed by the Germans and, in particular, in France, by collaborators keen to discredit the government that had unsuccessfully resisted German attack, and thus the entire Third Republic (1871–1940), does not inherently make the argument wrong. However, this point underlines both the partisan nature of many contemporary analyses, and the extent to which they have almost subliminally affected subsequent interpretations.

In contrast, an emphasis on specific, but far from inevitable, strategic and command flaws in the French campaign in 1940 leads to a downplaying of the argument about cultural weakness. These flaws can be matched by other problems in the French war effort including inadequate prewar economic preparations and low levels of industrial production once the conflict had begun; although France alone did not face such problems.

Crucially, the lack of French military and political will once defeat had occurred was important, especially as Winston Churchill, the new British Prime Minister, made a major and dramatic effort to keep France in the war. This effort included the offer of a union of the two states, an unprecedented step for the two countries in modern times. The British government planned, under similar circumstances of successful German invasion, to fight on from Canada, whence George VI, the fleet and the gold reserves were to be dispatched. In contrast, Marshal Pétain, who became Prime Minister, and Maxime Weygand, the newly-appointed Supreme Commander, were unwilling to continue the war from French North Africa, as was urged by Pétain's predecessor, Paul Reynaud, and by the Undersecretary of War, Charles de Gaulle. Instead, Pétain and Weygand were increasingly more concerned about social and political order within France, or rather maintaining and advancing their concept of this order. In part to help further this goal, Pétain was willing to negotiate a settlement with Hitler.[39] Northern and western France became a German occupation zone, part of eastern France was annexed by Germany, and a rump was left under the control of a government based in the town of Vichy and presided over by Pétain. The size and sophistication of the Vichy military were limited.

This willingness to negotiate a settlement, one, moreover, that entailed co-operation and a degree of collaboration, was very important to the politics of the war, and understandably has played a significant role in its subsequent discussion. French surrender, as opposed simply to defeat, greatly magnified German battlefield success in 1940, and thus its impact on European and world geopolitics. Germany did not face large-scale resistance in France after its victory. Indeed, the Resistance, the scale and impact of which were much exaggerated by postwar French commentators, took time to get going, while, until November 1942, Vichy France was not occupied by German forces, but rather by those of Vichy.

The Germans and their allies also did not face opposition from the French empire. France controlled the world's second biggest empire, and the fourth largest fleet. Even had it not proved possible to support opposition to German forces in southern France, a hostile North Africa, where France was the colonial power in Morocco, Algeria and Tunisia, backed by the French fleet, would have challenged not only the Germans but also the Italian position in the central Mediterranean, and would have made it easier for Britain to protect and pursue its regional and imperial interests. An additional help to Britain would have come had Syria and Lebanon, both French colonies, been opposed to Germany, instead of, as was to be the case, ready to follow Vichy and resist Britain.

French surrender secured the German triumph. Victory in the West in 1940 brought Hitler great popularity in Germany and with the military and enhanced self-confidence, and was the prelude to his onslaught on the Soviet Union in 1941. Germans felt that the *Wehrmacht* was invincible and this triumphalism combined with Nazi assumptions. The thrill of easy victory proved very heady. The euphoria felt by Hitler was important in his decision to move towards world domination as well as what he saw as the 'Final Solution' of the 'Jewish Question'.[40]

Victory in the West in 1940 also ensured that the eventual defeat of Germany would require large-scale American and Soviet participation, participation that in practice marked the end of European ascendancy.

It is worth noting that the collapse of France did not occur because troops were unwilling to fight. Indeed 92,000 French servicemen were killed in 1940. This point should be underlined because in 2003 when France (partly due to President Chirac's links with Saddam Hussein) refused to support the American–British invasion of Iraq, much was made in the USA about France's inglorious recent military history, and the collapse of 1940 was frequently mentioned. 'Surrender monkeys' was a term much used in the American public. In 2014, conservative commentators in the USA sought to disparage their Democrat opponents by comparing them to French generals in 1940.[41]

Yet, if any states took an inglorious role in 1939–40, the list was headed not by France, but by the Soviet Union, which actively collaborated with Hitler in dividing up Eastern Europe. American neutrality was less reprehensible, but also far from praiseworthy. This neutrality maintained the marked American non-involvement already seen in the Munich Crisis of 1938.[42]

War with Vichy

With France's surrender, there was no longer the prospect of a main-force conflict with the Germans on the Western Front, as in World War One. Instead, there was now the need to limit the consequences of France's surrender and of Italy's entry into the war. A key characteristic of Churchill's strategy was a determination to attack. He responded to the threat that the French navy, now in Vichy hands, would be taken over by the Germans, or would co-operate, by ordering action against it. This remains a controversial step.

Moreover, driving the Vichy French from their possessions was regarded as a crucial way to win the global struggle for power. On 18 September 1940, Churchill wrote to Sir Samuel Hoare, the Ambassador to Spain, explaining his support for the Free French attempt to capture Dakar, the capital of Senegal, the leading French colony in West Africa. Churchill presented a classic account of the indirect approach, observing that if Charles de Gaulle was to establish himself in Dakar and become 'master of Western and Central Africa, Morocco is next on the list'.[43]

In the event, due to firm resistance, the expedition failed. Churchill was very upset, and for his wife Clementine, looking back on the war, it was 'the progressive and sickening disappointment' she remembered most.[44] Fortunately, the port of Douala and, with it, the French colony of Cameroon, fell to the Free French in October 1940. Churchill greeted the news by promising de Gaulle 'We shall stand resolutely together'.[45]

Italy enters the war

In June 1940, the Italian dictator, Benito Mussolini, an ally of Hitler in the Pact of Steel, joined in the war. He did so once the French had been clearly defeated by the Germans, yet while the conflict with France was still continuing, because he feared that he would otherwise lose the opportunity to gain glory and territories from France and Britain. Longer-term ambitions also played a major role. German victory in 1940 brought to a head Mussolini's ideological affinity with Hitler, his contempt for the democracies, and the inherent violence and aggressive expansionism of his regime, and overcame his awareness of the poor financial and military situation of Italy and his realisation of little popular support for war.

Mussolini had already taken a very brutal role both in suppressing resistance in Italy's colony of Libya and, in 1935–6, in the conquest of Ethiopia. This was a conquest that flew in the face of the League of Nations' commitment to a peaceful settlement of disputes.[46] The idea that Italy was more benign (as opposed to weaker) than Germany appears very questionable from the perspective of Libya or Ethiopia. In Ethiopia, Mussolini authorised the large-scale use of poison gas in breach of the 1925 Geneva Gas Protocol. On 7 April 1939, Italy pressed on to invade Albania, an independent state where Italian influence was already strong. Albania rapidly fell and Victor Emmanuel III of Italy was declared King of Albania.

War with Britain and France, however, was conflict in a very different league for Italy, matching the process of escalation also seen with Germany and Japan. Feeling that his vision of Italian greatness required domination of the Mediterranean and, therefore, British defeat, Mussolini, who had built up a large modern fleet to that end,[47] sought gains from France and the British Empire. This policy, which entailed overcoming the pronounced pessimism of his service chiefs, destroyed the conviction in the British Foreign Office that Italy would remain neutral[48] and the linked illusion that Mussolini could be a moderating 'back-channel' to Hitler. This had been hoped by those on the Right in Britain keen to see a negotiated end to the war.

Italian expansionism in the late 1930s and 1940 represented a continuation of Mussolini's breach with both Britain and France and, instead, alignment with Germany as a result of the Ethiopian Crisis of 1935–6. In November 1938, the Italian Chamber of Deputies had echoed to calls for acquiring 'Tunisia, Corsica, Nice, Savoy',[49] all from France. Mussolini

judged Corsica as traditionally Italian,⁵⁰ but did not have the same view
of Savoy.⁵¹ In his forceful report on 4 February 1939 to the Fascist Grand
Council, he showed a clear opposition to France. Even though relations
were close with Hitler, notably with the Pact of Steel signed on 22 May
1939, this depended on a verbal understanding that neither Germany nor
Italy would provoke war before 1943.

Mussolini's son-in-law and Foreign Minister, Count Galeazzo Ciano,
opposed this alignment. He claimed that Mussolini was furious with Hitler
for not consulting him about the invasion of Poland. Mussolini appreciated that Hitler, rather than being Mussolini's equal, was becoming more
prominent. The invasion of the Low Countries and France made Mussolini
conclude that he could not remain neutral. He was convinced that war
would be short and that Germany was powerful enough to win.

Assisted by the alpine terrain and by prepared defences, the French
mounted an effective resistance to Italian attacks in June 1940, and, in
the subsequent peace, signed on 24 June, Italy's territorial gains were very
modest. These terms reflected the success of the French resistance to Italian
attack, but also Hitler's concern to bolster Vichy France.

Whatever the arrangements that would have been offered by Germany
had Britain accepted peace (i.e. surrendered) in 1940, Britain fought on.
Aside from the subsequent air war over Britain (the Battle of Britain
and then the Blitz) and the U-boat (submarine) assault on its trade,
most of the initial fighting on the part of the Axis involved Italy because
the projected German invasion of Britain was not launched. Although
vulnerable British Somaliland fell rapidly, Italian campaigning in East
and North Africa was a humiliating failure. Mussolini's planned advance
on the Suez Canal, the vital axis of British imperial power, failed totally.
The defeat of the Italian invading force in Egypt in December 1940 owed
much to Churchill's decision to send to Egypt tanks that were a key part
of Britain's strategic reserve.

In turn, in 1940–1, Somalia, Eritrea, Ethiopia and much of Libya were
captured by British troops (many from the Empire). This failure led to a
major shift in the politics of the Axis, with Germany ever more dominant.
The British achievement was impressive, not least given the terrain and
distances concerned, the resulting logistical strain, and the variety of means
of conflict the British had to pursue. Furthermore, the Italian forces were
very numerous. However, the subsequent passing of Empire, as well as
the extent to which the war is remembered in Britain as a struggle with
Germany, have ensured that this achievement has been largely forgotten.

The same shift in Italian policy, from ambition to action, occurred in the
Balkans. Mussolini's reckless ambition for Balkan gains led Italy to attack
Greece in October 1940. The two powers had had poor relations from the
1910s, over rival territorial interests in the Balkans and the Aegean. Thanks
to the Italian colony of Albania, they also had a common frontier. In turn,
Italian failure in this conflict, failure that resulted in a successful Greek

invasion of southern Albania, ensured that Hitler decided to intervene in Greece. This operation, however, when launched on 6 April 1941, was an attack on both Greece and Yugoslavia, because an unexpected nationalist coup by the military in Yugoslavia on 27 March challenged German influence there.

The British defeat of Italian forces in Libya had already led Hitler, on 11 January 1941, to order the movement of troops to aid in the defence of western Libya, and, the following month, they were named the *Afrika Korps*. These troops were to be directed to conquer Egypt and invade Palestine, in part in order to ensure the slaughter of all the Jews there.[52]

Soviet expansion

A focus on German, Italian and Japanese expansionism in 1939–41 can lead to an underplaying of that of the Soviet Union, which, instead, sought to keep pace with that of Germany, not least to give effect to the division of Eastern Europe agreed in the Nazi–Soviet Pact in August 1939. There is a tendency to underplay this expansion, but for Poland, Finland, the Baltic Republics (Estonia, Latvia, Lithuania) and Romania, it was a brutal process. The Soviets only annexed part of Finland and part of Romania, but in eastern Poland (overrun in 1939) and the Baltic Republics (1940), their control was accompanied by the large-scale deportation of large numbers of those judged potentially hostile. They were sent to the *gulags*, the often-deadly Soviet concentration camps. This deportation was conducted by the cattle-trucks that were to leave a more prominent impression in the shape of their use by Germany to move Jews to the extermination camps.

To the Soviet Union, this expansion was in part a matter of re-creating the pre–1914 Russian Empire, which had included all these areas; rather as the Nationalist government of Chiang Kai-shek sought to do for China in Sinkiang, where (after autonomous government by a warlord, Sheng Shi-ts'ai) Nationalist control was reasserted in 1943. The Nationalists also sought to reassert control in Tibet, the latter a challenge to British support for Tibetan autonomy and thus for a buffer to British India.[53] For those affected by Soviet expansion, the situation was very different: sovereign states whose independence was internationally recognised were forced to surrender independence (the Baltic Republics and, in concert with Germany, Poland), or territory (Finland and Romania).

Germany attacks the Soviet Union

The causes of the war between Germany and the Soviet Union in 1941, the largest-scale land conflict of World War Two, can be firmly found on the

German side. There have been repeated claims that the Germans pre-empted plans for a Soviet attack, a claim initially made by Josef Goebbels, Hitler's Minister of Propaganda, in June 1941. Whatever the nature of long-term Soviet intentions and military expansion, this claim was not an accurate account of the situation in 1941.[54] Instead, Hitler's over-confidence and contempt for other political systems reinforced his belief that Germany had to conquer the Soviet Union in order to fulfil what he alleged was her destiny and to obtain *Lebensraum* (living space).[55] The earlier reversal, from 1933 to 1940, of the Treaty of Versailles, the Paris Peace Settlement of 1919, was secondary to the re-establishment of Germany's victory in the East in 1918, a victory rapidly overthrown as a consequence of Germany's defeat later that year on the Western Front.

Such a war would also permit Hitler to pursue the extermination of the European Jews that he had promised the *Reichstag* on 30 January 1939. To Hitler and his supporters, 'International Jewry' was an active worldwide force, responsible for Germany's plight, and therefore had to be destroyed in order to advance the German cause.[56] Hitler's meta-historical goal of racial superiority, especially over Slavs, and of the slaughter of all Jews, was not an outcome possible without a total victory on the pattern of the pyramids of skulls left by certain medieval Asian conquerors, such as Timur (Tamberlane), when punishing opposition. At the same time, success encouraged Hitler to make his ambitions more central, not least to move from an emphasis on revising Versailles, so as to ensure a Greater Germany, to creating, instead, a new European order, one in which there would be no Jews.[57]

Hitler was convinced that a clash with Communism was inevitable, as well as necessary. Soviet pressure, notably during the Molotov–Ribbentrop discussions in Berlin in November 1940, over the future of the Balkans encouraged this view. Although Britain in 1941 was still undefeated, and Germany deployed considerable forces in France and Norway, Hitler felt that Britain was no longer able to make any effective opposition to German domination of mainland Europe, and therefore that her continued resistance should not deter Germany from attacking the Soviet Union. Indeed, Soviet defeat was seen as likely to weaken Britain and to encourage it to negotiate. Furthermore, Hitler was convinced that the USA would enter the war on Britain's side. Indeed, on 25 August 1941, he told Mussolini that Roosevelt was controlled by a Jewish group. Hitler believed that an attack on the Soviet Union was necessary in order to win rapid victory before such an American intervention.

Hitler's adventurism and conceit were a reflection of his warped personality and also the product of a political-ideological system in which conflict and hatred appeared natural. Moreover, Hitler was confident that the Soviet system would collapse rapidly, and was happy to accept misleading intelligence assessments of the size and mobilisation potential of the Red Army. German optimism was enhanced by the successful conquest of Yugoslavia and Greece in April 1941.

Equally, distrustful of Britain and suspicious of non-existent schemes for an Anglo–German peace, Stalin totally ignored warnings from German opponents of Hitler via Soviet intelligence, as well as from Roosevelt, and from Churchill (derived from Enigma decrypts), about German invasion plans.[58]

German assessments drew on the flaws revealed in the Soviet invasion of eastern Poland in 1939 and, even more, in the initial stages of the Soviet attack on Finland in 1939–40, the 'Winter War', as well as on assumptions based on the effect of Stalin's extensive purges of the military leadership from 1937 to 1941, purges themselves fed by the German provision of forged information.[59] These assessments failed adequately to note the success of the Red Army in the last (successful) stage of the 'Winter War' as well as postwar improvements, while, anyway, there was a major contrast between weaknesses on the offensive and capabilities in defence.[60] Furthermore, Russian military defeat and political collapse in World War One in 1917 encouraged the Germans to feel that victory could again be had. Letters indicate that many German troops were confident that the war would be speedily over. Nevertheless, despite their misjudgment of the Red Army, appreciable casualties were anticipated by the Germans, who deployed as many troops as they could.

There is also the question of the German way of war, and whether a national culture of warmaking, with its emphasis on short wars characterised by offensive operations designed to lead to total victory, encouraged the resort to war and, indeed, helped cause German failure.[61] Academic interest in national cultures of warmaking, and in national strategic cultures, has developed over the last two decades.[62] This interest opens another field for discussion of the politics of the war because the political cultures of individual states were bound up with these distinctive goals and types of warmaking. Most German generals were confident that they had developed a military system able to defeat the Soviet Union.

Germany's allies

Allies of Germany were expected to support the attack on the Soviet Union, launched on 22 June, and indeed did so, although for their own reasons. The Finns were determined to regain the territories they had lost to the Soviet Union in 1940, and saw what they termed 'the Continuation War', of 1941–4, as a second stage of, and response to, the Soviet attack in the 'Winter War' of 1939–40. The same goal of recovering territory was sought by Romania, which aimed to regain Bessarabia and Northern Bukovina from the Soviet Union. Thus, Romania wished to reverse the consequences of the Nazi–Soviet Pact. In order to help overcome Communism, and under pressure from Germany, Hungary declared war on the Soviet Union.

Hungary's government had an explicitly Christian nationalist ideology[63] and was, by the early 1940s, moving the country towards becoming a racial state.[64] Moreover, in 1938–41, Hungary had benefited greatly territorially from alliance with Hitler at the expense of Czechoslovakia, Romania and Yugoslavia, recovering losses under the Treaty of Trianon of 1920.

Yet, as is inevitably the case, these explanations are far too brief. To take Romania, there was a complex interplay between King Carol II, the Fascist Iron Guard, liberal politicians, and General Ion Antonescu, the Minister of War, an authoritarian nationalist seen as above politics – with the Germans also playing a major role. Carol called in Antonescu as Prime Minister in 1940 as a way to contain the Iron Guard, and Antonescu, a nationalist who did not want to be a client of Germany, nevertheless turned to Hitler as he was convinced that Germany was going to win the war, which indeed seemed a reasonable conclusion in September 1940. In turn, although the SS backed the Iron Guard, the German government, influenced by its army and the Foreign Ministry, supported Antonescu because they saw him as a reliable ally and a source of stability, neither of which was true of the Iron Guard. In light of the forthcoming war with the Soviet Union, reliability was more desirable than the ideological affinity offered by the Iron Guard. At the same time, Antonescu and his government were to be murderously anti-Semitic.[65]

Underlining the interaction of domestic politics with foreign policy, Antonescu bullied the unreliable Carol into abdicating in favour of his son, Michael, on 6 September 1940. The following January, Antonescu saw Hitler, telling him that he was ready to support Germany in defence of Eastern Europe against a possible Soviet attack, and, eight days later, Antonescu was able to crush the Iron Guard without German intervention on behalf of the latter. In June 1941, Romania joined in the attack on the Soviet Union, declaring a 'holy war' to free Bessarabia. Antonescu saw Germany and the Soviet Union as the only alternatives.[66] This was an analysis that France's defeat and British weakness encouraged many to share.

War in the Pacific

The outbreak of the Pacific War in December 1941 is harder to study because, in part due to the nature of the surviving sources, Japanese policy-making has proved more opaque than that of Germany: it is less easy to see the precise role of individuals in discussions. Nevertheless, the general situation is clear. Alongside an expansionism based on the self-confident assumptions of the Japanese ruling élite, resource issues, particularly access to oil, were important precipitants to the decision for war.[67] These issues played a key role in clashing geopolitical priorities focused on South-East

Asia. The collapse of France and the Netherlands to German attack in 1940, and the weakening position of Britain, already vulnerable in the Far East (of which the Japanese were well-informed), created an apparent power vacuum in East and South-East Asia. This vacuum encouraged Japanese ambitions southwards into French Indo-China (Cambodia, Laos and Vietnam), British South-East Asia (Malaya, Singapore, north Borneo, Burma), and the Dutch East Indies, while leading the Americans to feel that only they were in a position to resist Japan.

Chiang Kai-shek, the Chinese leader, had argued in his diary on 2 September 1939 that it was crucial to link the Sino–Japanese War with the Allied cause in Europe.[68] Although this did not happen in the way he predicted, Chiang was correct in feeling that to move beyond checking Japan it was necessary for China to benefit from developments in the international system.

Furthermore, the unresolved character of the war between Japan and China, which entered a state of attritional stalemate in 1939,[69] not only embittered Japanese relations with America, which provided some support for China, but also exacerbated resource issues in Japanese military planning, as well as placing a major burden on Japanese finances. Thirty-four divisions were bogged down by 1939; by that September, Japan had lost 500,000 troops killed or badly wounded in China. Japan had had to settle on a policy of consolidating the territory it controlled in China and launching punitive expeditions into the remainder of China. Japanese economic weakness was such that her trade deficit was condemning her to the prospect of national bankruptcy in the spring of 1942. This was a repetition of the serious fiscal and economic strain that had confronted Japan during the militarily-successful and far shorter Russo–Japanese War of 1904–5, but it had proved possible to end that conflict more speedily.[70]

Germany's victory over France in 1940 encouraged Japan to revive relations with Germany that had been dimmed when Hitler concluded his non-aggression pact with Stalin the previous year: Japan was opposed to the Soviet Union for ideological and geopolitical reasons and had sent a large force into the Soviet Far East during the Russian Civil War as well as briefly fighting the Soviet Union in Mongolia and Manchuria in 1938–9. On 27 September 1940, in response to pressure from the military, Japan joined Germany and Italy in the Tripartite Pact. The Japanese government and military, although divided, were determined to expand at the expense of others, particularly, from 1940, into South-East Asia, which was, to Japan, the 'Southern Resources Area', a region rich in raw materials, notably oil, tin and rubber. From June 1940, the Japanese navy had begun full mobilisation, although the German failure to invade Britain in the autumn of 1940, as planned, discouraged ideas of a Japanese attack on Britain's colonies that year.

Continued Japanese aggression against China and, more particularly, expansion into southern French Indo-China in July 1941 helped to trigger

American commercial sanctions, specifically an embargo on oil exports to Japan. This was tantamount to an ultimatum because, without oil, the operations of the Japanese armed forces, notably the navy, would grind to a halt. The ultimatum provoked the Japanese to act against the USA, in order to protect their position and potential, because they were unwilling to accept limitations to their expansion in the Far East. In 1941, the Japanese increasingly focused on the raw materials to be gained from South-East Asia and the East Indies. They also planned to seize British-ruled Burma (Myanmar) in order to block Western supplies to China, a goal that had already led them to occupy the northern part of French Indo-China in September 1940. The Dutch East Indies (modern Indonesia) posed a problem for Japan as, despite the German conquest of the Netherlands in May 1940, the Dutch colonial officials rejected Japanese efforts to acquire oil, and, instead, sought to align policy with Britain and the USA.

Supplies for Japan and China had become far more of an issue with the development of American policy. The Americans considered themselves entitled to react forcefully to events on the other side of the Pacific, and also felt threatened by the Fall of France in 1940 and by the possibility that Britain would follow, thus completely exposing the Atlantic to German action and the USA to attack by a worldwide coalition.[71] These anxieties encouraged Congress to support a rearmament made necessary by the weak state of the American military, and also led Roosevelt, in part in order to demonstrate bipartisanship, to appoint Henry Stimson as Secretary of War on 19 June 1940. Stimson, a prominent Republican who had served as Secretary of War under Taft (1911–13) and Secretary of State under Hoover (1929–33), argued that American security required the maintenance of British power. The Neutrality Act was repealed, military equipment was sold to the British, and steps were also taken to confront Japan.

At the same time, there were strong divisions in public opinion and public politics. The isolationist America First Committee was formed in September 1940 to oppose intervention against Germany. The Committee to defend America by Aiding the Allies and, later, the Fight for Freedom Committee took a very different stance.[72]

The Two-Ocean Naval Expansion Act was passed on 19 July 1940 when Britain appeared defeated by Germany and certainly could no longer rely on the French navy. This Act, increasing the authorised total tonnage of American warships by 70 per cent and providing for a cost of $4 billion, served notice on the Japanese that the Americans were going to be in a position to dominate the Pacific. This fleet would enable the Americans to wage naval war against both Germany and Japan, a necessity that seemed increasingly apparent.

This build-up had an impact on Japan comparable to pre-1914 German fears of Russian military developments: the vista appeared threatening, but, in the short term, a window of opportunity seemed to be present. In turn, although it did not want war with Japan, the American government was resolved to prevent Japanese expansion, yet unable to make an accurate assessment of Japanese military capability. The latter issue was linked to an American exaggeration of the effectiveness of their air power.[73]

French Indo-China came to play a crucial part in the crisis. America registered responses to what she saw as aggressive Japanese steps there. After the fall of France, Japan ordered the closure of the border between China and Indo-China, in order to prevent the movement of supplies to China. Indo-China was also of strategic importance as an axis of Japanese advance to the 'Southern Resources Area'. From airbases in Vietnam, it was possible to threaten Thailand and the British colony of Malaya. The declaration, on 24 July 1941, of a joint Franco–Japanese Protectorate over all French Indo-China led to an American trade embargo and the freezing of Japanese assets in America. Under the Hull Note of 26 November, a memorandum presented by Cordell Hull, the Secretary of State, the Americans demanded that the Japanese withdraw from China and Indo-China. Longstanding Japanese fears of encirclement now focused on anxiety about the so-called ABCD group: America, Britain, China and the Dutch.

Within Japan, there were attempts to explore the idea of better relations with Britain and the USA, but these required an ability to restrain the military that did not correspond to the dynamics of Japanese politics. These explorations, already seen in 1939–40, were pursued in late 1941 in order to ascertain if the USA could be persuaded to lessen its support for China. Britain and China were anxious about this point, but, in November 1941, Roosevelt agreed that the USA could not sacrifice China in order to maintain relations with Japan. Thus, a Japanese recognition of Chinese independence became a key American objective, continuing a pattern of international restraint on Japanese expansion there seen episodically from the 1890s.

After staging war games in August 1941, the Japanese decided to launch a war if diplomacy failed to lead to a lifting of the trade embargo. On 17 October 1941, a hard-line ministry under General Hideki Tōjō gained power. At the same time, as a reminder that it is necessary to appreciate the divisions and strains within states and their governments, Tōjō rose to power against the background of longstanding tension within the army, notably between the Control and Imperial Way factions, as well as within the government. There were disagreements over policy, especially whether there should be compromise with the Chinese Nationalists, an option opposed by Tōjō; and also over the Neutrality Pact signed with the Soviet Union on 13 April 1941 so as to enable Japan to focus on war with Britain and the USA. This pact reflected Hitler's assurances to Japan that he would invade Britain in 1941. This apparently provided Japan with an opportunity to take over British colonies. The alignment of Germany–the Soviet Union–Japan apparently provided the necessary opportunity. This helped explain Japanese anger when Hitler attacked the Soviet Union in June 1941.

In late 1941, pressure from Admiral Yamamoto Isoroku, the Commander of the Japanese Combined Fleet, for an attack on the American naval base at Pearl Harbor in Hawaii (using the same military technique of the 'knock-out' blow as had been seen with Germany), as a prelude for covering Japanese invasions of Malaya, the Philippines and the Dutch East Indies was successful. This plan won the day on 3 November 1941.[74] The devastating (but also unfinished) surprise attack on Pearl Harbor on 7 December, 'a date which will live in infamy' according to Roosevelt next day, was to play a key role in American public memory.[75]

The Japanese suffered from the lack of a realistic war plan, a lack already apparent in the case of Japan's attack on China. As with Hitler in the case of both Britain and the Soviet Union, a misleading conviction of the internal weakness of the opposing systems led the Japanese to a failure to judge resolve accurately. In particular, there was a certainty that Britain and the USA lacked the willpower of Japan and Germany. The British and Americans were believed to be weakened by democracy and consumerism, an extrapolation of authoritarian views within Japanese politics onto other states. In the event, the initial Japanese ability to mount successful attacks, to gain great swathes of territory, and to establish an apparent stranglehold on the Far East and the Western Pacific behind a defensive perimeter, did not deter the Americans from the long-term effort of driving back, and destroying, Japanese power.

Germany and the USA

Hitler followed the unexpected blow at Pearl Harbor by declaring war on the USA on 11 December 1941, as (ludicrously, but necessarily as an ally) did Mussolini. Hitler claimed that this declaration was in accordance with German obligations under the Tripartite Treaty with Italy and Japan signed on 27 September 1940. However, strictly, the terms of the treaty did not require such a co-operation, and Japan did not declare war on the Soviet Union. Angered by American co-operation with the British against German submarine (U-boat) operations in the Atlantic, operations that had already brought the war to the seas off North America, Hitler claimed that his decision was in response to American 'provocations' in the Atlantic. Like Goebbels, Hitler also saw the USA as part of a global Jewish conspiracy directed against Germany, and Roosevelt as the key instrument of this conspiracy. Already, on 21 December 1940, Germany had claimed that American assistance to Britain constituted 'moral aggression'.

In practice, there was no real appreciation in Germany of the impact of American entry and no sign of any informed analysis of the likely trajectory of war between Japan and the USA, nor of the consequences for Germany of war with America. This was an aspect of the more general failure of

German Intelligence, and notably Hitler's unwillingness to consider the views and capabilities of his opponents other than in terms of his own ideological suppositions.

As in 1917, when the USA declared war in large part because of the attack on its neutral rights represented by German submarine warfare,[76] there was a mistaken confidence in Germany that the U-boats would weaken the USA, providing Germany with a weapon that could operate to strategic effect. This was a belief necessary to Hitler's attempt to regain the initiative by a bold step. In reality, the U-boats only provided an operational capability. In addition, this capability was gradually to be eroded by improved Allied anti-submarine warfare tactics and by the vast capacity provided by American shipbuilding and, in particular, by the development of the latter thanks to large-scale investment, the availability of raw materials, and labour flexibility. By the end of the third quarter of 1943, the Allies had built more ships than had been sunk since the start of the war.

Hitler, moreover, regarded the USA as weakened by deracination resulting from interbreeding, by consumerism and by democracy, and as lacking in martial spirit. He felt that Japan and the U-boats would keep the USA busy until after Germany had successfully settled the war with the Soviet Union. In January 1942, Hitler told Lieutenant-General Hiroshi Oshima, the Japanese ambassador, that he did not know how he would defeat the USA, but such lucid moments were overtaken by rambling fantasies.[77]

As a result of Hitler's declaration of war, the struggle was now truly global. The USA, in response, declared war on Germany on 11 December, and its influence was such that most of the world's remaining neutrals followed suit. Cuba, the Dominican Republic, Guatemala, Nicaragua and Haiti also declared war that day. Honduras and El Salvador followed the next day, and Panama, Mexico and Brazil in 1942. The declaration by Brazil, on 22 August, was influenced by German attacks on Brazilian shipping as well as by American pressure and the Brazilian determination to exploit America's need for support.[78]

These entries marked a major blow to German diplomatic and espionage attempts to build up support in Latin America. In part, these attempts reflected the desire to exploit opportunities, not least those presented by local German populations and by authoritarian governments, such as the Peron dictatorship in Argentina. In part, the attempts were a product of the global aspirations of key elements in the German government. As in the case of Mexico in World War One, there was also a desire to weaken the USA by causing problems in its backyard. Thus, there was a strategic intention underlying Germany's Latin American policy. This policy had many flaws, not least encouraging American hostility, and a central problem with implementation: the inability of Germany to give teeth to its hopes. This inability reflected British naval strength as well as the German focus on operations in Europe. Yet, despite the flaws of Germany's Latin American policy, there was a potential for causing trouble.

This potential was one of the victims of Hitler's decision to declare war on the USA. Instead, the Rio Conference in January 1942 saw the creation of the Inter-American Defense Board which was designed to coordinate military matters throughout the Western hemisphere. In effect, the USA assumed responsibility for the protection of the region. It, not Germany, benefited from Britain's declining role. As a symptom of this declining role, in 1942, an Argentine navy transport raised the Argentine flag in the South Shetland island group contested with Britain and left a bronze plaque to record the occasion.[79]

America's success in Latin America, nevertheless, had limitations, which, in part, reflected the appeal of the German authoritarian model. Indeed, many Latin American states delayed entry into the war: Bolivia and Colombia until 1943, and Ecuador, Paraguay, Peru, Venezuela, Chile and Argentina (in which there was much sympathy for Germany) until 1945. Although, once they joined the war, none of the Latin American states played a major, let alone crucial, role in the conflict, their experience as combatants and neutrals reflected the global impact and nature of the struggle, at once military, political, ideological and economic.

The state that played the leading military role was Brazil which sent 25,000 troops to fight in the Italy campaign. As a result, Brazil was to be angered by postwar American sales of warships to its regional rival, Argentina, and refused to send troops to take part in the Korean War (1950–3). North-East Brazil also played a staging role in the 1942 Operation Torch, an American amphibious attack on French-held North Africa. Mexico sent units to the Philippines in 1944.[80] Other late entrants into the war, all on the Allied side, were Liberia in 1944, and Saudi Arabia, Egypt and Turkey in 1945.

Moreover, the alliance between Britain, the USA and the Soviet Union led these three powers to declare war on those who were already at war with their allies. Thus, Britain and the USA went to war with Hitler's allies that had attacked the Soviet Union, while the latter went to war with Japan on 8 August 1945, two days after the first atom bomb was dropped on Hiroshima.

Neutrals

Some states, however, remained neutral throughout, notably Afghanistan, Eire (Ireland), Portugal, Spain, Sweden and Switzerland.[81] Some of these states, moreover, provided important support to Germany, that from Spain including not only raw materials but also the volunteer 'Blue Division' which fought on the Eastern Front.[82] Sweden and Switzerland provided important economic and financial assistance to Germany.[83]

During what was termed there the Emergency, the refusal of Eire (Ireland) to permit Britain the use of its ports increased the damage to trans-Atlantic trade from German submarine attack. Concern about the naval situation led to British planning for the invasion of Eire in order to ensure the use of the treaty ports – Cobh, Castletown Bere and Lough Swilly – that the British had retained the right to utilise when Eire gained independence in 1922, but which they had handed over in 1938. These ports could have helped British convoying, as had been the case in World War One. Eire's neutrality, the sole neutrality by a member of the Commonwealth, however, was a powerful affirmation of independence from Britain. Despite vitriolic press criticism in Britain and Churchill's anger over the ports, it was deemed prudent by the British government not to occupy Eire.

The contrast with German, Soviet and Japanese policy towards neutrals (in the case of Japan, towards Thailand and both Vichy and Portuguese colonies) was readily apparent. However, outside Europe, Britain took a firmer stance. This was shown in the case of both Iraq and Iran, each of which was successfully invaded in 1941 in order to overthrow pro-German governments.

The anti-British IRA was repressed by the Irish government, while many Irish citizens volunteered to fight in the British forces, a key instance of the transnationalism to which, alongside more intense nationalism, the war gave rise.[84] However, the policy of the Irish government reflected a moral bankruptcy not least in treating the combatants and their political systems as equally valid. When, in accordance with this rubric, Éamon de Valera, the Taoiseach (Prime Minister), called at the German Legation in Dublin on 2 May 1945 to offer condolences on the death of Hitler, Sir John Maffey, the British High Commissioner, called it 'an act of conspicuous neutrality in the field'. In addition, at least a few prominent Irish nationalists saw British defeat as a means to pursue Irish unity and, as a consequence, were willing to consider helping Germany.[85]

The neutrality of Portugal and Spain included their colonies, which were mostly in Africa. Portugal also had colonies in Asia, and Japan occupied those of Macao and East Timor. In 1943, in response to the war moving in the direction of the Allies, Portugal permitted the Allies to establish air bases on Terceira and Santa Maria in the Azores. Opened that October, these bases provided a crucial capability in closing the mid-Atlantic 'air gap' in Allied air cover against U-boats, notably what the Germans termed the 'Black Pit' west of the Azores. More generally, the key role of air power in operations against U-boats meant that the acquisition of air bases was an important aspect of the international politics of the war, as with America's ability to develop bases in north-eastern Brazil.

The politics of the neutral states were an important aspect of those of the war, and one that tends to be underplayed, if not neglected. Many states had their neutrality infringed or ended by intimidation or conquest by major powers, as happened to the Baltic Republics, Denmark and Norway in 1940. Whether or not their neutrality lasted, the neutrals are interesting in themselves, and also throw much light on the goals and fortunes of the combatants. In a broadcast on 9 February 1941, Churchill declared 'One of our difficulties is to convince some of these neutral countries in Europe that we are going to win'. The previous month, in a speech on 17 January, he had defined the aim of 'Hitlerism' as 'little less than the subjugation of Europe and little more than the gratification of gangster appetites', both of which posed a serious threat to neutrals.

The nature of the pressure brought to bear on neutrals for support by both sides, and how the goals of the combatants changed in this regard, are instructive. Neutrals registered the changing politics of the war. Thus, Afghanistan maintained its links with Germany despite British opposition: if British India was a neighbour to Afghanistan so also was Germany's Soviet ally. However, Afghanistan ended these links under pressure after Germany attacked the Soviet Union in 1941. In June 1944, determined Allied pressure, notably from Brazil, led to Portugal stopping its important supply of tungsten, used for alloying steel, to Germany. The Vatican City was an instance of a very different type of neutral, and one whose wartime role has been, and continues to be, highly contentious.[86]

The neutrals provided channels for real or attempted communication between the combatants. Thus, in 1944, the British asked the Swiss diplomat Alfred Escher to negotiate the surrender of Athens with the Germans, so as to ensure that it was kept out of Communist hands; while, in 1945, Japan made limited approaches to the USA via Switzerland.[87]

The politics of the war were closely registered by, and in, the neutrals. Their subsequent very varied accounts of the war serve as a reminder of its complexity. The circumstances of the war interacted with those of postwar politics.[88]

CHAPTER TWO

Alliance Politics and Grand Strategy

In relaxed poses, Churchill and Roosevelt amiably share a bench on New Bond Street in London, or at least they have done so since the sculpture *Allies* was displayed there from 1995. Commissioned to commemorate 50 years of peace, and largely paid for by the luxury businesses on the street which serve many foreign tourists, prominently Americans, the sculpture testifies to the desire to propagate a memory of wartime co-operation. This co-operation is a memory much used by those who emphasise the value of alliance between the two powers, and, in doing so, see this wartime alliance as an important lesson for modern Britain, and, indeed, the USA.[1]

The reality was of a far more troubled relationship.[2] Indeed, Roosevelt, who could be very harsh to Churchill, notably at the Teheran conference of Allied warleaders in December 1943, carefully avoided visiting London during the war. Nevertheless, the many problems of alliance politics were a subject kept well from the eyes of contemporaries. Instead, these politics were particularly prone to propaganda designed to make alliances appear natural and strong. This was especially so of Anglo–American propaganda about the Soviet Union during 1941–5, and of German propaganda about the value of alliance with Mussolini, an implausible claim at the best of times.

Axis alliance politics

Most of the scholarly work on alliance politics has been on the Allied side, in part because these politics proved less prominent and important for the Axis, which failed as an alliance. This failure was a matter both of planning and of execution. Hitler's inability to direct his allies led to serious problems for him, most especially with their attacks on other powers, that of Italy on

Britain and Greece in 1940, and of Japan on the USA in 1941. Moreover, as a result of the total failure of Italy's attack on Greece, Hitler's timetable for launching an attack on the Soviet Union in 1941 was overtaken and the attack postponed to late June. In this, and as a result, the gap between his determination to impose his will on events and the pressures of reality became ever stronger.

The implementation of the Axis as a military alliance was also a serious problem. Germany and Japan were unable to create a military partnership, nor to provide mutual economic assistance that in any way matched that of the Allies, seriously strained as relations among the latter were. Hitler seems to have underestimated Japan's potential as an ally, probably because he was both focused on Europe and a racist. German plans for war with the USA made little of the remote prospect of Japanese assistance and preferred to centre on the possibility of using German naval power alone, and, to that end, on Atlantic naval staging bases, such as the Canary Islands. Subsequently, when that possibility ceased to be even remotely plausible, the Germans, as part of their development of advanced weaponry such as jet fighters, rockets and new-type submarines, considered the prospect of further advances, notably with long-range bombers, multi-stage rockets, space bombers, and submarine-launched missiles. These schemes included plans for attacks on New York City and Washington.[3]

Germany and Japan fought what were in essence two separate wars, and there was little in the way of coordination or co-operation between them, and still less between Italy and Japan. In Somalia, Italy had a colony on the Indian Ocean, with a port at Mogadishu, while destroyers were based in the Italian Red Sea port of Massawa (in Eritrea). However, both were conquered by the British (on 25 February and 8 April 1941 respectively) before there was any prospect of co-operation. Moreover, the large, and modern, Italian navy was essentially deployed in the Mediterranean, although Italian submarines took part in the Battle of the Atlantic from 1941.

The highpoint of German–Japanese coordination was Germany's decision to declare war on the USA after Pearl Harbor, an attack Hitler had sought to encourage by pressing forward military operations against Moscow. He had done so in part because he was concerned about the possible outcome of the negotiations between Japan and the USA in late 1941. This declaration of war, however, did not lead to any concerted attempt at grand strategy, not least because, despite German pressure early in the war, Japan had chosen not to attack the Soviet Union and, instead, maintained the neutrality agreement.

The only sphere in which an attempt at Axis grand strategy might have been possible was the Indian Ocean, with German pressure on the Middle East interacting with Japanese advances on India and in the Indian Ocean. British policymakers indeed feared pressure on South Asia, with, for example, the Germans possibly advancing through Turkey, prior to the launching of Operation Barbarossa in June 1941, and/or, subsequently, through the Caucasus. These concerns were a second tranche of earlier fears about the Germans exploiting support in Iraq and (Vichy) Syria. They had indeed sought to do so, although the British, who invaded Iraq in May 1941, underrated the extent to which nationalism, rather than support for the Axis, was the key element in Iraqi politics and policy.[4]

A German advance into the Middle East did not materialise. The Germans did not attack Turkey and, had they done so, they would have found the Turkish army capable of mounting a formidable resistance. Moreover, any advance through Turkey would have encountered serious logistical and transport limitations and problems. Pressuring Turkey into granting transit rights would have been a different question, but the situation would have had to be more dire for such pressure to succeed.

In the event, the planned German advance to the Caspian Sea oilfields near Baku in late 1942 was thwarted by Soviet resistance and by Hitler's focus on the capture of Stalingrad. By then, anyway, the British and Soviets had occupied Iran, overthrowing the Shah whom they suspected of Axis sympathies. As a consequence, British India was provided with defence in depth in the event of German success in the Caucasus and/or the Middle East. The occupation of Iran in August 1941 thus supplemented the earlier British conquest of Iraq, as well as providing control over strategic oilfields.

With their conquest of Malaya, Singapore, Sumatra and Burma in early 1942, and notably of the naval bases of Singapore (February) and Rangoon (March), the Japanese were well placed to advance into the Indian Ocean region, and far better so than the Germans. However, the Japanese naval raid into the ocean in early April 1942 with five carriers was not the prelude to further action; although the Japanese then inflicted serious losses on the British, including a carrier (the *Hermes*) and two heavy cruisers (the *Cornwall* and the *Dorsetshire*), and obliged the outmatched Eastern Fleet to retreat to East African waters.

Instead of persisting, so as to attack further British targets, the Japanese fleet launched the Pacific operations that led first to the Battle of the Coral Sea (7–8 May) and, subsequently, to disaster at the hands of the Americans at Midway. The loss of Japanese offensive capability as a consequence of the sinking of four of their carriers and the destruction of many planes (the two comprising much of their fleet strike force) at Midway on 4 June 1942 made thoughts of joint action with the Germans, or of further Japanese advances in the Indian or Pacific oceans, implausible. This development was significant because the major role that Japan played in the war was an important aspect of the war's novelty. As a result, Allied planners were obliged to confront challenges on a far greater scale than in World War One. However, there was no repetition of the threat mounted in April 1942 to the strategic resource and depth presented by British control of the Indian Ocean.

The sense of concern then was clear; General Sir Alan Brooke, the phlegmatic Chief of the Imperial General Staff, noted in his diary for 6 April
1942:

> On reaching COS [Chiefs of Staff] I discovered that most of the Japanese
> fleet appeared to be in the Indian Ocean and our Eastern fleet retiring
> westwards. Up to present no signs of [invasion] transports. I don't like
> the situation much as we are very weak in the Indian Ocean. I have been
> trying to get First Sea Lord to fix up with the Americans some counter
> move towards Japan to cover this very predicament that we are in, but
> he has failed to do so up to present.

Brooke was even gloomier next day:

> COS at which we looked into the unpleasant situation created by
> entrance of Japanese fleet into Indian Ocean ... I suppose this Empire has
> never been in such a precarious position throughout its history.

On 10 April 1942, Brooke added, 'usual COS meeting, mainly concerned
in trying to save India from the Japs. A gloomy prospect with loss of
command of sea and air'.[5]

As a result of the threat of a renewed Japanese incursion into this
vulnerable region, American victory at Midway can be understood as a
crucial element in the broader geopolitics of the war, and as a vital contribution to coalition politics and warfare. It was a part with the movement
of American aircraft to northern Australia from 17 March 1942. This
deployment countered the vulnerability revealed by the Japanese bombing
of Darwin, the capital of the Northern Territory, as well as the threat of a
Japanese invasion of Australia. Moreover, the checking of a Japanese fleet
at the Battle of the Coral Sea (7–8 May) also helped strengthen the defence
of Australia by blocking Japanese plans to attack Port Moresby, the port
on the coast of New Guinea opposite to Australia.

Thanks to Midway and the American–Japanese War in the Pacific,
on which the Japanese navy concentrated until the end of the war, the
British thereafter were able to deploy only limited naval strength against
Japan until the closing year of the war when British naval strength
was transferred to Pacific waters after D-Day. Whereas the British had
had two carriers to cover the attack on Diego Suarez, the main port in
Madagascar, in May 1942, from January 1943 there were none in the
Indian Ocean until October, when an escort carrier arrived. No British
warship was lost in the Indian Ocean in 1943 and the Royal Navy
focused on the Mediterranean and the Atlantic, with significant consequences in both.

The British had feared that the Vichy-governed French Indian Ocean
island of Madagascar might become a Japanese submarine base and, in

March 1942, signals intercepts indicated that Germany was urging Japan to occupy the island. These fears were ended by the British conquest of the island between May and November 1942. Although German and Italian submarines did link up in that ocean with the Japanese, they did not mount any large-scale concerted operations.[6]

The trade-off was not simply between the war in the Pacific and that in the Indian Ocean. Thanks to Japan's major commitment to China, and the Chinese refusal to stop fighting, Japan had more limited resources to deploy elsewhere,[7] whether against the Western Allies or the Soviet Union. At the same time, this approach to the war assumes a more ready transference of resources than is generally the case.

Axis alliance politics focused not on Japan and Germany, but on bilateral relations between Germany and its European allies. Hitler sought to treat them as clients, with peremptory demands for troops and other resources, the attempted imposition of anti-Semitic policies, and assumptions that their territory could be used for operations, and be reallocated to suit German diplomatic goals. Thus, in 1940, Transylvania was transferred from Romania to Hungary (of which it had been part until the Treaty of Trianon of 1920, part of the Versailles Peace Settlement), and the southern Dobrudja, also long a region in contention, was transferred from Romania to Bulgaria. Among Germany's allies, however, there were serious tensions exacerbated by such territorial changes, as well as hostility or opposition to German requirements.[8]

This situation, for example, led Finland to resist German direction of its war against the Soviet Union from 1941 to 1944 and, finally, to switch sides and attack the Germans.[9] The Finns were more effective militarily against the Soviets than Germany's other European allies, but the Finns also refused a full-scale commitment against partly-besieged Leningrad, despite repeated requests from the Germans. This issue represents one of the many 'what ifs?' of the war, as such an advance might well have cut the supply route across Lake Ladoga and brought the siege to an end, enabling the Germans to concentrate their forces further south. The distant Finns were helped by their separate sphere of military operations, as well as by their control of raw materials, which made it possible to bargain with Germany from a position of some strength. Despite pressure from Himmler, the Finns were also able to ignore German pressure to hand over Jews: only eight foreign Jews were handed over.[10]

Tensions in the German alliance system would have existed anyway, but they were not eased by the character or content of German alliance politics. Instead, Germany's allies were kept in the dark, there were no summits equivalent to those of the Allies, Intelligence was not shared, and there was a general failure to sustain co-operation.[11] This failure was a part of a more general one in Hitler's concept of Germany and Europe, namely his preference for a racial chimera over an acknowledgement of the legitimate political aspirations of others.[12]

Tensions between German allies, as well as their particular goals, looked back to prewar issues. These issues were exploited by the Germans, but could also restrict their options. For example, the *Ustasha* regime in Croatia was a product of prewar tensions within Yugoslavia, notably Croat opposition to its highly-centralised, Serb-dominated, government and constitution. Five Croat deputies were assassinated in the legislature in 1928 and, the following year, King Alexander I suspended the constitution, while Croat nationalists formed the *Ustasha* (Insurgent) organisation which launched a terrorist campaign for independence. In 1932, Alexander introduced a constitution considerably lessening democratic options, and the main Croatian party denounced this constitution in the Zagreb Manifesto. Yet, in 1939, in a new constitutional settlement, an autonomous Croatia was created within Yugoslavia.

This agreement was overthrown in 1941. The German invasion provided an opportunity for the creation of a separate Croat state, ostensibly ruled by an Italian prince, but in practice run by a *Ustasha* government determined to ensure ethnic homogeneity and willing, to that end, to slaughter Jews and Serbs. These policies, however, made it harder for the Germans to win support and to lessen backing for the Yugoslav Resistance.

There were serious problems within the German alliance system. Most particularly, the degree to which Italian resources were mobilised was insufficient to maintain the Italian empire, let alone to support Mussolini's expansionist ambitions against Greece, Egypt and the vulnerable British colonies bordering Italian East Africa: Sudan, British Somaliland and Kenya. Conscription was readily evaded in Italy, rationing was limited, and the economy, which was anyway weak in key industrial sectors, was not militarised. Mussolini, however, rejected German dominance of the Axis until after Italy was defeated in Greece and North and East Africa. These defeats helped ensure that Italy thus became a drain on the German military, notably as a result of Allied advances in the Mediterranean from late 1942. This situation coloured Mussolini's view on the strategic situation in 1943: he urged Hitler to negotiate with Stalin and to concentrate on defending Western Europe, a policy designed to protect his own position.

There have been suggestions that the Germans under-valued their Italian allies militarily and that the latter fought well in some areas, including the Soviet Union in 1941–2.[13] Nevertheless, the Italians failed to make a successful effort commensurate with their resources. This failure was readily apparent with the substantial Italian fleet in the Mediterranean, which was unable to inflict serious damage on its British counterpart, nor to threaten the British position in the eastern Mediterranean. On 28 March 1941, off Cape Matapan, in Britain's last major high-seas fleet battle, the British navy sank three Italian cruisers and damaged a battleship, thanks to the use of torpedo aircraft, battleship firepower and ships' radar.[14]

There were also major problems in coordination between the Italians and Germans. These problems were seen across the range of operations, for example in the failure to coordinate attempts to block Allied relief to the besieged British garrison in Tobruk in Libya in 1941, although this failure was as much a matter of poor co-operation between the Italian navy and air force.[15]

Such limited co-operation was not only true of the Italians, for the German air force and navy had very poor relations, which greatly affected the assault on British maritime trade routes. In contrast, good co-operation between the German air force and army was important to the tactical and operational success of *Blitzkrieg*. There were also serious problems on the Allied side, for example air–land coordination in France in 1940.

Although their potential was less than that of Italy, military, political and economic support from Bulgaria, Croatia, Hungary, Romania and Slovakia also proved to be of limited value to Germany. This support largely evaporated when the war went badly and the assistance might therefore have proved most valuable. Prior to 1944–5, the Germans had already found their allies' support frequently conditional. By 1943, the Hungarian government was seriously considering how best to switch to the Allies. The military consequences of this lack of support were clear, even in the defence of the Hungarian homeland. Thus, in the defence of the capital, Budapest, against Soviet attack in 1944–5, German morale, in this closing stage of the war, was high, in part due to conviction in an existential struggle for survival against Soviet Communism, while Hungarian morale was low.[16]

Elsewhere, outside their alliance system, Germany was able to benefit from military success in 1939–41 by securing a measure of collaboration and, more widespread, passivity[17] and, in doing so, to draw on widespread anti-Communist and anti-Russian sympathies. The Germans also drew on opposition to the Allies in the Arab world, for example by the anti-Semitic Mufti of Jerusalem, Hadj Amin el-Husseini, in a continuation of the prewar Arab Rising in Palestine against British rule. However, the Germans failed to exploit these opportunities, in part due to the flow of the conflict and in part, in Europe, due to the brutality and racism of the German military and occupation. The Japanese were equally culpable.

These were failures in goals as well as in means, and the failures in realistic goals were integral to the Axis war effort. The key Japanese goal – a number of client regimes in a divided China – was advanced without any real sense of how it was to be achieved, maintained and made effective.[18] As so often with war, there was a mismatch between goal and process as well as between ends and means. More generally, despite talk of a Co-Prosperity Sphere in Asia, Japan did nothing that would consolidate support in captured territory. Nor did she even make the most of the raw materials that could be extracted. In part, this failure was due to Allied submarine attacks, notably on shipping from Singapore to Japan, which, in disrupting the articulation of the Japanese system, had an impact comparable to that of the Allied air assault on Germany. There were also serious weaknesses in the Japanese war economy.

In the case of Germany, it proved impossible, and unsurprisingly so given Hitler's attitudes and policies, to ground the new empire in popular support from the conquered peoples, to persuade Britain to end resistance, to win much effective backing in conquered areas for Germany's conflict with Britain and the Soviet Union, or to define the basis for a settlement with the Soviet Union. This multiple failure was more important than the tactical and operational successes best summarised as *Blitzkrieg* because this failure helped to ensure a weakness in the German position. This weakness could be exploited from 1942 by the superior resources and, eventually, much improved fighting effectiveness of Germany's opponents.

If these points demonstrated the primacy of politics, then it could also be seen in more specific matters. Thus, the determination to focus on the capture of the Soviet city of Stalingrad (now Volgograd) in late 1942, in large part rested on its significance for Hitler. He had assumed supreme command of the *Wehrmacht* on 19 December 1941 in response to the initial successes of the Soviet counter-offensive launched that month. Stalingrad's significance was political, as a symbol of triumph over an alleged icon of Communism, as much as military, in so far as the two could be separated. Hitler hoped that Stalin would commit his forces to hold the city. However, Hitler's obsession with Stalingrad squandered German advantages in mobile warfare and the pursuit of the open flank, and, more particularly, the advantages of Soviet vulnerability in the Caucasus region.

Hitler's plans in the early years of the war focused on German efforts but included an expansion of the German alliance system, an expansion believed necessary in order to facilitate war with Britain, conflict with the Soviet Union, and confrontation with the USA. In 1940, Hitler was interested in the idea of a league of Germany, Italy, Spain (then a Fascist dictatorship under Franco) and Vichy France – although his commitment to the interests of the last two was greatly limited. Franco's victory in the Spanish Civil War (1936–9) had been considerably aided by German and Italian military co-operation in providing armaments and troops.

Spain's entry into World War Two could have led to an attack on the British base of Gibraltar. If successful, such an attack would have destroyed the British ability to operate in the Western Mediterranean, not least as the Germans would also have gained air bases in southern Spain. Furthermore, such an alliance would enable the Germans to gain submarine bases on Spain's Atlantic coast and in the Canary Islands, a Spanish territory, making the Allied task of containing the U-boats in the Atlantic even more difficult. Hitler met Franco at Hendaye on 23 October 1940. Although Franco was a keen supporter of Hitler's cause, a point played down after the war, Spain stayed out of the conflict. This was because Franco's demands for armaments, food and territorial gains from French North Africa were seen as excessive by Hitler, and as likely to weaken Vichy France, which was regarded as more important politically and militarily.[19]

There was, nevertheless, German interest in acquiring Atlantic naval bases, from where it would be possible to threaten the convoy routes that brought Britain crucial supplies, notably food and fuel, as well as to increase German influence in South America, and to challenge American power. This interest was an aspect of the goal of the Naval Staff in Germany of becoming a power with a global reach provided by a strong surface navy. The German naval build-up helped drive American preparations, encouraging a determination to expand the American navy, and also defensive preparations around Norfolk, Virginia, the main American naval base on the Atlantic. These preparations included the deployment of land-based guns capable of outfiring the *Bismarck*, the leading surface ship in the German navy, in the event of the latter trying to approach the Chesapeake. Roosevelt took great interest in the eventual defeat by the Royal Navy in 1941 of the *Bismarck*'s sortie into the Atlantic. Moreover, in May 1940, Roosevelt requested planning for support to Brazil in the event of German attack on it.

However, although Hitler hankered after global domination, and wanted Germany to regain the African colonies it had lost to Britain, France and their allies in World War One (an aspect of his general desire to reverse the losses and humiliations of that conflict), the latter goal was tangential to his central concern with creating a new Europe. Apart from gaining glory, it was not clear, not least to himself, what Hitler would have done with overseas German colonies. Instead, his concern with a new Europe involved Hitler in having to consider the trade-off between beginning war with the Soviet Union and, on the other hand, continued confrontation with Britain and the prospect that it might win American support.[20] Yet, from another perspective, Hitler sought a Europe dominated by Germany in order better to challenge Britain and the USA.

British concern about German oceanic intentions led to the occupation of the Danish colonies of Iceland and Greenland in 1940 once the Germans conquered Denmark. This concern also resulted in planning, in early 1941, for landings (not in the event carried out) on the (Portuguese) Azores and the (Spanish) Canaries to pre-empt possible German moves. Similarly, anxiety about Vichy, and the possibility that the Germans would be able to take over the French fleet, led to the contentious British attack on the Vichy fleet at Mers el Kébir in Algeria on 3 July 1940, in which one French battleship was sunk and two were damaged, as well as a subsequent, mishandled and unsuccessful attack on 23–5 September on the main Vichy base in West Africa, Dakar. Readers should pause at this point, because it illustrates the importance of nomenclature and the difficulties in defining alliance systems. The warships attacked in Oran and Dakar were French, but to call them French ignores the key point that they were attacked because they were supporting Vichy rather than the Free French. The attack helped provide the Vichy government, which had a better constitutional claim than the Free French to be the legitimate government of France, with an excuse for stirring up anti-British sentiment. Support in France for Charles de Gaulle and the cause of continued resistance to Germany was weakened. The attack remains contentious in France to this day. At the same time, the attacks demonstrated British resolve at a time when that was unclear to American commentators.

Allied alliance politics

On the Allied side, attention has focused on relations between the 'Big Three' – the USA, the Soviet Union and Britain. This focus, however, underrates other powers, notably China. Moreover, prior to late 1941, there was no 'Big Three', as neither the Soviet Union nor the USA was then directly involved in the conflict. Instead, once France had been conquered by Germany in June 1940, alliance strategy and grand strategy were largely a matter of the British Empire.

This is a field in which much valuable work has been produced in recent decades, not least in showing the importance of the war as an imperial struggle, with the responsibilities, routes and alliances of Empire all playing key roles,[21] albeit with some important hesitations about support for the war effort, notably in South Africa.[22] It was seen as significant that visiting Commonwealth Prime Ministers were treated as *ex officio* members of the War Cabinet in London.

Most of the work on the Empire is bilateral, and differences in the politics of alliance within the Empire emerge clearly. For example, Anglo–Canadian relations proved less contentious than those between Britain and Australia. Canada provided vital financial and military support to Britain, although the Canadian government insisted that its troops should not be sent to the Middle East, which helped explain the prominent Canadian role in the unsuccessful Dieppe attack in 1942: the Canadian government wanted their troops to be seen to be active.[23] Earlier, the VII Canadian Corps, formed in Britain in July 1940, was crucial to the GHQ Reserve south of the Thames, the key element in repelling any German invasion. Canadian troops were sent to Hong Kong in 1941 as part of a political demonstration of British imperial commitment to the cause of China. These troops were to be lost in the Japanese conquest of Hong Kong in December 1941 and, since the 1990s, the deployment has been a source of controversy in Canada.

By 1942, 500 Canadian ships were in commission. Indeed, whereas in the spring of 1939 there were 10,000 men in the Canadian armed forces, by the summer of 1945 more than one million men had served (a formidable number given the size of the population), and Canada had the third biggest navy in the world after the USA and Britain.

Anglo–Australian relations, in contrast, had to adjust to serious differences in opinion over the need to respond to Japan or to concentrate on

Germany, a more politically-charged version of the Germany First or Japan First debate in the USA. In large part, this issue focused on the allocation of Australian military resources and, in particular, on British assumptions that, as part of a world-wide distribution of the Empire's resources in response to multiple challenges, the Australian forces should help protect the Middle East.[24] In Australian eyes, however, there was a British unwillingness to heed the Japanese threat and to respond to it appropriately.

This issue has proved part of a more general discussion of the politics of the failure to defend the Empire in the Far East, and notably the relationship between politics and strategy. Brian Farrell has concluded that 'the politics of imperial defence made it impossible to base' the defence of Singapore on 'sound military principles'.[25]

Allowing for this, the response to the Japanese invasion of Malaya in December 1941 was very badly handled. Failure, which culminated in the surrender of Singapore and 62,000 troops on 15 February 1942, led to a major loss of British prestige. This proved disastrous in the long term to the reputation of the British Empire in Asia and devastating in the short term to Anglo–Australian good relations. Discussion of the failure remains vexed to the present day, notably with a continuing tendency by many Australian commentators to neglect the faults of their own troops. The dispute over priorities had serious political consequences for Anglo–Australian relations, and helped lead Australia to look to the USA. Writing in the *Melbourne Herald* on 27 December 1941, John Curtin, the Australian Prime Minister, observed:

> The Australian government regards the Pacific struggle as primarily one in which the United States and Australia must have the fullest say in the direction of the Democracies' fighting plan. Without any inhibitions of any kind I must make it quite clear that Australia looks to America, free of any pangs as to our traditional links with the United Kingdom.

In the short term, the consequences of the disputes over priorities for Anglo–Australian relations were serious before Japan's entry into the war and acute thereafter. Indeed, these disputes were one of the most important political results of the emphasis on the Middle East that followed Britain's defeat in Western Europe and Italy's entry into the war in 1940. The minutes of the Australian War Cabinet made clear anxieties about British priorities in goals and force allocation, and these anxieties were shared by the New Zealand government. In July 1942, the Australian War Cabinet cabled Churchill, 'superior seapower and airpower are vital to wrest the initiative from Japan and are essential to assure the defensive position in the Southwest Pacific Area'.[26]

A number of developments can be discerned. When, after the 1942 crisis was long over, the newly-formed British Pacific Fleet reached Australia in February 1945, en route for operations against Japan, the public response in Australia was highly enthusiastic.[27] This fleet was very much an imperial one, including Australian, Canadian and New Zealand ships. By then, the Empire had been transformed, in large part as the Dominions gained international recognition, national pride, and an independent stance toward British direction. In place of the Dominions had come a British Commonwealth which provided a new political context for military planning, one that greatly affected Britain's postwar situation.[28]

Wartime pressure in, and on, Anglo–Australian relations can be related to the more general discussion of British strategy, which has been the subject of much scholarship, with the significant variant that the aggrieved party becomes the USA rather than Australia.[29] In particular, there has been discussion of whether the British focus on an indirect strategy,[30] designed to defeat Italy and to attack Germany where it was weakest, led to a mistaken concentration, from 1940, but, more particularly, 1942, on the Mediterranean that failed to inflict serious damage on Germany. Moreover, this strategy culminated, between 1943 and 1945, in the difficult and costly Allied attempt to fight the way up the length of Italy against relatively small-scale, but still highly effective, German opposition. The issue has been accentuated by suggestions that the British sought a Mediterranean focus because they wished both to protect imperial interests and to fight in an area where they could still wield control, and not be dependent on the USA, goals that were reasonable in British, but not American, terms.

The politics of grand strategy was part of its contentious character at the time, and has greatly affected subsequent discussion. In particular, there was widespread disquiet about Soviet intentions concerning Eastern Europe, disquiet that was most pronounced in the British government. As a consequence, after America had entered the war in December 1941, Churchill sought to direct Anglo–American strategy in order to ensure that the scope of the eventual Soviet advance against Germany and its allies was limited by Anglo–American moves into the Balkans. This was a key aspect of his Mediterranean strategy. He also aimed to restrict Soviet control in parts of Eastern Europe that could not be reached by Western forces.

The focus was Poland, its government, and the extent to which the Soviets were to be able to annex eastern Poland anew, as they had done in agreement with Hitler in 1939. From the Polish perspective, Poland was an ally betrayed to the interests of the Soviet Union.[31] It was certainly an ally that it was difficult to assist, not least due to distance and to Soviet policy.[32] As a reminder of the extent and impact of domestic politics discussed in the next chapter, British views on the Soviet Union, however, were very varied.[33]

The central part taken by the Red Army in the defeat of Germany ensured that the Soviet Union would play the dominant role in Eastern Europe, as the Russian army had not been able to do in the closing stages of World War One or thereafter. Moreover, Stalin's assumption that the alliance with Britain and the USA could not be sustained after the war, itself almost the definition of a self-fulfilling prophecy, left him determined

to extend the Soviet sphere of influence, as well as to obtain direct territorial control through annexations. Stalin, who was paranoid (although not
about Hitler in 1939–41), exaggerated British commitment to the cause of
hostility to Communism, indeed discussing in the autumn of 1942 whether
Churchill wanted a separate peace with Germany so as to leave the latter
free to oppose the Soviet Union.[34] The purging of Soviet diplomats who did
not support a firm Communist line ensured that the only advice received
by Stalin was that which treated the Western allies critically and with
suspicion. This was a serious weakness, for the Soviet Union and the anti-
German cause; a weakness both in the short term, notably with the failure
to appreciate the threat from Germany in 1941, and over the long term.[35]

America's move towards war provides another impact of the developing
nature of alliance politics. Prior to December 1941, there had already been
a serious deterioration in relations between America and both Germany
and Japan. This deterioration had led to closer links between Britain and
the USA, the latter taking an increasing role in Atlantic security. After
Germany conquered Denmark in April 1940, Iceland – a state under the
Danish crown – had declared independence and, to prevent a German
intervention, the British landed troops there. These included Canadian
units, for British as a term is frequently employed to include imperial
troops. In an important extension of commitment, which also captured
acute geopolitical sensitivity about the Atlantic, the Americans established
airfields in Greenland – a Danish colony – in April 1941. Three months
later, American forces replaced the British in Iceland as part of their
attempt to protect the Western Hemisphere, a policy outlined at the Havana
Conference of July 1940.

Meanwhile, on 3 September 1940, the USA had agreed to provide
50 surplus and elderly destroyers (seven of them to the Canadian navy),
in return for 99-year leases on British bases in Antigua, the Bahamas,
Bermuda, British Guiana, Jamaica, Newfoundland, St Lucia and Trinidad,
bases that enabled Roosevelt to claim to be supporting the defence of the
Western Hemipshere. In practice, the deal was of limited value as the largely
obsolete ships took time to prepare. However, aside from the considerable
psychological value at a time when Britain was vulnerable, no other power
was in a position to provide such help. More generally, the critical importance of American supplies was exaggerated by the British for political
reasons, so as to make Britain appear stronger to both domestic and
international audiences. Moreover, even the quantity of American supplies
agreed was not delivered, while there was a counter-flow of high quality
British supplies to the USA and of initiatives from the British that helped
the USA in particular to develop better aircraft than they would otherwise
have done.

Roosevelt, nevertheless, sought to give effect to his vision of America as
an 'Arsenal of Democracy', a theme outlined in a 'fireside chat' carried by
radio on 29 December 1940. Nine days earlier, the Office of Production

Management, under William Knudsen as Director, had been established by Roosevelt to coordinate the production of military *matériel* and to help provide aid, 'short of war', to Britain and other opponents of the Axis.

On 6 January 1941, Roosevelt, in his annual message to Congress, recommended Lend-Lease for Britain and also enunciated 'Four Freedoms' which stigmatised the Axis and linked the war to domestic American policy: freedom of speech and expression, freedom of worship, freedom from want, and freedom from fear. In March 1941, the passage by Congress of the Lend-Lease Act granted the American government the right to sell, lend or trade military *matériel* to any state vital to American security, opening the way for the shipping of American military supplies to Britain. Managers of business in the House of Representatives numbered the Lend-Lease Bill HR 1776[36] to make it look more patriotic.

In a major attempt to secure these supplies in the face of the growing threat from German submarines, Churchill and Roosevelt, during the Placentia Bay Conference of 9–12 August 1941, agreed to allocate spheres of strategic responsibility, with the Americans becoming responsible, alongside the Canadians, for escorting convoys in the western Atlantic. Moreover, this conference recorded and enhanced symbolism in Anglo–American relations. As part of the process, the conference saw a religious theme, centred on a joint Sunday service, advanced as part of the opposition to Germany.[37]

Any American focus on the Atlantic was challenged by Japanese action against the USA, but Roosevelt was able to develop his policy because Hitler promptly followed Pearl Harbor by declaring war. This declaration let Roosevelt off the hook, since he agreed with Churchill that Hitler was a greater menace than the Japanese. However, not all of American opinion shared this view. There were complaints from the American navy that Roosevelt neglected the Pacific theatre, and some admirals refused to fly flags at half-mast on his death. In addition, Chiang Kai-shek was very much opposed to the emphasis on Germany. In practice, considerable resources, notably, but never only, naval resources, were devoted throughout to the Pacific.[38]

The German declaration led to the enunciation of the 'Germany First' strategy, which was to see the bulk of American land and air assets allocated to preparing for the invasion of Europe. Such a strategy had already been outlined in the American Rainbow 5 War Plan and the Anglo–American–Canadian ABC-1 Plan talks in early 1941, which had envisaged a defensive strategy in the Pacific in the event of conflict with the three Axis powers. Roosevelt had supported this emphasis because of his concern that Britain might otherwise collapse in the face of German pressure. Such a collapse would have increased American vulnerability to Japan as well as Germany, which indicated the relationship between different spheres of the conflict. Roosevelt, however, was also concerned about the prospect of China collapsing, which indeed was a factor in American policy towards Japan in 1941.

The 'Germany First' strategy led the American army manoeuvres in 1941 to focus on preparing for European-theatre conflict, and was confirmed by the Washington Conference that began on 22 December 1941, when Churchill reached Washington. This conference also resulted in the creation of an Anglo–American planning mechanism based on the Combined Chiefs of Staff, as well as the establishment of the Anglo–American Combined Raw Materials Board, a significant indication of joint planning. On 1 January 1942, the United Nations Declaration was signed at Washington. Affirming the principles of the Atlantic Charter, this declaration promised vigorous opposition to the Axis and no separate armistice or peace.

An emphasis on fighting Germany also greatly helped the Soviet Union by diverting German resources to resist American attacks and the potential of such attacks. The movement of American forces across the Atlantic greatly magnified the strategic challenge to Germany from Britain, not least by giving Britain offensive capability as far as Atlantic Europe was concerned. If less help was provided to the Soviet Union by this diversion than the Americans and British imagined, it was still considerable. The declared American focus on Germany also accorded with the need to destroy the stronger adversary first.[39]

The declared emphasis on Germany still left American, and thus Allied, strategic preferences unclear, particularly the extent to which it was prudent to mount an invasion of France in 1943, or even 1942. In an echo of debates in Britain from 1939, the Victory Plan, the statement of American strategy drawn up in late 1941 by the War Plans Division of the War Department General Staff, and principally by Albert Wedemeyer, an able officer who had attended the *Kriegsakademie* in Berlin from 1936 to 1938, had argued that sea blockade and air attack would not defeat Germany. Instead, the plan pressed for a land attack, and for it to be mounted speedily before Germany benefited from its extensive conquests:

> time is of the essence and the longer we delay effective offensive operations against the Axis, the more difficult will become the attainment of victory ... we will be confronted in the not distant future by a Germany strongly intrenched economically, supported by newly acquired sources of vital supplies and industries, with her military forces operating on interior lines, and in a position of hegemony in Europe which will be comparatively easy to defend and maintain.[40]

In October 1944, Wedemeyer replaced the cantankerous 'Vinegar Joe', Joseph Stilwell, as Chiang Kai-shek's Allied Chief of Staff, commander of American forces in China (most of whom were advisors), and administrator of American aid.

American policymakers were opposed to what they saw and decried as the Mediterranean obsession of British policy and, in 1943, were reluctant to support British plans for an Allied invasion, first, of Sicily and, subsequently, of mainland Italy. The Americans feared that such an invasion would detract resources from the invasion of France (the army's prime concern) and from the war with Japan (the navy's), and also be a strategic irrelevance that did not contribute greatly to the defeat of Germany. Instead, the Americans pressed for an attack on the German army in France, an attack seen as the best way to use Anglo–American forces to defeat the Germans, and to assist the Soviet Union.[41]

British strategic concerns in the Mediterranean, however, were a product not simply of imperial concerns and related geopolitical interests, but also of the legacy, since 1940, of conflict with the Axis in the Mediterranean where the Germans, moreover, could be engaged as they could not then be in Western Europe. The British had military resources in the region, as well as territorial and strategic commitments to protect, notably the Suez Canal; and, not least due to serious pressures on shipping, these resources could not be readily reallocated.[42] Strategic speculation and political commentary are apt to overlook this point.

The employment of imperial military resources was particularly notable in this respect. The sensitivity about the deployment of Australian and New Zealand forces in the Middle East while the two countries were threatened by Japan had underlined the need for political care in the use of imperial units, and a focus of efforts on northern France could not be permitted to weaken Britain in the Mediterranean. Britain's position in the Mediterranean was, in part, seen as a forward-defence for the Indian Ocean, as were the occupations of Iraq and Syria in 1941, and that forward-defence was important to the politics of imperial commitment. Moreover, until July 1944, Britain and the Empire had more divisions than the Americans in fighting conflict with the enemy.

The British preference for an indirect approach, weakening the Axis by incremental steps as a deliberate preparation for an invasion of France, was also important. The indirect approach was an aspect of longstanding British strategic culture, powerfully fortified by the lessons of World War One, notably the extremely costly struggle on the Western Front, one that the British did not wish to repeat. There were also concerns about the manpower available: with a smaller population than the USA, the Soviet Union or Germany, Britain's potential to field as many divisions was limited. The indirect approach also drew on the benefits of naval power and amphibious capability.

Interest in the indirect approach was not restricted to Britain. In the winter of 1939–40, there was support in France for an expedition to Salonika in northern Greece in order to maintain Allied influence in the Balkans. The British were then opposed to such an expedition, for both military and political reasons, notably the risk of starting a war with Italy.[43] In 1940, the fall of France and Italy's entry into the war dramatically took forward the indirect approach. It faced a major failure, however, in April 1941 when forces were sent to Greece in an unsuccessful attempt to help resist German invasion. Churchill backed the policy for political reasons, in order to show that Britain was supporting all opposition to the Axis, but he swiftly recognised it as an error. The dispatch of forces there greatly weakened the British in North Africa.

The indirect approach was also a response to the specific military circumstances of 1942–3. The British were concerned that a direct attack across the English Channel would expose untested forces to the battle-hardened Germans. Their experience of fighting the Germans in 1940–1, in Norway, France, Greece and North Africa, in each of which British forces had been defeated, had made British policymakers wary of such a step until the Germans had been weakened. The bloody failure of the Dieppe Raid on the North French coast on 19 August 1942 underlined the problems and uncertainties of amphibious landings on a defended coastline, as well as the prior need to acquire air superiority. Allied success in amphibious operations in the early stages of the war was limited, with the British invasion of Madagascar in 1942 mounted against a far more vulnerable target than occupied France, and benefiting in particular from surprise and good planning.[44]

Later in 1942, the British were successful with the Eighth Army at El Alamein in Egypt, but Bernard Montgomery's victory over the German–Italian force under Erwin Rommel in the battle fought from 23 October to 4 November was greatly assisted by superior air power, and was characterised by a deliberative, controlled style of attack supported by clear superiority in artillery. This was a variant of Allied offensives in 1918. To replicate this style in an amphibious assault on France would not be easy. As far as the alternative was concerned, the difficulties of campaigning in Italy, however, were not appreciated, those posed neither by the terrain nor by the German defenders.

Moreover, the amphibious operation mounted to secure the formerly Italian-held Dodecanese Islands in the eastern Aegean in late 1943 proved a disaster, with the Germans successfully regaining the islands in October-November. The Americans had opposed the commitment. It appealed to Churchill's interest in bold steps, his commitment to action, his interest in the Mediterranean, and his longstanding belief in the importance of Turkey. Indeed, he hoped that the operation would lead to partial control of the Dardanelles and to Turkey entering the war on the Allied side. Turgut Özal, Prime Minister (1983–9) and President (1989–93), was to argue that Turkey should have done so, and captured and annexed the Dodecanese,[45] but caution prevailed in Ankara, and Greece gained the islands in the postwar peace settlement. The British lost about 4,800 troops, six destroyers and 113 planes in the operation.[46]

As much in fear of a repeat of the Russian collapse of 1917 as anything else, Churchill declared in Washington on 19 May 1943, 'we must do everything in our power that is sensible and practicable to take more of the weight off Russia in 1943'. Indeed at the Casablanca Conference that

January, the British and Americans agreed on the Combined Bomber Offensive. It was seen as a way to show Stalin that the Western Allies were doing their utmost to weaken Hitler, and thus to aid Soviet operations. This was a key justification of the air assault. The Allies were moving over to the offensive, not as a series of counterattacks, but as part of a planned attempt to regain Axis conquests, and then to take the war to the Axis states themselves.

Italy, in contrast, was a contentious goal, and remained so for the rest of the war, affecting Anglo–American politics and planning as a result. The Americans argued throughout that Italy was a strategic irrelevance that would dissipate military strength. Formidable forces were indeed devoted to Italy, including, in the eventually-successful fourth Battle of Monte Cassino in May 1944, 25 divisions, 2,000 tanks and over 3,000 aircraft.

Instead, the Americans sought a focus on the direct approach, particularly an engagement with the major German forces in Western Europe, and an advance into Germany. German weaknesses in 1943 suggest that such an invasion might have been an option that year. Many key German units were allocated to the unsuccessful Kursk offensive on the Eastern Front, an offensive, launched on 5 July, designed to re-establish German operational superiority, but, in the event, their last major attack on the Soviets. Good intelligence, in part provided by the British ability to read German cyphers, ensured that the Soviets were forewarned. Already thwarted by the Soviet defence, the operation was cancelled by Hitler on 13 July, in part due to the Allied invasion of Sicily on 10 July. Moreover, the Germans lacked the build-up in munitions production that 1943 was to bring, and their defensive positions in France were incomplete.

Public discussion of the war in the Soviet Union criticised the failure of Britain and the USA to invade France. Moreover, the Soviets mentioned their suspicion of their allies' failure to open a Second Front to the Germans when secretly probing the possibility of a separate peace with Germany. These probings led to a peace offer in September 1943, but Hitler was not interested in pursuing it. Nevertheless, the possibility of such a development indicated the potentially unfixed nature of alliances as well, more specifically, as the possible relation between strategic decisions, alliance dynamics and geopolitical alignments. This potentially unfixed nature also helps explain the extent to which contemporaries engaged in counterfactual (what if?) speculations.

Discussion of Anglo–American wartime strategy continues to be contentious to the present, not least because it is linked to counterfactuals relating to postwar geopolitics. This is particularly so with the claim that more commitment to a Mediterranean strategy might have restricted subsequent Soviet control of the Balkans, and that greater success in Italy could have been obtained had American pressure to allocate resources, instead, to an invasion of southern France in 1944 been unsuccessful. The British certainly hoped that a presence in Italy would encourage resistance in Yugoslavia, hold down German forces in the Balkans, and serve as the basis for advancing into Austria and southern Germany; and it was also expected that a forward policy in the Mediterranean would affect the postwar situation. This argument, however, did, and does, not take sufficient note of the military and political realities on the ground in Yugoslavia, both during and after the war; although it was true that the Hungarian government thought of joining the Allies in 1943–4 if their forces invaded the Balkans, while Romania and Bulgaria also switched sides in 1944 when the Soviets advanced.

The British were correct to draw attention to deficiencies in Allied preparedness that argued in favour of caution in launching an Anglo–American invasion of France. There is a strong argument for considering that an invasion of France before 1944 could have failed. At the beginning of 1943, reflecting prewar assumptions about needs, there was only limited equipment for, and experience in, amphibious operations.[47] There was no reason then to assume that a large-scale invasion of France would be necessary.

Moreover, it was still unclear in early 1943 how far, and how speedily, it would be possible to vanquish the U-boat threat, and thus control the Atlantic shipping lanes. Aside from the need to build up forces and experience for an invasion of France, there was also the requirement of assured air and sea superiority to support both landing and exploitation. In 1943, the Allies did not yet have sufficient air dominance to seek to isolate an invasion zone. This was a task that the Anzio (south of Rome) and Normandy landings, both in 1944, indicated was, in practice, extremely difficult.

Yet, this task of isolating a zone was very necessary for, with an invasion, the key issue was not so much the initial success (which should be assured by the local superiority provided by surprise), but, rather, the consolidation of a bridgehead and the subsequent break-out. There was an echo of the difference between break-in and break-out in the trench warfare on the Western Front in World War One. For World War Two, consolidation and break-out were still to be very difficult in Normandy, as also from Anzio. Even the operations on D-Day itself could have gone badly wrong, not least if Allied deception schemes had failed. Moreover, delaying the invasion until 1944 enabled the Allies to benefit from the problems that hit the Germans in 1943: failure at Kursk, and subsequent large-scale Soviet advances in southern Russia and Ukraine, chewed up part of the German army and air force.

War goals

Strategy was related to war goals. Anthony Eden, the British Foreign Secretary, made it clear to Parliament in December 1942, well before Hitler had been overthrown, that a fundamental change in Germany was being sought: 'It will be the first and imperative duty of the United Nations to establish such a settlement as will make it impossible for Germany to dominate her neighbours by force of arms. It would be sheer folly to allow some non-Nazi government to be set up and then trust to luck'.

After the Casablanca conference of Allied leaders of 14–24 January 1943,[48] a summit that was part of a series that charted the respective influence of the powers, a policy of unconditional surrender was announced, and it was one that was not abandoned. This policy was regarded as a way of maintaining Allied unity, notably by pre-empting separate negotiations with Germany, and thus blocking the option of divide and rule for the latter. Unconditional surrender was also seen as the way to prevent Germany from repeating the experience of World War One, namely moving from defeat in the war in 1918 to renewed hostilities in 1939.

The policy of unconditional surrender, however, made it more difficult to allow Italy to change sides briskly once Mussolini was overthrown in 1943. It was also to be condemned by some commentators as making it difficult to encourage German resistance to Hitler, and thus as undermining the chance for a shorter war and, even, for a resolution of the conflict in the shape of a postwar alliance of the USA, Britain and Germany directed against the Soviet Union. This condemnation is misplaced. Unconditional surrender might be criticised as a policy on the grounds that a fundamentally political goal made a compromise peace impossible: the Allies would fight on and the Germans, whatever the nature of their regime, would not be able to bring the war to a negotiated end even when it was clearly lost; but this goal was an accurate response to the politics of German power during the war. The Allies sought to destroy not only the Nazi regime and Nazism, but also Prussian militarism and the potential for Germany to cause trouble anew. These aims were seen as requiring the occupation of all of Germany, the destruction of the Nazi regime, and the dismantling of the German military. To ensure this outcome, unconditional surrender appeared necessary, and, indeed, this conclusion still appears well-founded. The myths of German power propagated by Hitler had to be destroyed, as indeed they were not only by the Allies, but also as a consequence of Hitler's actions.

Hitler, for whom a stalemate peace was unacceptable,[49] realised that final victory was out of reach. However, he was determined to fight on in order to destroy Europe's Jews, as well as to achieve what he regarded as a moral victory for his concept of the German people. As a consequence, a notion of heroic self-destruction, which had arguably always been present, became a decisive part of the regime's ideology.[50] The war, always a struggle of the will in Hitler's eyes, was increasingly organised in those terms. The *Volkssturm*, a Nazi-run, compulsory, local defence militia for men between sixteen and sixty, was ordered in July 1944. It was designed to inflict casualties on the advancing Allies such that their morale could not tolerate, and also to indoctrinate the German civilian population for a total struggle.[51] Thus, the politics of the war became a matter of will, as, in Hitler's view, it had been throughout.

The policy of unconditional surrender made a compromise peace with a regime led by German generals, the goal of the July Bomb Plot against Hitler in 1944, unacceptable. After the Bomb Plot, in which a group of German officers tried and failed to kill Hitler and to overthrow his regime, the bulk of the military command rallied to Hitler. Nazification was pushed by General Heinz Guderian, the new Chief of the Army General Staff. Officers were increasingly promoted on the basis of their Nazi zeal.

The repression of disaffection and any sign of 'defeatism' by the Nazi surveillance system presided over by Heinrich Himmler, the head of the SS, helped ensure that there was no repetition of the German collapse of 1918, and that despite the situation becoming far more bleak than it had then been. Instead, it was a very different German regime and society that waged World War Two. On 18 January 1945, Churchill told the House of Commons:

> I am clear that nothing should induce us to abandon the principle of unconditional surrender, or to enter into any form of negotiation with Germany or Japan, under whatever guise such suggestions may present themselves, until the act of unconditional surrender had been formally executed.

The British, whose role in the formulation of policy was eroded by the greater economic strength and military power of their allies, as well as by Soviet successes in Eastern Europe and American advances in the Pacific, were determined not only to keep the Soviet Union in the war, but also to ensure that the USA sustained the peace settlement, unlike after World War One. In turn, Roosevelt wanted to make certain that Stalin was committed, in the short term, to conflict with Japan, and, in the long term, to the eventual peace settlement.[52]

Commitment in the short term of the remainder of the war was also seen as an important factor by Hitler. He hoped that German success in the Ardennes offensive in December 1944, the Battle of the Bulge, would lead Britain and the USA to negotiations. Moreover, Goebbels recorded that, on his visit to Hitler on 11 March 1945, the latter had argued that, due to what he saw as Churchill's determination to exterminate Germany and his refusal to ally against the Soviets, and what he claimed was Roosevelt's wish that the Europeans destroy themselves through war, it was necessary for Germany to fight sufficiently well to lead Stalin to seek a separate peace.

This prospectus was a foolish illusion, but one that indicated the arithmetic of alliance rearrangement that came to pass for German strategy. Hitler was delighted when he heard of Roosevelt's death on 12 April, believing that this offered a proof of providential salvation leading to a change in the political situation, rather as Frederick the Great of Prussia had been saved in the Seven Years' War (1756–63) by the death of his enemy, Tsarina Elizabeth of Russia in 1762, and by the consequent unravelling of the hostile coalition. The remorseless pressure of the Allies swiftly ended these hopes. The Soviets launched their final offensive on 16 April and Hitler committed suicide on 30 April as Soviet forces conquered Berlin.

Looking to the future

Indeed, the reality of the Soviet advance also vitiated subsequent claims that Roosevelt and Churchill had 'sold-out' Eastern Europe to Stalin at their conference in Yalta in early February 1945. In practice, Poland was already occupied when the leaders met, and eastern Germany soon would be.[53] Geography could scarcely be reversed: Poland was vulnerable to an expansionist Germany and an expansionist Soviet Union. At Yalta, it was also agreed that the Soviets, after they had attacked Japan, would have an important presence in Manchuria including the naval base of Port Arthur. China was not consulted and the Soviets occupied Port Arthur until after Stalin's death in 1953.

As in 1814–15, when the future of the European world was negotiated at the Congress of Vienna in the aftermath of Napoleon's defeat, Russian/ Soviet power and success were key factors that could not be wished away from the negotiating table. Indeed, in some respects, the diplomatic position in 1944–5 was similar to that in 1814–15. The most significant difference was that the role of the victorious oceanic power was now played by the USA, or by an uneasy Anglo–American condominium dominated by the USA and not, as in 1814–15, by Britain alone.

In 1814–15, there was a de facto delimitation of spheres of influence, with Russia dominant in Eastern Europe. Crucially, this meant Russian rule over most of Poland. The Russian gain of Bessarabia and Finland in recent wars with the Ottoman Empire/Turks (1806–12) and Sweden (1808–9) was also part of the post-Napoleonic order, just as the Soviet gain of Bessarabia and Karelia and control over key aspects of Finnish policy were part of the post-Hitlerian order. Russia in 1814–15 also played a central role in determining the fate of the defeated kingdom of Saxony, and in the face of opposition from Austria, Britain and France; and this role also looked towards the situation in 1944–5. Saxony was the southern part of the Soviet occupation zone in what became East Germany.

In many respects, what was unusual was the assumption, in 1944–5, as in 1790–1 during the Ochakov Crisis, when there had been an unsuccessful effort to put pressure on Russia to hand back wartime gains from the Ottoman Empire, that Britain could play a major role in determining the fate of Eastern Europe. This assumption, however, reflected the sense that World War Two could, and must, lead to a new and more benign international order: if there was to be a United Nations, there should also be self-determination for the peoples conquered by Germany, notably the Poles.

For the Allies, the postwar world was a key issue throughout, and not only in the closing stages of the war. This concern with the future linked public with politicians. In October 1943, *Life*, a leading American publication, declared 'Of one thing we are sure. Americans are not fighting to protect the British Empire'; a stance the USA would later regret in some areas as it faced difficulties with nationalist movements and states that resisted or replaced the European empires. At the Teheran conference of Allied leaders that December, there were bitter differences over the fate of European colonial empires. Roosevelt was opposed to colonial rule (although not by the USA in the Pacific) and, instead, in favour of a system of 'trusteeship' as a prelude to independence. The Americans had already promised to give the Philippines its independence when the war began, and was to do so after the war ended. The USA was still imperial, but argued that it was using a different political model.

Willing to satisfy Stalin at the expense of Eastern Europe and over Manchuria, Roosevelt pressed Churchill on the status of both Hong Kong (which he wanted returned to China) and India, and British officials were made aware of a fundamental contradiction in attitudes. Roosevelt told Churchill that Britain had to adjust to a 'new period' in global history and to turn their back on '400 years of acquisitive blood in your veins',[54] although he did not press the point on India. Roosevelt's opposition to French and Dutch imperialism in Asia was also very strong.

The two powers competed over Middle Eastern oil, with America successfully developing links with Saudi Arabia[55] and over economic interests elsewhere.[56] There was also strong American support for a Jewish state in British-ruled Palestine, a policy opposed by Anthony Eden, the British Foreign Secretary. Roosevelt's opposition to key aspects of British policy was shared by significant advisers such as Sumner Welles, Under-Secretary of State from 1937 until September 1943.[57] This opposition was also seen with other prominent politicians. Highly conscious of his Irish antecedents, as well as an isolationist, Joseph Kennedy, ambassador to Britain from 1938 to 1940 and a politician with ambitions to be the Democratic Party presidential candidate, had scarcely been supportive to Britain and was criticised by George VI for defeatism in 1939.[58]

More serious in the long term was American opposition to imperial preference, the commercial adhesive of the British Empire. Article seven of the Lend-Lease agreement of 1942 stipulated the eventual end to such preference, and this was followed up as a result of the loan from the USA that Britain was obliged to seek after the close of the war.

There is a balance to be struck here. Roosevelt's treatment of Churchill at the Teheran conference on 2–7 December 1943, and his refusal to have any truck with re-establishing Britain's empire, have to be set alongside both his open-handed support of Britain in very problematic circumstances in the USA in 1940, and his subsequent 'Germany First' policy.

Nevertheless, Churchill's determination to save the Empire in what, in one respect, was a War of the British Succession, was directed at the USA, the Soviet Union and China, as well as Germany, Japan and Italy. The decline in British power he felt so keenly made him clear on the need to retain the Empire as well as imperial preference in trade; although, in 1943, Britain and the USA signed treaties with China ending the extra-territorial rights they had acquired with the Treaty Ports system of the nineteenth century.

Alongside ignoring pressures for decolonization and trying to save their empires, France and Britain indeed had territorial ambitions on the Italian colony of Libya, which bordered British and French colonies. Churchill was also interested in the Kra isthmus in southern Thailand, which would provide a continuous land route between the neighbouring British colonies of Burma and Malaya. The Japanese had used this isthmus in the invasion of both. At present, there are Chinese plans for a canal across the isthmus in order to shorten maritime routes from China to the Indian Ocean.

In the event, the colonial empires of Britain and France were to be largely gone within two decades. Instead, a prime result of the war was the spread of American influence, not only military and power, but also potent economic and cultural models underpinned by financial strength. This process affected not only Europe's empires, but also Europe itself.[59]

The familiar focus on the Big Three risks underplaying the extent to which there were more players on the Allied side. Despite Chiang Kai-shek and Roosevelt playing up the role of (Nationalist) China, however, there were no other players at the level of the Big Three. Indeed, all the other allies were heavily dependent on the assistance of the Allied superpowers. This was a case for example of the Free French under Charles de Gaulle.

It was also true of the Poles resisting German occupation, both the London-based government-in-exile and the pro-Soviet Polish National Liberation Committee, which became the provisional government as the Soviets advanced into Poland. Nomenclature as ever can play a key role, as the government-in-exile can be disparaged by reference to the London Poles.

China received help by air 'over the hump' from India, a difficult route which encouraged American and Chinese pressure for the re-conquest of Upper Burma from Japan; whereas the British preferred the idea of an amphibious invasion of Lower Burma, a course that would permit the use of naval assets. The British command in India clashed repeatedly with the Chinese over operational planning in Burma.

The Americans, eventually, came to be disillusioned with Chiang's conduct of the Chinese war effort, although Roosevelt did not express Churchill's contempt for the idea of China as a great power. By 1944, there was serious tension as Chiang resisted pressure for Lieutenant-General

Joseph Stilwell to become commander of all Chinese forces, and also American demands that Chiang seek a coalition with the Communists in order to put pressure on the Japanese. The failure of these plans, combined with major Japanese successes in the Inchigo offensive in southern China that year (which eventually created a Japanese land route from Korea to Vietnam), ended American hopes of China as a key partner.

Assistance from the superpowers to their allies was to be underplayed in postwar recollection and commemoration by these allies, as a key aspect of the politics of such discussion. Even at the time, the receipt and use of assistance was readily compatible with a determination by these players to assert independence and to follow a distinctive line.

For example, de Gaulle, who had flown to England on 18 June 1940 and was condemned to death *in absentia* by the Pétain government, was determined to ensure that the French Empire was maintained and that the French played a key role in liberating France. However, he was disliked and distrusted by the Allies because of his arrogant wilfulness. Moreover, there was a reasonable suspicion that de Gaulle's pretensions – as a self-proclaimed and unelected leader – would make it harder to win over Vichy elements, notably, but not only, in North Africa. Indeed, in July 1941, the Vichy High Commissioner in Damascus, Henri Dentz, an ardent anglophobe, insisted on surrendering to the British rather than to de Gaulle.[60] Suspicion of de Gaulle led to serious antagonism between de Gaulle and Roosevelt in 1942, especially over the successful American wooing of other French leaders, including Vichy figures, before and during the Anglo–American invasion of North Africa, Operation Torch, which began on 8 November. There were also Anglo–American differences over Vichy and the Free French.

The overhang of Free French activity for postwar relations between France and the Allies was considerable, notably when de Gaulle was President (1959–69) and in favour of France following an independent line on foreign and military policy: de Gaulle twice kept Britain out of the European Economic Community, the forerunner of the European Union, and, in 1966, took France out of NATO's military structure. This was the reality of the warning, by Churchill and others, that de Gaulle would never forgive Britain for saving France.

Moreover, a reminder of the multiple currents of autonomy and animosity that made up the weave of the war was provided in 2009 when research in the British public records revealed that, during interrogations in London, the Free French in 1942–3 had tortured suspected French opponents of de Gaulle, and possibly been involved in murder. This activity led to the issue of a High Court writ by a French detainee against de Gaulle in 1943, much to the anger of the latter.[61]

The role of lesser players was intertwined with that of the great powers as, in part, the latter pursued their interests, or sought to define them, by the sponsorship of protégé movements and by doing down those of others.

Thus, for example, in some occupied states, notably Poland and Yugoslavia, there were strong cross-currents in the Resistance to Axis occupation, with particular groups looking to different authorities in exile each of which, in turn, sought to advance its interests by securing the backing of a great power. Studies of the Cold War have indicated the extent to which the great powers could be led, committed or compromised by their weaker protégés, for example the USA by Israel; and the same factor was an element in World War Two.

Alongside discussion and dissension over how best to conduct the war, there were also efforts to address the nature of the eventual peace as far as the defeated were concerned.[62] A number of factors came into play, including punishment and retribution, the path to which was eased by a belief in collective responsibility. Yet, there was also a wish to avoid creating a discontented population that might serve as the basis for a subsequent revival of German aggression, as well as the need to consider how best to respond to the apparently menacing stances of wartime allies. Alongside de-Nazification and the end to wartime militarism, British military policymakers were already envisaging the postwar requirement for alliance with Germany against a threatening Soviet Union. Such an alliance indeed was to occur, at least with West Germany.

Looking to the future linked the successful victors to those accommodating themselves to victory, whether Axis initially, or Allied subsequently. This process underlined the linkage between the war and the periods on either side, a linkage that provided a central political context for the war and for subsequent consideration of it. Thus, for example, in Belgium, German conquest impacted on already divisive ethnic politics and on a public opinion fragmented on the issue of national identification. The work of wartime historians reflected this impact in Belgium[63] and elsewhere. Moreover, subsequent scholarship can be considered in this context.

More generally, a crucial strategic element in the closing stages of the war was that of preparing for the aftermath, in particular by determining areas of advance and thus occupation zones. The crucial element in 1944–5 across most of Eastern Europe was that of Soviet, as opposed to Anglo–American, advance. This was an advance motivated by the search for Soviet security, as well as by the quest to extend the Communist revolution, and this advance looked towards the Communist seizure of power there.[64]

In contrast, British intervention played a key role in Greece after the departure of the Germans. By 18 January 1945, there were 75,000 British troops in Greece. A month earlier, they had become involved in conflict in Athens with the National Popular Liberation Army (ELAS), the Communist Resistance force that had already fought the anti-Communist Resistance in the winter of 1943–4. The British presence led to the defeat of ELAS and, by the Varkiza Agreement of February 1945, to an agreement for its demobilisation and for a British-guaranteed plebiscite about the constitution. The

Cold War in Greece appeared won for the West, although it was to resume in the summer of 1946.

Yet again, the role of the great powers was not the sole issue. For example, it was very important to postwar Yugoslavia that Tito's Communists, rather than the Red Army, played the central role in the liberation in 1944. This role was directly responsible for the ousting of the monarchy that year, and for Yugoslavia becoming a Communist state in 1945. Tito was to be in a stronger position than the other Communist leaders in Eastern Europe, and, alongside the lack of a contiguous border with the Soviet Union, this made it possible for him to break with Stalin in 1949. This break helped ensure that, deprived of bases in neighbouring Yugoslavia, the Communists lost in the Greek Civil War, although American intervention on the royalist side was also significant.

It was also important for Albania that it was not liberated by the Red Army. Divisions among the Resistance had been eased by the formation of the Albanian United Front in 1940, but the Communists, under Enver Hoxha, broke with the Front in 1943 and focused on defeating the Balli Kombetar, a more conservative Resistance movement. As a result, civil war engulfed southern Albania. This conflict spread into central and northern Albania, as the Communists attacked tribal Resistance groups there.

The Communists won, helped by the extent to which British support was increasingly channelled through them. The extent to which this decision reflected left-wing sympathies among British policymakers (which definitely existed, notably amongst those in Cairo and Italy) is unclear, although there was this tendency. This point can also be made for the development of American links with the Chinese Communists in 1944: the key individual there was John Paton Davies, political advisor to General Stilwell.

To end this chapter by mentioning Albania may appear ironic. Albania, first conquered by Italy in April 1939, then, in 1943, when Italy surrendered, occupied by the Germans, and, finally, taken over by the Communist Resistance movement, was scarcely the most important combatant, nor the leading sphere of contention. Yet, it is appropriate to underline the extent to which the war was an umbrella conflict encompassing a large number of diverse struggles. Ask the question, 'Which of Mongolia, Thailand, Iraq, Syria and Madagascar saw conflict during the war?'. The answer is all of them. As a result, there are multiple narratives of the war as a whole, with, indeed, a periodisation of the war differing from country to country. This diversity needs to be understood if the subsequent and present political aftermath of World War Two is to be appreciated.

CHAPTER THREE

Domestic Politics

Domestic politics were an important element of the war, both in the conventional understanding of the operation of political systems and in a wider sense of the role of the state. Indeed, the coming of a war more global in its scope than World War One, as well as longer, gave a renewed boost to the role of states and the control of societies, as the mobilisation of national resources led to state direction of much of the economy. The net effect was that of a transformation in, and by, the state, and one that remains a benchmark for government spending, as with comparisons between government spending in 1945 and 2014. This chapter serves to consider these issues, not least as a bridge to the next chapter, on the explanations for Allied victory, because domestic politics are involved alongside the alliances, strategies and warmaking of the Allies.

Home Fronts, the setting for national politics, conjure up an image of reassuring domesticity. This is an image frequently referred to in subsequent talk of national identity, notably in Britain. However, the reality was frequently bleaker. Moreover, the situation on Home Fronts was very varied, not least in their interaction with other aspects of the war.[1] Home Fronts stretched round the world, more so indeed than zones of conflict, as these Home Fronts included people and areas not directly touched at all by combat.[2] The absence of fighting did not prevent a range of effects. These included the loss of manpower and resources through conscription, allocation and taxation. Individual and collective suffering, often very painful, through casualties and the dislocation of life, was also significant.

So, moreover, were developments with less dramatic consequences. For example, sport was cancelled or curtailed. Players, even in areas distant from combat and bombing, such as the USA, were affected by military service and travel restrictions. The timing of games was influenced by limitations on night fixtures.[3]

A key aspect of politics in the broadest sense was provided by the creation and sustaining of structures and systems necessary to ensure the wartime mobilisation of society and economy. The context was very different by state, in large part, but not solely, as a result of differing prewar political systems. In non-totalitarian countries, such as Britain, the USA, Australia, Canada and New Zealand, there had been important developments in military preparedness prior to the war, for example the introduction of conscription in Britain in April 1939.[4] However, these developments had been within existing political, economic and social structures, notably the practice and precepts of limited government, and there had not been a large-scale prewar moulding of state and society to further the goals of conflict.

When the war broke out, economic regulation and conscription were introduced more rapidly and comprehensively, and less contentiously, in non-totalitarian countries, than in World War One. There was none of the bitter division over conscription seen in Britain and Australia in that struggle;[5] although there was not a prior mobilisation of resources on a scale akin to that in the Soviet Union. This absence led to the question, raised by the future President John F. Kennedy in 1940, in his book *Why England Slept*, whether there was a structural factor inherent in democracies that made it harder for them to prepare. His description was of Britain, but he also addressed the question to the USA. Kennedy served in the Pacific during the war, while one of his brothers was killed in the air war against Germany, preparing for the Normandy invasion of 1944.

World War Two would also pose questions about the comparative nature of domestic politics. For example, did the USA, where elections, notably Congressional in 1942 and Presidential and Congressional in 1944, affirmed domestic support for the government, have an advantage over Britain where there were no wartime general elections? Or, over the Soviet Union, which coerced domestic support, but at the cost of relying on nationalist, rather than Communist, ideology? Or, over Germany, where Nazi ideology limited female participation in the economy? Or, over Japan and its divine Emperor?

Germany

Whatever the apparent deficiencies of democracies, the German economy failed to adapt to the needs and strains of world war as successfully as that of the USA. At the same time, the Germans also had the disadvantage of a much smaller and less modernised prewar industrial base. They also had to cope, eventually, with the impact of heavy Allied air attack. In the event, the Germans were able to rearm sufficiently well to win a one-front war in France in 1940, but not to confront both the Soviet Union and the USA (each more formidable powers) from the winter of 1941–2. As far as the criteria of mechanisation were concerned, the German army on the Eastern Front indeed became less mechanised and less 'modern' in the latter stages of the war.

After the war, the devastation of a bombed and defeated country and a discredited ideology created problems in assembling material on how the German state had operated in practice.[6] Nevertheless, much excellent scholarship was eventually produced. It has revealed that serious deficiencies in German warmaking, many of which reflected the structural weaknesses of the Nazi state, were also, in part, a product of a systemic failure to understand the situation. It has also been argued that Hitler was preparing for a major war to break out later than it did.

The multiple inefficiencies in the German war economy were more than the inherent problems of a totalitarian regime lacking the efficiencies of market discipline. There were also the issues of the particular flaws of the Hitlerian regime, notably the organisational chaos it spawned. The duplication of agencies, in turn divided between competing ministries, as well as the party, army, SS and air force, led to serious rivalry, both institutional and personal, and resulted in acute confusion in policy implementation. For instance, German intelligence was affected by the systemic rivalry between the Abwehr, a branch of the military, and the SD, which was the SS Security Service. There was no war cabinet to provide coherence. In Japan, there were also serious divisions in policy and the war economy, notably, but not only, between the army and the navy.

In Germany, rivalry and confusion focused decision-making on Hitler, who was seriously unable to provide clear, coherent and systematised direction. His failure included a lack of understanding of economic issues, as well as confused responses to the issues and structures involved in economic mobilisation and, indeed, planning.

Many of the preferences of the German war economy, however, reflected more than the weakness of Hitler's position or his poor leadership. For example, the focus on quality in weaponry, rather than on quantity, proved a mistake, as did the division of production among a large number of types, rather than the mass production of a smaller number of durable models pursued by the Allies. Will was no substitute for sensible planning processes, and violence was part of an expedient of hasty improvisation that could not act as a replacement for the rational and effective crisis management required by the Germans.

Albert Speer, who, as Armaments Minister from February 1942, became effective head of the war economy, sought to provide rational crisis management, not least through improving the allocation of raw materials and labour. However, aside from the serious personal deficiencies he overlooked in his highly-misleading postwar memoirs, he faced not only major problems in resource availability but also multiple sources of opposition to his control of allocation. Some of this opposition was systemic to the regime, but part of it was due to the attitudes of the army. Tensions over the availability and use of manpower repeatedly emerged. The resulting problems, and the role of individual conjunctures and leaders, highlight the impact of particular decisions on military capability, as well as the failure to contain problems within efficient structures able to appreciate and respond to the wider implications. Thus, in early 1942, Admiral Raeder, the head of the navy, decided to meet the shortage of shipyard workers for U-boat maintenance by drawing on labour engaged in new U-boat construction. As a consequence, a useful short-term increase in the number of operational U-boats for the Battle of the Atlantic was achieved at the cost of cutting new production, and thereby sustaining that battle.[7]

Furthermore, alongside complicity with the murderous purposes and policies of the regime,[8] notably, but not only, the location of manufacturing plant at Auschwitz and other concentration camps, individual German companies followed their own economic policies in a manner that lessened central direction of the war economy. Thus, Daimler-Benz was unwilling to commit itself too heavily to armament production before or during the war, as the conflict was expected to lead to victory, or, later, to defeat, and, in either case, it was necessary for the company to plan for peace.[9] More generally, the economy in Germany 'failed to rise to the challenge of a large-scale war as it did in Britain and the USA'.[10] Structural reasons played a role, but so also did issues of management. The deficiencies of the latter throw much light on the political weaknesses of the Nazi state and the serious flaws in managerial terms of its vicious ideology, at once murderous, bombastic and rhetorical.

In a wider perspective, the politicised nature of the German wartime economy helped compromise German military success and strategic dominance by making German control over conquered territories oppressive, if not vicious, for large numbers of their people,[11] as well as by lessening the value of their economic assets.[12] Thus, the forced employment of millions of foreign workers, especially, but not only, Soviet, Polish and French, who were brought to Germany and generally treated harshly, if not murderously, was not a way to ensure labour commitment or efficiency, while it also greatly compromised the appeal of co-operation with Germany.[13] Both Germany and Japan failed to make the best use of their conquered territories. Germany would have, if it had followed policies which showed more consideration for the conquered nations, gained far more in terms of economic support from them. Germany would also have found more military support in Eastern Europe, if, for example, Ukrainians had been offered a better deal.

This was a key instance of the degree to which Hitler had a chance of welding together a united Europe, or, at least, a new European order with considerable support, under his hegemony in 1940–1. This new order could have drawn on a range of tendencies including anti-Communism, conservatism, authoritarianism, anti-Semitism, anti-liberalism, and interest in a new-model European future.

However, enlightened self-interest was scarcely one of Hitler's characteristics. From the moment at which serious preparations began to be made for Operation Barbarossa, the invasion of the Soviet Union launched on 22

June in 1941, notions of economic co-operation with occupied areas took a decidedly second place to an economic exploitation that was particularly harsh.[14] The remnants of the social order in the areas of Russia that were occupied remained recognisably Soviet and the collaborators with the German occupation were too weak to overcome this.[15]

German policy was a key strand in the politics of Soviet resilience. Hitler did not offer terms likely to open the way to a compromise peace, the course followed with France in 1940, although, in the Soviet Union, there was no agency for negotiation comparable to that which led to the establishment of the Vichy régime. For Hitler, war with the Soviet Union, which he saw as a land of Slavs and Jews, was as much an end as a means, and, indeed, was a metahistorical and existential struggle for supremacy that was to be waged without finish, let alone compromise.

This central political goal, at once objective and context, helps explain the way in which the war was fought by the Germans. This goal was also linked to domestic policies such as the attempt to produce a healthier race, with health understood in explicitly racial terms. Thus, the women receiving the Honor Cross of the German Mother from 1939 for having numerous children[16] were under the would-be panoptic vision of a regime for which the Home Front was truly a front line of racial conflict and where Joseph Goebbels's Ministry of Propoaganda was one of the more effective institutions. Similarly, alongside the creation of a *Judenfrei* [Jew free] panorama,[17] Germanisation, as a key element in ethnic reorganisation and cultural extension was a theme in some occupied territories, for example (albeit to very differing extents) Bohemia-Moravia, Slovenia, Crimea and Belgium.

An emphasis on racial struggle invited a key theme of postwar consideration, notably how far the war would have been different without Hitler. World War One indicated that authoritarian politics and the apparent logic of war meant that it was not necessary to have a leader of Hitler's megalomaniac fanaticism in order to ensure that a bitter war was for long intractable. Nevertheless, Hitler's racial paranoia and prospectus gave German policy in World War Two a distinctively murderous character. However easy it is to think of the two world wars as part of one longer conflict, there were crucial differences in ideologies and methods, as well as alignments and events.

Some members of the German military in World War Two tended to be less concerned with Nazi ideology and/or less subject to Nazi control than civilian administrators, but the treatment of much of Eastern Europe and the Soviet Union by the Germans, and of China by the Japanese, were aspects of total war. As a result, the slaughter of civilians was particularly acute in both regions. Thus, the Japanese were murderously brutal to the Chinese population of conquered Singapore. Straits Chinese believed to be sympathetic to the Nationalists (Kuomintang), Communists or simply unwelcome, were slaughtered, many being machine-gunned on the beach, while women were coerced into prostitution, and the economy as a whole was ruined.[18]

Such occupation practices on the part of all the Axis powers undermined the possibility of winning local support and encouraged large-scale resistance in some areas,[19] but not in others. In turn, resistance led to further brutality, which was deliberately totally disproportionate. This brutality could help contain opposition,[20] but it also ensured that support for the occupiers was limited. *Wehrmacht* officers might complain about what they saw as the excessive violence towards civilians shown by allies, for example the Croats and the Hungarians, but the *Wehrmacht* idea of maximising violence against supposedly insurgent-controlled areas in order to eradicate resistance was brutal, and linked to Nazi ideology and racism. The *Wehrmacht* policies were generally unsuccessful.[21] Axis occupation practices also fed through into the attitudes that sustained the war on the part of those not occupied.

The consequences of Hitler's views and position help direct attention to the significance of German resistance to Hitler. This resistance failed, but, even had it succeeded, the consequences would have depended greatly on circumstances, notably timing. The situation on 20 July 1944, the date of the unsuccessful Bomb Plot to kill Hitler and overthrow his regime, was very different to that four years earlier.[22]

Discussion of the German resistance was greatly affected by postwar politics. Efforts to integrate West Germany into the West as the front line against Communism led, from the 1950s, to the reformulation of German nationalism, with the creation of a 'new' free West Germany and, in particular, a new West German army. This process required an acceptable presentation of recent history in which Nazism was seen as an aberration, and regarded as restricted to a minority of 'devout' members of the party, while resistance to Nazi policies was emphasized.

There was a particular stress on the July 1944 bomb plot, which seemed appropriate as it had been mounted by conservative elements, presented as 'moderate' Nazis, and not by Communists (whose resistance role, in turn, was stressed in East Germany). More generally, the part of the latter in the resistance was underplayed in West Germany[23] and is still underplayed today. Indeed, the 'National Committee for a Free Germany', the Seydlitz Committee of prominent German prisoners of war in Soviet hands who produced propaganda at the behest of the Soviets, had scant impact on the conduct of the *Wehrmacht*. However, the same was true of the Bomb Plot: the failure of the military plotters to kill Hitler on 20 July 1944 was seriously compounded by the refusal of sympathisers, such as Field Marshal von Kluge, to stop fighting the Allies.

Despite a number of plots and a range of other forms of opposition, resistance to Hitler in Germany was patchy.[24] Instead, reflecting the extent to which the war, as much as Nazism, brought major changes in Germany, the cumulative pressure of defeats, and of a failure brought home by Allied bombing, led to social dissolution, rather than resistance.[25] Yet, in Germany from the outset, alongside the sense of destiny that helped give force to Nazi plans, governmental confidence in popular responses was, in practice, less pronounced than might be suggested by a focus on the wartime propaganda of togetherness; a situation that matched that in other states. Indeed, the Nazis had to confront the lack of popular celebrations when war broke out.

Alongside fanatical support which continued until the very end of the war, failure in war, and a disillusionment on the Home Front that led to a fall in morale as well as to dissidence, resulted in an intensification of repression and terror. Repression was facilitated when Heinrich Himmler, the head of the SS, became Minister of the Interior from 1943, a classic instance of the nature of the Nazi state with its empire-building and duplications.

Nevertheless, the extent to which Nazi rule of Germany rested on fear, rather than consent, has been questioned.[26] The weakness of popular resistance on behalf of the Nazi regime during and after the Allied conquest of Germany was a demonstration of its *eventual* unpopularity and sense of failure, although the formal surrender of the German regime after the death of Hitler was also important in undermining the legitimacy of any resistance. However, this unpopularity did not mean that there was a lack of support or, at least, consent earlier.

A side-effect of fanaticism and failure was the suicide of Nazi leaders in 1945. However, these suicides, like the determination of many (but not all) German soldiers to fight to the death, also reflected anxiety about the consequences of surrender to the Soviets whom they had brutalised, as well as fear of dishonour. In addition, for the soldiers, there was fear of the literally deadly military discipline practised by the Nazi regime.[27]

Britain

Any attempt to draw a clear contrast between the Allies and the Axis in terms of freedom and totalitarianism collapses in the face of the Soviet Union and, to an extent, British imperial rule. The often harsh treatment of Soviet labour, both male and female, has been underplayed in many accounts of the conflict. In the democracies, on the other hand, there were problems with labour freedom, while the mobilisation of labour was constrained by the liberal assumptions of these societies. For example, British trade unionists went on strike without being arrested. Trade union dissatisfaction proved a particular problem prior to the German attack on the Soviet Union in 1941, as many left-wing activists propagated the Communist critique of 'the bosses' war'. This was an attitude and an activity they subsequently found it useful to forget. The contrast between subsequent mention of Far-Right sympathy for Hitler, and of interest (and not just on the Far Right) in peace with Germany in 1940, and a lack of subsequent mention of the sometimes ambivalent stance on the Far Left is striking.

More than politics was at stake. Churchill complained in the Commons on 7 May 1941 about the strength of the 'negative principle ... in the constitution and the working of the British war-making machine ... the difficulty is to get more impetus and speed behind it'. Indeed, the institutional freedom of the trade unions was preserved alongside central planning and wage restraints. Strikes were not only a problem in Britain, as disputes in the Australian dockyards in 1945 affected warships based there and indeed the planning for British naval operations against Japan.

Yet, in Britain, despite strikes and other aspects of labour unrest that, at least in part, were a symptom of disillusionment, labour relations were far better than in World War One. From 1940, union leaders, such as Walter Citrine, the General Secretary of the TUC, played key roles in what was very much a corporatist state. Ernest Bevin, General Secretary of the Transport and General Workers from 1921, instead, became a Member of Parliament (MP) and Minister of Labour in 1940. During the war, trade union membership rose from about 6,250,000 in 1939 to nearly 8,000,000 in 1945, in part because union membership was officially encouraged.

This was a case of trade union backing for a Conservative-dominated government, from 1940 a government that was supported by all the established political parties. It is unclear what would have happened had there been no war – no general election was due until 1940 – but, despite some Labour by-election successes in 1938–9 and the possibility of Liberal–Labour co-operation in many seats,[28] most observers, prior to the outbreak of war, were confident that Neville Chamberlain would win re-election at the head of the Conservative-dominated National government that had come to power in 1931, and that had easily won the 1935 general election. Indeed, in public opinion polls, Chamberlain won approval rates of 55 per cent and above until March 1940.

However, the political situation was transformed by Hitler's growing aggression and the outbreak of war, for, besides having been proved publicly and seriously wrong over Appeasement, Chamberlain was not capable of energising the war effort and conveying determination as David Lloyd George had done in World War One once he became Prime Minister in 1916. During the winter of 1939–40, in what was later called the 'Phoney War', the government attempted to wage war with as little disruption to society as possible. It was hoped that the British blockade, combined with the strains of maintaining a war economy, would weaken Germany and lead to Hitler's overthrow or to a major change of German policy. This 'long war' strategy, however, unsuccessful in itself, was also not one that brought good news. Chamberlain, who was intolerant of criticism, moreover mishandled Cabinet reshuffles and failed to unite the Conservative Party.

The government's war strategy was totally swept aside by Hitler's successful *blitzkrieg* in Western Europe in the spring of 1940. The complete and humiliating failure of the attempt to prevent the German conquest of Norway resulted, in the context of a continuation of adversarial party politics, in a Labour censure motion in the Commons. This motion attracted enough Conservative support to lead to the search for a coalition that could encompass Labour: 41 Conservative MPs voted against the government, and many more abstained.

Chamberlain still had the backing of most Conservative MPs, many of whom regarded Churchill, a vocal and bitter critic of Appeasement, as a dangerous maverick. However, Conservative divisions were growing and becoming more public, Chamberlain, possibly suffering from the cancer that was to kill him that November, was losing heart, and the Labour and Liberal leaders, who had been unprepared to establish a Coalition government under Chamberlain at the start of the war, remained unwilling to serve under him. Hitler's aggression, not just the invasion of Denmark and Norway but more particularly that of the Low Countries and France, made Chamberlain all the more determined to hang on, but he needed a coalition to demonstrate unity and ensure war production, and Labour refused to join a ministry under him.

The search for an alternative became urgent. Viscount Halifax, the Foreign Secretary, was seen as a possible Prime Minister, one whose views were in keeping with the majority of the Conservative parliamentarians, but, aware of his own deficiencies, not least his position in the Lords, his linkage with Appeasement, and a lack of Labour support, he did not push himself as much as Churchill. The latter had not had a particularly good 'Phoney War', and the Royal Navy, of which he was First Lord, although energetic against German surface raiders (notably the *Graf Spee*) and U-boats in what was very much a real war, had failed to prevent the German conquest of Norway. Nevertheless, Churchill conveyed determination, had war experience, and, whatever the reservations of some generals, gave the impression he could do the job.

Churchill was asked to form a new government on 10 May 1940. This was to be a coalition government. A War Cabinet of five, including two Labour members as well as Chamberlain as Lord President of the Council, was made responsible for policy. Chamberlain, who acted in an honourable fashion, was not to serve as the leader of a Conservative opposition to Churchill, and Churchill became more powerful when the now-ill Chamberlain resigned as leader of the Conservative Party that September and was replaced by him. Chamberlain soon died (on 9 November 1940), and no-one took the role of leader of a Conservative opposition group.

The Labour leader since 1935, Clement Attlee, proved an effective Deputy Prime Minister. His appointment was intended to highlight the notion of national unity. Other prominent Labour figures obtained major posts, Herbert Morrison as Home Secretary, Ernest Bevin as Minister of Labour, and Albert Alexander as First Lord of the Admiralty.

A key change was Churchill's appointment also as Minister of Defence, which gave him complete control over running the war. Churchill's appointment as Minister of Defence was not entirely unprecedented. In 1936, Sir Thomas Inskip was appointed Minister for Co-ordination of Defence, and he was followed by Lord Chatfield in January 1939. However, they were minor figures who were appointed to mute the growing demand for Churchill to be given a key defence role. The power and authority that Churchill obtained as Minister of Defence in May 1940 (and, arguably, earlier as the key figure in Chamberlain's War Cabinet) was much greater.

The Fall of France in May–June 1940 hit the new British government hard, leading to a crisis of credibility that was seen in the debates within the War Cabinet in May. Moreover, a number of ministers and ex-ministers, including Halifax, who kept the spirit of Appeasement alive until 1941, R. A. Butler and Lloyd George, were willing to consider negotiations with Hitler via intermediaries, especially Italy. However, the would-be negotiators were unable to build up a dynamic, in part because they lacked traction within the government; while Italy's entry into the war in June ended the chance of presenting Mussolini as an intermediary. Halifax remained Foreign Secretary until Anthony Eden, who had held the post in 1935–8, regained it in December 1940. Butler, the Under-Secretary of State in the Foreign Office (a post that was made more important because Halifax was in the Lords), and an enthusiastic supporter of Chamberlain, was moved to be President of the Board of Education in July 1941.

Lloyd George's hopes of office after Chamberlain's resignation were thwarted due to the latter's opposition, and when, on 4 June 1940, he was at last offered a Cabinet post by Churchill, he refused to serve as long as Chamberlain remained in office. Chamberlain saw Lloyd George as a potential Pétain, and Lloyd George was certainly convinced that Churchill was foolish to fight on. That October, he said he would enter office when 'Winston is bust'.[29] Lloyd George, who had met Hitler in 1936, considered himself as a possible leader, saving the country from the consequences of disaster. He also regarded Churchill as junior to him, and felt that he had a better claim to lead the country having been Prime Minister in 1916–22, for some of which Churchill had served in the Cabinet.

Churchill, who very much took charge on 10 May 1940, was convinced that Hitler was untrustworthy and a mortal threat to Britain and the world. There was to be no alliance of expedience with Germany comparable to the Nazi–Soviet Pact of 1939, which helps explain why the British account of the politics of their war record is justifiably a good one. Instead, Churchill's determination led to a surmounting of the pressure for negotiation, and steadied both government and nation for the challenges of the summer and autumn of 1940, notably the German air-assault known as the Battle of Britain. He was able to explain the need to fight on and the purpose of doing so, although, in practice, there was a degree of waiting for something to turn up in order to derail Hitler.

Churchill's ascendancy was completed by his brave and firm stance during the Battle of Britain that August and September, but also by the convenient death of Chamberlain that November. Chamberlain's cancer opened the way for Churchill to become leader of the Conservative Party. In his speech of 9 October accepting the leadership, Churchill offered an account of his broadest concerns: 'I have always faithfully served two public causes which I think stand supreme – the maintenance of the enduring greatness of Britain and her Empire and the historical continuity of our Island life'. Churchill was strong enough politically to send his major Conservative political rival, Halifax, to be ambassador to Washington. Thereafter, although criticised, both in public and in private, Churchill's position was unassailable until the end of the war.

The unprecedented and deadly air assault on the civilian population in 1940–1 did not really produce criticism of the government. Instead, following on from the Battle of Britain which had produced a significant boost to British civilian morale,[30] air attacks on cities fortified hostility to Germany and strengthened the idea that Hitler had to be defeated and removed. The German hope that the British people would realise their plight, overthrow Churchill, and make peace, proved a serious misreading of British politics and public opinion. The German bombing offensive led, British intelligence reports suggested, to signs of 'increasing hatred of Germany' as well as to demands for 'numerous reprisals'.[31]

From 7 September until mid-November 1940, the Germans bombed London every night bar one. There were also large-scale daylight attacks between 7 and 18 September, as well as hit-and-run attacks. Film helped ensure that London's Blitz was widely dramatized. Photographs of St Paul's Cathedral surrounded by flames and devastation, for example that by Herbert Mason of the raid on 29 December 1940, acquired totemic force. Documentaries included *London Can Take It* (1940), shot during the Blitz and featuring iconic shots of St Paul's; *Christmas Under Fire* (1941), which included a tracking shot down an escalator to people sheltering on an Underground platform; and *Fires Were Started* (1943), which featured location shooting in the docks.[32]

The major divisive consequence of the Blitz was that there was a degree of anger about the extent to which some of the wealthy could lessen their vulnerability by leaving London. Moreover, Londoners from the much-bombed dockside district of Silvertown, where there was a lack of shelters, forced their way into the Savoy Hotel's impressive shelter. Yet, the air assault did not lead to serious contention.[33] Instead, there was a phlegmatic and fatalistic response, one captured by the Listener Research Report organised by the BBC in 1941. The previous autumn, a Special Enquiry by the BBC into air raids and listening to the radio established that the radio was often seen as an alternative to the sounds of air attack.[34]

The air assault made the Home Front far more significant. It became the focus of government effort, in the shape of civil defence, and of activity by the public, such that Britain was both a welfare and a warfare state. The bravery of the civilians became a key theme, a bravery in which women played the central role. The emphasis on a stoical response to suffering was designed to preserve morale.[35]

The combination of an effective coalition, a popular wartime leader and the support of the Empire, helped the country and its politicians bear wartime problems and serious and humiliating setbacks without debilitating division. This was particularly so of total defeat in Greece and Crete in April–May 1941, of the humiliating loss of Singapore in February 1942, and of the ability of the *Scharnhorst* and the *Gneisnau*, two major German warships, to sail successfully from Brest to the North Sea the same month. Although his speeches were not always received favourably,[36] Churchill's rousing oratory, egotistical determination, bulldog spirit, interest in war,[37] and sheer capacity for work, all the more remarkable in a man born in 1874, made him the motive force as well as the public face of the government. Through the War Cabinet, he was able to exercise a degree of central control which had eluded Lloyd George in 1916–18. Moreover, unlike Lloyd George, Churchill was a member of the largest parliamentary party in the coalition, the Conservatives.

Furthermore, as in World War One, there was no general election during the war. In addition, as far as by-elections made necessary by deaths and retirements were concerned, the parties declared an electoral truce. This truce, however, was rejected by unofficial left-wing challengers, who won four seats from the Conservatives in 1942, and by the Common Wealth Party, an idealistic left-wing party established in 1942 by Sir Richard Acland, Liberal MP for Barnstaple. Common Wealth set out to contest by-elections against 'reactionary' candidates, and won three by-elections in 1943–5. A flavour of Acland's views can be seen in the motion of no confidence he tried to lay before the Commons in 1943. Acland noted that Churchill 'deservedly enjoys the personal affection of the overwhelming majority of his fellow citizens', but continued that, 'for the sake both of early victory and lasting peace', it was necessary for British policy to show 'greater understanding of the fact that this war is part of a world-wide revolution, out of which must emerge a new civilisation firmly based on the common ownership of all major productive resources'.

The appeal of the Common Wealth Party was not the only source of pressure on the government. There were also demands for a commitment by Churchill over the December 1942 Beveridge Report, which advocated a compulsory national insurance scheme designed to provide 'cradle to grave' security, a measure that would greatly extend the scope of the state. Churchill's unwillingness to give any immediate commitment to legislation based on the Report had significant political results. On 16 February 1943, 119 MPs went into the division lobby against Churchill on the issue of the Report being implemented. Moreover, in the 'little General Election', as the press called the six by-elections in January and February 1943, the Conservatives' vote dropped in four of the six, and the Conservative candidate was lucky to hold the North Midlothian seat against a Common Wealth challenge.

The contrast with totalitarian Germany in that period was readily apparent, not least as, on 18 February 1943, Goebbels called for total war and total mobilisation in a key speech at the Sports Palace in Berlin that was broadcast nationally and listened to by millions. No other views were acceptable in Germany. The context of Churchill's rhetoric was very different, not least with the obsessive emphasis on the *Führer* (Leader) in Goebbels's speech and other propaganda. Churchill's effective deployment of the monarchy as a symbol of nation and empire was very different in tone and content. As another instance of contrast, Churchill disliked Ronald Giles, the critical cartoonist in the *Sunday Express*, regarding him as a Trotskyist, but Giles remained at work. Churchill was also no Tōjō. The latter not only accumulated ministerial positions in Japan, but also, in April 1942, called a general election that was very much stage-managed.

Yet, in Britain, despite this relative freedom, the war was conducted with less public criticism and ministerial dissension than World War One, let alone the French Revolutionary and Napoleonic Wars, when there had been both elections and several changes of government. Two Labour left-wingers, Aneurin Bevan and Emanuel Shinwell, were the only serious parliamentary critics with whom the Churchill coalition had to contend, although, also from the Left, Sir Stafford Cripps saw himself as an alternative Prime Minister. An able lawyer, Cripps was Ambassador to the Soviet Union in 1940–2, and then Lord Privy Seal and a member of the War Cabinet. He was popular on the Left and proposed the formation of a War Planning Directorate, which was intended as a body to circumvent Churchill. Field Marshal, Lord Milne, a former Chief of the Imperial General Staff, who dined on 19 March 1942 with General Sir Alan Brooke, then holder of that post, was recorded by the latter as thinking: 'Winston is drawing near unto his end and … he won't last much longer as PM. Predicts that Stafford Cripps will succeed him soon'.[38]

Cripps, however, proved to have limited traction, while his willingness to propitiate Stalin was shown by his response to the seizure of the Baltic States, which was more conciliatory than that of Churchill. Cripps's mission to India in 1942 failed to solve political tension in the sub-continent, a blow to his reputation, while eventual victory in North Africa vindicated Churchill's strategy there. Moreover, Churchill remained very popular in the country and easily won the two votes of confidence he faced in Parliament, that on 2 July 1942 by 476 to 25 votes.

This debate was touched off by the humiliating surrender on 20 June of Tobruk, with 33,000 prisoners, to the *Afrika Korps* under Rommel, and the resulting search for causes. The debate revealed that parliamentary critics of the government held differing views, lacked coordination, and found it difficult to voice criticism without causing offence. There was no equivalent to the Shell Shortage issue of World War One, one that had led to serious and well-founded public attacks on the government, and, indeed, helped provoke the fall of the Asquith ministry and the rise of Lloyd George in 1916.

After victory at El Alamein on 23 October–4 November 1942, Churchill was able to demote Cripps, and his political position was far less vulnerable. Churchill announced on 10 November 1942 that recent successes signified not 'the beginning of the end' but the 'end of the beginning'.

There was criticism of Churchill within both the government and the coalition. Moreover, there was good cause for criticism. Churchill bore some of the responsibility for the humiliating failure in 1941–2 of the strategy for confronting Japan, and Alan Brooke's diary made it clear that, throughout the war, he could be very difficult as far as military planning was concerned. Although his ideas were good enough to be taken seriously, Churchill's interest and attempted intervention in operational matters irritated the Chiefs of Staff.[39] Moreover, his judgment of individual generals could be flawed because he tended to focus on their alleged lack of drive and moral fibre rather than the constraints posed by the nature of the forces under their command.[40]

However, Brooke's overall judgment was that Churchill was crucial to the winning of the war, while repeated command failures in Malaya and Singapore, notably by the naval commander, were in large part responsible for disaster there. Churchill could also correctly refute military advice, as in September 1941 when he responded to a plan by Charles Portal, Chief of the Air Staff, for victory by mass bombing, by pointing out that not only were the effects problematic, but also that the plan downplayed, what actually occurred, the German ability to improve their air defences. More generally, Churchill's main objective was to get the Americans to fight the Germans and then defeat the Japanese later; and that was how the situation turned out.

Churchill benefited not only from being Prime Minister in wartime, but also from the weakness of his Conservative rivals and critics. Moreover, despite criticisms from some of its members, notably Aneurin Bevan, Labour provided largely consistent support. However, the British intervention in Greece at the expense of the Communists in 1944–5 led to serious strains, in large part because anger over British military support for the Royalists interacted with tensions within the Labour Party.[41]

Yet, mostly as a consequence of his focus on the war and his own self-confidence, Churchill was insufficiently sensitive to shifts in the public mood towards attitudes and policies associated with Labour. The consequences were to be made brutally clear in 1945, when he and the Conservatives were rejected by the electorate. The wartime coalition was not maintained, as, in contrast, it had been after World War One, with Lloyd George continuing as Prime Minister, with Conservative support, until 1922, an alignment seen with the 'Coupon Election' of 1918 in which the Conservatives had co-operated with the Lloyd George Liberals.

In May 1945, the Labour Party conference turned down Churchill's suggestion that the coalition be maintained until Japan was defeated. Instead, Labour left the coalition that month, and Churchill formed a new caretaker government that lasted until the general election. This was a coalition government overwhelmingly centred on the Conservatives, but including the remnants of National Labour and National Liberal support that had backed the 1931–40 National Government. Labour thus insisted on a return to party politics which Churchill had done his best to avoid. Moreover, he discouraged the Conservatives from preparing for a partisan election.

On 5 July 1945, when the war with Germany was over, although not yet that with Japan, a general election removed the Conservatives. The results were announced on 26 July so that the votes of the military could also be counted. The shift to Labour was far more abrupt and sweeping than had been predicted. Already, in April, the Common Wealth party's candidate had won Chelmsford from the Conservatives, under the banner 'A Vote for Common-Wealth is a vote for the people'. In the general election, Labour strengthened its working-class support, which was not seriously challenged by the Communists. The election in 1945 was the first since the universal male franchise was granted in 1918 in which working-class Conservative support (difficult as that is to measure) dipped to come close to 30 per cent, while Labour took a majority of the working-class vote. The *Daily Mirror*, the most popular newspaper in the country, supported Labour, but presented it in a non-partisan, wartime spirit; and not as a working-class, still less a Socialist, party. Unlike in 1935, the year of the last general election, Labour also indeed gained a large portion of the middle-class vote. Labour took 393 seats (in a house of 640 members) on 47.8 per cent of the votes cast, to the Conservatives' 213, the most miserable Conservative result since 1906, although their share of the poll was still 39.8 per cent. Conservative organisation had been poor, notably in the decline in the system of constituency agents, but it was too easy (and convenient) to blame this factor: the Conservatives' lack of attractive policies was more important. The Liberals took 12 seats on 9.1 per cent of the vote. With its percentage of the vote rising by 10 per cent, the Labour net gain was 227 seats to give it its first parliamentary majority.

Aside from doing very well in industrial constituencies, Labour also took such southern seats as Cambridgeshire, St Albans, Taunton, Wimbledon and Winchester. Having won none of the 12 Birmingham seats in 1935, Labour now took ten of the 13 available. Aside from maintaining unity, Labour also dominated the Left. The Independent Labour Party (ILP) had only three MPs, the Communists only two, and the Common Wealth only one, Ernest Millington for Chelmsford. He subsequently joined Labour, as did the ILP MPs.

Labour's victory, in what the left-wing Labour MP Michael Foot (co-author of *Guilty Men* (1940), a bitter attack on Appeasement) was later to call 'the blissful dawn of July 1945', reflected political, social and cultural shifts during the war. State control, planning and Socialism increasingly seemed normative. Millington declared that the result showed 'that the people are tired of the old order and want a new plan'. During the war, the cost of living had been subsidised, taxation rose, and attitudes towards what was quintessentially British changed. A language of inclusiveness and sharing became important, and achieved visual form in the celebration of ordinary people in the documentaries made during the war, for example *Listen to Britain* (1942).[42] Widely-held wartime aspirations were focused by the Beveridge Report. This formula for postwar reconstruction, a formula that in practice could not be afforded, encouraged the sense that the war had to lead to change, and that Labour offered the best chance of such change. The expansion of state activity provided a new impetus for opinion-formers who argued that such activity postwar could transform society.

An indication of the support for state-directed reform was provided by the passage of the 1944 Education Act, which was introduced by R. A. Butler, the Conservative Minister of Education who, in 1940, when a Foreign Office minister, had been interested in negotiations, via Mussolini, to secure peace. This Act obliged every local education authority to prepare a development plan for educational provision, while the Ministry of Education was to impose new minimum standards in matters such as school accommodation and size. The minimum school leaving age was to be raised to 15 from 1947, and fees in state-supported secondary schools were abolished. The abolition of fee-paying grammar schools would, it was hoped, encourage the entry of children from poorer families. Entry into schools was on the basis of the new '11 plus' examination.

Trade union membership had risen considerably during the war, while the role of the Labour Party in the wartime coalition was important to its revived standing, and also provided an apprenticeship in power. This role confounded claims that Labour was inexperienced and therefore unfit for government.

Yet, the Labour landslide in 1945 owed just as much to the unpopularity of the Conservatives as it did to an upsurge in positive support for Labour. Memories of the past, of mass unemployment and Appeasement, were as potent as any hopes for the future which the electorate may have had. The Conservatives were not willing, nor able, to offer the more optimistic scenarios proposed by Labour, many of which indeed were to prove naïve and damaging to the economy. However, the Conservatives were also associated with privilege and seen as opposed to the workers.

USA

In the USA, preparations for war were stepped up in 1940 in response to the startling nature of Axis success. Yet, this was not a state-run military mobilisation: economic regulation was relatively light, and numerous failings in the quality of munitions produced by the private sector were exposed by the Truman Commission in 1941. Interagency disputes were also an issue. However, the Americans benefited from their already-sophisticated economic infrastructure, which helped in the adaptation of the economy for war production, a process that became better organised as a result of the establishment of the Office of War Mobilization in May 1943.

Already responsible for 31.4 per cent of world manufacturing in 1938 (compared to 12.7 for Germany, 10.7 for Britain and 9.0 for the Soviet Union), the USA was the key to the out-production by the Allies of the Axis.[43] The absence of a need to defend America's industrial capacity from air attack was a contributory factor to the ability there to focus so many resources on production for overseas operations, including the application of new advances in the mass production of improved weaponry. There was also a labour dimension. The American emphasis on a mechanised and relatively high-tech military entailed (by relative standards) a stress on machines, not manpower, in the American army. As a consequence, a larger percentage of the national labour force worked in manufacturing than in the case of Germany or Japan. Cultural factors also played an important role, as the Americans (like the Soviets and British) were far readier to use women in manufacturing than either the Germans or the Japanese. American agriculture was also more mechanised than its German and Japanese counterparts. Furthermore, the speedy expansion of the fiscal strength of the federal government played a significant role in encouraging an unprecedented surge in war production.

Truly the 'arsenal of democracy' as Franklin Delano Roosevelt, the President from 1933 to 1945, had promised his radio-audience in December 1940, the USA produced 297,000 planes and 86,000 tanks during the war, as well as more aircraft carriers than all the other combatants. The sophistication of weaponry also rose greatly, a process that culminated with the development of the atom bomb. The pursuit of corporate, competitive and individual advantage brought great benefits for the national economy. For American companies, gross corporate profits rose markedly, helping fund investment in production. Workers benefited from a rise in real wages which ensured both labour mobility, including the large-scale movement of African-Americans from the South, and good labour relations. Greater prosperity provided a growing tax base for rising federal expenditure that, in turn, led to economic expansion.[44]

There was no shift in political control in the USA (nor in the Soviet Union) comparable to that in Britain in 1945, although for very different reasons. Roosevelt was elected President for an unprecedented third term in office in November 1940, running on a misleading pledge to keep the USA out of the war. He received 27,244,160 votes compared to 22,305,198 for the Republican candidate, Wendell Willkie (the largest popular vote for a defeated candidate up to then), taking 449 electoral votes in the Electoral College compared to Willkie's 82. The other candidates – Norman Thomas (Socialist), Roger Babson (Prohibitionist), Earl Browder (Communist) and John Aiken (Socialist Labor) – managed only 221,516 votes in total. The Republicans attacked Roosevelt running for a third term as well as aspects of the New Deal, but Willkie, who had moved from supporting the Democrats in 1940, was leader of the left-wing element in the Republican Party. Both candidates backed the national defence programme as well as hemispheric defence (the defence of the Americas), but both opposed participation in foreign wars, while Willkie criticised the New Deal.

As President during the war, Roosevelt faced no equivalent to the uncertainty facing Abraham Lincoln in Congressional elections of 1862, and the Presidential election of 1864. In part, this was because of the course of the campaigning. In the American Civil War, there was a clear relationship between Robert E. Lee's successes and Union (Northern) war-weariness. Thus, in the autumn of 1862, there was a possibility that the Democrats might capture the House of Representatives and press for peace. Had Lee's invasion of Maryland maintained its initial dynamism that September, and Lee and the Confederate Army of Northern Virginia outmanoeuvred George McClellan and the Union's (North's) Army of the Potomac, instead of dividing his army in the face of the Union forces who had managed to acquire a copy of Lee's orders, then the Congressional elections might not have gone for the Republicans. Again, Lincoln had a particularly strong political need in the early summer of 1864 for an appearance of success. The heavy casualties in Grant's unsuccessful 'Overland' campaign, and the initial failure to capture Atlanta, hit civilian morale in July and August. Lincoln feared that he would not be re-elected. His opponent, McClellan, wanted reunion by the Confederacy as the price of peace, but McClellan's running mate, George Pendleton, was a Peace Democrat, and the platform pressed for an armistice. However, a series of Union (Northern) successes, in the Petersburg and Atlanta campaign and the Shenandoah Valley, let Lincoln back in.[45]

Roosevelt faced no such problems. First, although America's direct participation in the war did go very badly in the early months, notably with Pearl Harbor and the fall of the Philippines and Wake Island to Japanese invasion, the charge of poor preparation and planning was not brought home on the government, as, in part, it should have been. There were accusations of neglect in the aftermath of Pearl Harbor, accusations that led to controversy, to government enquiry, and to Congressional hearings, notably the Roberts Commission and the Congressional inquiry of 1945–6. However, it was the commanders on the spot who took the criticism. Attempts to argue that the President had been culpable lacked traction.

Later failures were short-term, for example the German victory over American units in their first major clash, in the Battle of the Kasserine Pass in Tunisia in February 1943, and also the initial success of the German surprise attack at the expense of the defending Americans in the Battle of the Bulge in December 1944. In each case, the Americans recovered and were victorious. Moreover, controversies, for example over the risky conduct of the navy in the Battle of Leyte Gulf of 23–6 October 1944 – dividing its strength in the face of Japanese attack, or over the need for the very costly attack on the Japanese-held island of Iwo Jima in February and March 1945, were neither particularly prominent at the time, nor brought home on the government. This was helped by the fact that the over-complicated Japanese attempt in the Battle of Leyte Gulf to attack the American landing fleet was thwarted with the loss of four carriers, three battleships and ten cruisers.[46] Moreover, Iwo Jima was captured.

Thus, there was no equivalent in the USA to the consequences of the fall of Norway for Chamberlain in 1940, nor the fall of Tobruk in 1942 for increasing parliamentary criticism of Churchill. The timing was very different: in 1940 there was already considerable dissatisfaction over the Chamberlain government's conduct of the 'Phoney War'. In contrast, the lack of American preparedness at Pearl Harbor was covered by the shock of the Japanese surprise attack, and the devastating nature of this surprise attack encouraged a rallying round the government, which was further aided by Hitler's declaration of war on the USA.

Within five months, moreover, the conflict in the Pacific had been stabilised at the Battle of the Coral Sea (7–8 May 1942) and, on 4 June, the American navy achieved a major and obvious victory at Midway. Thereafter large-scale Japanese offensives in the Pacific ceased and the flow of the war was clearly in America's direction. Thus, the Congressional elections in November 1942 took place against a more benign background than if they had been held earlier in the year. Indeed, the Americans had landed on Guadalcanal in the Solomon Islands on 7 August and, although that proved a difficult campaign, their navy checked the Japanese off the island that November and the remaining Japanese troops were evacuated in January 1943.

Pearl Harbor had destroyed the logic and force of the isolationists' critique of Roosevelt. More specifically, the direct attack on the USA undermined the isolationists' argument that Roosevelt was in fact propping up the moribund British Empire by offering assistance against Germany. Indeed, isolationism was the last major instance of anti-British sentiment in American public culture,[47] although it amounted to much more than that. The cultural and political sources and manifestations of isolationism were very varied and drew on both Left- and Right-wing views, for example liberal concern that war would hit domestic reform, as well as xenophobia. The Japanese preference for operational rather than strategic thinking was shown by the treatment of Pearl Harbor solely as a military target, and the failure to appreciate the political consequences of the attack for the isolationist cause within the USA.

In the November 1942 Congressional elections, criticism of Roosevelt focused on the New Deal. The campaign centred on mundane domestic issues, notably taxes, high prices, rationing and the efficiency of war agencies. In particular, the Republicans benefited from opposition in the Farming Belt to the regulation of farm prices under the Stabilization Act of 1942. Indeed, throughout the war, the bulk of the political critique of Roosevelt was directed at domestic policies, and a coalition of Republicans and conservative Democrats dismantled aspects of the New Deal during the war. The 1942 elections led to a marked shift in Senate representation, but, despite the strengthened Republican position (from 28 to 37 Senators), the Democrats retained the majority. The Republicans also gained 44 seats in the House of Representatives, and, if the Democrats also retained the majority there, Roosevelt no longer had one. Indeed, this result represented a loss of his margin for domestic reform. In turn, the Democrats tried, and failed, to use the issue of isolationism against the Republicans.

In contrast, Roosevelt had faced little criticism over foreign policy during the 1942 campaign. Having been defeated in 1940, Willkie, who was an opponent of isolationism, travelled the world representing Roosevelt in the Middle East, the Soviet Union and China.[48]

By the time of the presidential election in November 1944, the question was really how soon the war would end. The Americans had conquered the islands of Saipan, Tinian and Guam earlier in the year, bringing Japan within bombing distance, and, in October, invaded the island of Leyte in the Philippines, defeating the Japanese navy in the Battle of Leyte Gulf. As a further instance of the folly of the Pearl Harbor assault, the Americans benefited in 1944 from deploying battleships sunk in that attack: although the *Arizona* had exploded, several battleships had gone down in the mud in what was a relatively shallow anchorage and could therefore be salvaged. In Europe, France and Belgium had been speedily liberated by Anglo–American forces from June, and, although the Germans had mounted strong resistance on their borders, notably to the Americans in the Huertgen Forest, it was clear that they had lost. The British failure at Arnhem in September 1944 did not challenge this impression of inevitability, no more than the German counter-attack in the Battle of the Bulge was to do (after the election) in December.

Roosevelt won the 1944 election, held on 7 November. If the results were less satisfactory than in 1940, or indeed 1932 and 1936, there was no comparison with Churchill's defeat the following year. Indiana, Ohio, Wisconsin, Iowa, the Dakotas, Nebraska, Kansas, Colorado, Wyoming, Vermont and Maine went Republican in 1944, compared to Indiana, Ohio, Iowa, the Dakotas, Nebraska, Kansas, Colorado, Maine and Vermont in 1940. Thus, the Republicans carried two more states, Wisconsin and Wyoming. The Mid-West was the centre of isolationism. Willkie was regarded as too left-wing by many Republicans and he was not selected as the Republican presidential candidate in 1944. He also refused to endorse the candidate, Thomas Dewey, Governor of New York. Dewey gained 22,006,278 votes, compared to 25,602,505 for Roosevelt (a lower number than in 1940): the figures in the electoral college were 99 to 432. Norman Thomas (Socialist), Claude Watson (National Prohibition), and Edward Teichert (Socialist Labor), had a combined vote of 200,152, indicating that there had been no move towards fringe parties comparable to the Common Wealth Party in Britain. As an indication of the extent to which the military was a citizen army, 2,691,160 ballots were cast by the military. The Democrats also retained control of both Houses of Congress.

In the 1944 campaign, Dewey focused on domestic issues, not least on the argument that a younger generation was needed in government. There was criticism of Roosevelt for standing for a fourth term. Dewey presented himself as vaguely internationalist, thus nullifying foreign policy as a big issue. The approaching end of the war enabled the Republicans to argue that, since the Americans were nearly across the stream, the argument about not changing horses in midstream was not valid. This argument was far less successful than the Labour critique of Churchill's Conservatives in 1945.

Dewey was less ideological than focused on competence. He had made his name, as District Attorney for New York from 1937, as a crime-buster, becoming Governor in 1942, and was not comfortable centring his political attack on foreign policy.[49] Indeed, after the 1948 presidential election, in which Dewey, the favourite, was surprisingly defeated by Harry Truman, the incumbent, Dewey was to be criticised in Republican ranks for failing to attack Truman over foreign policy.

The 1944 election had been most notable for the unexpected selection of Truman, a relative unknown at the national level, as Vice-President. This was not a selection that was directly related to foreign policy issues, although the decision to replace Henry Wallace, a New Dealer and the current Vice-President, was in part a function of his reputation as someone who was too Liberal, even Socialistic and potentially sympathetic to Communism, which had foreign policy implications. This decision also reflected the Democratic consensus that, while Roosevelt remained personally popular, the electorate had moved to the Right during the war. Truman was known within the Senate as a keen and sharp member of the Armed Service Committee; so his selection was in part based on defence considerations.

The shift away from isolationism was shown by the bipartisan commitment to a new international order. The House of Representatives adopted a measure introduced by J. W. Fulbright, supporting 'the creation of appropriate international machinery with power adequate to establish and to maintain a just and lasting peace' and American participation 'through its constitutional process'. A similar resolution passed the Senate

by 85 votes to five, and, on 28 July 1945, the Senate ratified the United
Nations Charter by 89 to two votes. There was to be no repetition of
America's failure to join the League of Nations after World War One.

Nevertheless, a sense that the Democrats had not been put under sufficient pressure over foreign policy in the 1944 campaign played a role in
the development of McCarthyism, which in part was, like isolationism, a
product of the Mid-West. By the end of the war, there were intimations of
a linkage by some Republican critics of the strong opposition to the New
Deal (lambasted by the hostile as Socialism) with a foreign policy allegedly
overly favourable to the Soviet Union. For critics, Roosevelt could thus
serve as a link between a much decried domestic policy and a new focus of
foreign policy concern: in place of isolationist criticism of interventionism
came hostility to an alliance with Communism. This critique looked
towards the subsequent argument that the Democrats 'lost China' by failing
to support the Nationalists (Kuomintang) against the Communists during
the 1946–9 civil war, an argument that was to be highly significant to the
development of an influential strand of Republican thought.

In 1944, aside from Roosevelt being helped by good war news, the
creation of a war economy had brought great prosperity to the bulk of the
American work force, with an increase in employment, company profits,
personal incomes and living standards. Popular support for the war was
also encouraged by government effort. Norman Rockwell was one of the
many artists enlisted to help by producing posters that were deployed to
assist the military and to persuade all Americans to help the war effort;
while Frank Capra produced the *Why We Fight* series of public education
films. Posters and photography[50] were used for recruitment, to boost
production, to motivate, and to assist rationing and the conservation of
resources, for example oil; and they linked the Home Front to the front line.

In the '90-division gamble', which forced an intensity of conflict that
placed an enormous strain on army manpower in 1944–5, the army was
kept relatively small (although the air force and navy absorbed large
numbers), and economic growth that involved large numbers of workers
brought much prosperity on the Home Front. Partly as a result, the USA
was less traumatised than other, economically-weaker powers that experienced greater mobilisation, although the latter were also more exposed to
attack. Yet, to argue that, as a result, the USA fought a modern war, and not
total war, risks pushing these definitions too far, and also runs the danger
of underplaying America's fundamental commitment and contribution to
Allied victory. Mobilization, furthermore, was in part a matter of attitude
of mind. A sense of being under threat was important in the USA, although
it was not sufficiently challenging to conventional racist assumptions to
ensure that due use was made of African-Americans in combat.

The possibility of contrasting judgments about the nature of the
American war effort is shown by the internment of more than 120,000
Japanese-Americans, which can be seen as a symbolic act of total war in

a society fighting what was, as far as its home base was concerned, a less threatening conflict. Yet, this internment also reflected anxiety about their loyalty, combined with fear of Japanese capability. Anger about internment leaves its legacy in the Japanese American National Museum in Los Angeles, alongside pride in the heroism of the Japanese-Americans who fought. At the same time, there are indications that some Japanese-Americans from Hawaii were willing to co-operate with the Japanese military.[51]

There is a tendency in the USA to forget that such internment, as well as surveillance,[52] and a more general abrogation of the rights of refugees and citizens of German, Italian and Japanese descent, was also seen in other combatants, for example Britain and Australia. Canada's history of Japanese internment was harsher than that of the USA. The situation was far harsher in the Soviet Union, and not only for people of such a 'foreign' background. Thus, on 14 June 1941, there were mass deportations to Siberia of about 43,000 Balts, allegedly for 'counter-revolutionary activity'. Most of these deportees died within a year in the harsh Soviet *gulags*.

What may seem the paranoia of the war years can be located in particular political and social circumstances. In part, alongside a concern about a fifth column of subversives, there was the sensitivity in nation states to those judged aliens, especially if they had an ethnic inflexion. With a certain parallel to the USA, the Soviet Union was a federal state of many nationalities, but ethnic groups judged suspect, such as the Kalmyks, the Crimean Tatars and the Volga Germans, were treated very harshly. The Tatars were deported to Uzbekistan once Crimea was reconquered in 1944.

There was also an economic challenge: modern societies, in the shape of industrial economies, depended on reliable workforces, and sensitivity about the latter was increased by the threats seen to lie in trade unionism, left-wing activism and the challenge of Soviet power. Paranoia played a role, and sometimes understandably so. In February 1941, when the Soviet Union was allied to Germany, the Australian War Cabinet was concerned about Soviet subversion, specifically 'the continued state of industrial unrest in the community'.[53] Two months earlier, in his talk on the theme of the USA as 'The Great Arsenal of Democracy', Roosevelt claimed that Axis 'secret emissaries' were trying 'to turn capital against labor, and vice versa. ... The nation ... expects and insists that management and workers will reconcile their differences by voluntary or legal means, to continue to produce the supplies that are so sorely needed'.

In the USA (as in Australia) success helped ensure that the war did not end with any transformation in the political system to match that in the scope of government. Thus, Roosevelt, who died in office in 1945, was succeeded by the Vice-President, the inexperienced Truman, in an orderly and constitutional fashion. Indeed, this succession seems unremarkable in American history, which itself indicates the extent to which, during the war, a combination of political culture and military success produced a governmental continuity that was notable.

Possibly, the maintenance of constitutionalism alongside initial serious failure was more remarkable in the case of Britain. However, as in World War One, and both reflecting and affecting the situation in Britain, there was no wartime general election and no foreign invasion. There were more serious divisions within some of the Allies' second-rank powers, notably China, where the Nationalists and Communists remained bitter rivals, and South Africa. The Nationalists in South Africa opposed the war and were to benefit postwar from its unpopularity. In Québec, the example of Vichy was important in challenging support for the war in 1940–2, including the willingness to serve in the military; but the German occupation of Vichy France in November 1942 affected Québecois views.

Soviet Union

The politics of the war were very different in the totalitarian states. There the key issues were grip and success. The strong grip of the totalitarian system could help overcome serious, indeed traumatic, military failure, as in the Soviet Union in 1941 and Germany in 1944. Nevertheless, the pressure was still severe. The July Bomb Plot indicated this in Germany, as did manoeuvrings among the Nazi leadership.

In the Soviet Union, Stalin had a nervous collapse of will on 28–30 June 1941, when the rapidly advancing Germans reached Minsk, the bombed capital of White Russia (Belarus). Indeed, there was possibly consideration on his part of a settlement with Germany, similar to the Treaty of Brest-Litovsk accepted by Lenin in 1918, a treaty that had enabled the Communists to consolidate their own position. This treaty might have been used to vindicate such an agreement in 1941. As another turning point, there was also a panic, involving popular disturbances, in Moscow in mid-October 1941, as ministries and factories were moved in the face of German advance; but Stalin decided not to flee, and the ruthless NKVD (Secret Police) was used to prevent anarchy and restore order.

The lack of Soviet collapse in late 1941 was a key moment in the politics of the war, and one that brought together a number of strands. Stalin's attitudes were a crucial element, and help explain his subsequent and present-day eulogisation by Soviet apologists and Russian nationalists in a Stalin cult.[54] However, these eulogies ignore the extent to which, in trusting Hitler, he was largely responsible for the plight facing the Soviet Union in 1941, as well as for much else that ruined the life of his contemporaries.

The role of the prewar purges, and of continuing and large-scale wartime slaughter and repression, in ensuring that Stalin was able to pursue his course – first alliance with Hitler and then resistance to him – was important, but is difficult to evaluate, not least as all sorts of counterfactuals come into play. Nevertheless, in the absence of political collapse at the top, the state maintained its control. With the exception of the early days of the war, when there was resistance to the Soviets in advance of the German conquest, for example in Lithuania, where members of the Lithuanian Activists' Front seized the city of Kaunas, this control generally only broke down in areas occupied by the Germans. Communist cadres in these areas found it difficult to inspire and lead resistance until German atrocities helped provide them with support.

The emptiness of German claims, at the time and subsequently, to be leading Europe against Communism was shown by the situation in Lithuania. The provisional government established by the Lithuanian Activists' Front on 23 June 1941 restored the administration before the Soviet occupation in 1940, but was expected by the German occupiers to act as a puppet government and swiftly disbanded. Instead, German rule meant the exploitation of the population for the cause of the war effort. For example, the property nationalised by the Soviet Union when Lithuania was occupied was not restored. After the initial stages of the German advance, there was no comparable development to that in Lithuania. In part, this was because, with the exception of Ukraine, the Germans largely advanced into areas with a Russian majority. In addition, the ruthless determination of the Soviet system came into play after the initial shock was over. For example, on 4 October 1941, Marshal Georgi Zhukov, the commander of the Leningrad Front, announced that the families of all those who surrendered would be shot. Stalin approved of this declaration.

Soviet (and Allied) propaganda made much of the resolve of the Soviet population, as also of that of the Red Army, each of which faced appalling circumstances.[55] Indeed, the Soviet Union lost about 27–28 million people in the war, 14 per cent of the prewar population. Moreover, there was extraordinary devastation to its western lands, notably Belarus which lost about a quarter of its population.

Resolve was doubtless a factor, not least due to Stalin's skill in playing on nationalist themes, although there has also been scepticism about the effectiveness of Soviet propaganda.[56] Stalin evoked memories of Russian nationalism, including in film, even though this nationalism entailed a patriotism that did not centre on Communist ideas and, indeed, involved respect for tsars, especially Ivan IV (the Terrible), Peter I (the Great) and Alexander I, the opponent of Napoleon. Ivan's cruelty, not least his use of the *oprichnina*, his private army, for harsh repression, was presented as necessary patriotism in order to protect Russia, a parallel apparently justifying Stalin's Purges.[57]

The brutality of German occupation politics, a brutality integral to German policy and far from 'collateral damage',[58] also contributed to Soviet resolve. Yet, these arguments can be pushed too hard. For example, the heroic stereotype of the Red Army soldier bore scant reference to the reality, not least to the marked contrast between nationalities: the Central Asian recruits had little understanding of the causes or purposes of the war effort.[59] As with the Germans, the Soviets, due to distrust and a measure of racism, made insufficient use of the subordinate peoples within their empires: a similar point can be made about African-Americans.

Helped by the coercive powers of his brutal state, Stalin proved an effective war leader. A dictator, he took a significant role in strategy, but was even more important in the mobilisation and production of resources, notably through the State Defence Committee.

The Soviet economic system indicated that totalitarianism was not incompatible with effectiveness, although it is important not to forget the extent to which the Soviet war effort depended on the supply of British and American *matériel*. This theme was very much downplayed in Soviet-era history, but this *matériel* was crucial at the key moment of the Battle of Moscow in December 1941, when the Soviets made extensive use of British tanks.

More generally, Soviet mobility greatly depended on the supply of American lorries, and this mobility was important as the Soviets advanced, because they were not able to rely on rail links in reoccupied areas. The rapid Soviet advance in 1944, an advance that played a key role in the German defeat, owed much to such mobility, although, like the Germans, the Soviets also made extensive use of horses for transporting supplies. Large numbers were deployed when Germany was invaded in 1945, although the Soviets did not put such horses in their celebratory parades and films. Lend-Lease helped the Soviet Union to focus on what it did well – building T-34 tanks and artillery barrels – by giving it what it could not make. Food, a product of the efficiency of American agriculture, was also a significant part of Lend-Lease.

The importance of Allied aid ensured that the routes by which it was supplied became key elements in the geopolitics of the conflict. These routes were from Alaska to Siberia, from Britain by sea to Murmansk and Archangel on the White Sea, and via Persia (Iran). Although German sea and air attacks from occupied Norway inflicted heavy losses on the Arctic convoys from Britain, the Germans were unable to cut the supply routes. Moreover, the absence of a German strategic bombing capability ensured that the movement forward in the Soviet Union of this *matériel* was not blocked. Similarly, the routes by which aid entered China were an important geopolitical element in the war.

Despite the significance of Allied aid, most Soviet military *matériel* was produced within the Soviet Union. In this production, there were important comparative advantages over Germany. The state control of Soviet industry was more thorough and longer-established than that in Germany. Combined with prewar planning, this control helped considerably in the large-scale relocation of manufacturing made necessary by the deep and rapid German advance in 1941, a relocation for which there was already considerable preparation.

More generally, the Soviet Union proved better able to cope with the demands of mobilising resources than its German rival, which, of course, also had to support the war against the Western Allies and to cope with strategic bombing. Once relocated beyond the range of likely German advance or air attack, in areas where there had already been considerable investment in the 1930s, Soviet industries turned out vast quantities of military *matériel*, out-producing the Germans for example in tanks and artillery. The Soviet commitment to quantity, rather than quality, which in part was more generally true of the practice of Soviet government, proved particularly well-suited to the equipping of the large Soviet armies, and, crucially, to their re-equipment as *matériel* was destroyed.

Moreover, the aftermath of the Communist destruction of intermediate institutions and the brutal treatment and cowing of the population in 1917–41 helped ensure that the economic system responded to the particular requirements of state-directed mobilisation. One symptom was the production of large quantities of *matériel* by the inmates of Soviet *gulags* or concentration camps. This, again, is an instance of the use of nomenclature not only in a descriptive fashion but also to make a political point relevant to the situation during the war and to subsequent memorialisation. Of course, such a use depends upon the knowledge that there was a distinction between German concentration camps – murderous by intention and focusing on compulsory labour extorted in murderous circumstances – and extermination camps, such as Auschwitz II and Treblinka, where the intention was the slaughter of all. As the war closed, Stalinist controls were to be harshly re-imposed in the Soviet Union, weakening the sense of national unity that had developed in the furnace of the war.

The strength of the Soviet state, including a centralised system for allocating resources, combined with its substantial military industrial complex, ensured that the Soviet military system had more durability than that of Russia in World War One. This durability was shared by Britain, which also had an effective military industrial complex and government. In addition, Britain was able to draw on an international commercial system as well as on accumulated foreign assets. These assets included investments that could be sold, notably to American companies. Dominion and colonial military co-operation also proved highly significant to Britain's war effort.

In contrast, Italy, Germany and Japan lacked this range of resources. Their economies did not make the transition to American-style mass production seen in Britain and the Soviet Union, and were also not joined in, and to, a global system of economic and military co-operation.[60]

Japan

Japanese politics and society were affected by greater militarism from the beginning of the 1930s. Hit in the Great Depression by a collapse in vital exports, and mass unemployment, Japan became more bellicose.

In part, this bellicosity arose because sections of the military followed autonomous policies ignoring civilian restraint, and in part because the military supported a militarism that challenged civil society and affected government policies. After the civilian government in Tokyo had failed to support unsanctioned expansionist acts by the army in Manchuria in 1931, a young naval officer assassinated the Prime Minister, Inukai Tsuyoshi, on 15 May 1932; and a cabinet of 'national unity', including military leaders and bureaucrats, was formed. Party politics continued, but became less significant from 1932.

Expansionism was linked to a sense of imperial mission, a sense that for some, but far from all, was related to a radical Shintō ultranationalism and, in particular, a belief in a divine providential purpose of Japanese superiority. Hirohito, who became Emperor in 1926, proved a supporter of the military, although the Emperor was not expected to voice an opinion or make decisions on military matters. The expectation was that he would accept the advice of his professional officers and officials. Only when they came to a complete impasse, as in the 1936 revolt by young army officers, was there space for the Emperor's intervention.[61]

The 1936 attempted coup, although unsuccessful, not least in the face of the Emperor's imposition of martial law, resulted in the fall of the government and the rise to power of Prince Fuminaro Konoe, who became Prime Minister in June 1937. In November and December 1938, he issued declarations that outlined a New Order for East Asia, ending Western imperialism and Communism there.[62]

After the violence of 1930–6, it is difficult to speak of moderates in the Japanese government. Whether they were army officers, like Senjuro Hayashi, or civilians, like Konoe, ministers generally agreed that Japan could not afford to compromise in international relations and that a war between Japan and either, or both of, the USA and the Soviet Union was probably unavoidable. Faced by criticism of the impasse in China, Konoe resigned in January 1939, only to return to power in July 1940. Clashes with the military over war or peace led Konoe to resign in October 1941, being replaced by the bellicose General Hideki Tōjō.

The attitude of the government matched that of the army which, in turn, reflected a society that was more militaristic than its opponents. Martial values were widely diffuse. On the part of recruits, there was a dread of disgracing family and community. Training destroyed individuality. Soldiers were abused and beaten. Recruits were indoctrinated to believe that the Chinese were inferior to Japanese, indeed below pigs. The process of dehumanisation continued with the war in China. At Nanjing in December 1937, soldiers were forced to torture the Chinese and, if they refused, were beaten hard. Dazed Westerners did not expect such cruelty in modern times. The consequences were to be apparent in the determined resistance by the Japanese to Allied operations and in the treatment of their own troops as well as Allied prisoners and civilians. Having caused famine and economic collapse across the territories they occupied, Japanese garrisons resorted at times to cannibalism.

In Germany, the regime remained in control until the close of the war, but the situation was different in the other Axis powers. In Japan, the course of the war caused a change in the government. Both Japan and the USA had seen Saipan, the island in the Marianas best-suited as a bomber base against Japan, as vital. Its fall on 7 July 1944, after bitter fighting, led to the resignation of Tōjō and his cabinet on 18 July. This major military defeat had a serious political effect in part because, due to the role of the Emperor, Hirohito, and the absence of a governing party equivalent to the Nazis, no Japanese politician enjoyed dominance equivalent to that of Hitler. Tōjō had not wished to resign, and in 1943–4, influenced by Mussolini's overthrow in July 1943, had sought to strengthen his position by sending political opponents away from Tokyo. However, in 1944, he was faced by pressure from opponents in the governing system, notably from the navy, and from senior statesmen and imperial princes, both influential groups. His assumption of the position of Chief of Staff of the army that February, a step taken to try to produce coordination in military policy, had angered many already concerned about his accumulation of posts, and he was made to take personal responsibility for failure.

The weak government under General Koiso Kuniaki that took power after the fall of Tōjō had no realistic plan. In a parallel with Hitler's dreams of a transformative rift among his opponents, Koiso wanted to divide China from Britain and the USA, but this scheme lacked traction. He resigned on 5 April 1945 after the army rejected his plan also to become War Minister, an attempt to overcome the continuing divisions in military command. In practice, alongside hopes of peace, the government assumed that the Japanese military would die heroically and was also willing to accept the loss of large numbers of civilians to American bombing. The ministers felt unable to explain to the public that all had gone wrong and, like the Tōjō government, were very worried by the possibility of domestic opposition, from both Left and Right.

Most of the Japanese civilian population supported the war and wartime propaganda was relatively successful.[63] However, the principal impact of the war on the Home Front was the speed with which resources began to run out (well before 1941) and, at least in 1944–5, the eradication of the urban landscape, taking with it the entire tangible wealth of the middle class.[64]

The American air assault gathered pace in late 1944. Initially, the American raids were long-distance and unsupported by fighter cover, as fighter range was less than that of bombers. This situation led to attacks from a high altitude which reduced their effectiveness. The raids that were launched were hindered by poor weather, especially strong tailwinds, and by difficulties with the B–29 reliability, as well as the general problems of precision bombing within the technology of the period. From February

1945, there was a switch to low-altitude night-time area bombing of Japanese cities. The impact was devastating, not least because many Japanese dwellings were made of timber and paper and burned readily when bombarded with incendiaries, and also because population density in the cities was high. Weaknesses in Japanese anti-aircraft defences, both planes and guns, eased the American task and made it possible to increase the payload of the B–29s by removing their guns. Although the Japanese had developed some impressive interceptor fighters, especially the Mitsubishi AGM5 and the Shiden, they were unable to produce many due to the impact of American air raids and of submarine attacks on supply routes, and they were also very short of pilots. American bombers destroyed over 30 per cent of the buildings in Japan, including over half of the major cities of Tokyo and Kobe.[65]

Nevertheless, although different to German and Soviet-style totalitarianism, Japan was ruled by an authoritarian system, with Emperor-worship, or at least pronounced deference, proving an important factor, and the military was determined to fight on. At the same time, by 1945, there was anxiety that, if the war continued, it might lead to a Communist revolution, and that, therefore, peace was necessary in order to protect the position of the imperial family. This was a position taken by Konoe, now an imperial advisor. Koiso Kuniaki was succeeded by the elderly Suzuki Kantarō, a retired admiral who was a member of the Privy Council. While seeking peace through intermediaries, he failed to provide any real lead. The determination of the military to fight to the finish lessened his options.

In the event, Emperor Hirohito had to play a major role in August 1945 in ensuring that Japan surrendered in the aftermath of the dropping of the atom bombs on 6 and 9 August. The apparently inexorable process of destruction seen with the dropping of the second bomb, on Nagasaki, had a greater impact on Japanese opinion than the use of the first atomic bomb. The limited American ability to deploy more bombs speedily was not appreciated. There was considerable reluctance from within the military in Japan and Manchuria to accepting this surrender, as well as a measure of opposition that had to be overcome. Hirohito's role was crucial. An Imperial Rescript broadcast on 15 August announced the end of hostilities. It followed Hirohito's intervention at the Imperial Conference on 9 and 14 August. Ashamed of surrender, and as a form of atonement, many of the Japanese military leaders committed suicide. So also did some of the civilian leaders, including Konoe.

Italy

A year prior to the fall of Saipan, an Allied attack on another island had already forced a change in the Axis. Allied forces landed in Sicily on 10 July 1943. This precipitated a growing crisis of confidence in Mussolini among the Fascist leadership, as well as among other Italian leaders, particularly the King, Victor Emmanuel III, who had offered Mussolini the premiership in 1922. Having promised totalitarian efficiency and national modernisation, Mussolini had only delivered failure.

The surrender of the large Axis forces in North Africa that spring, as Anglo–American forces, advancing from both Egypt and Morocco/Algeria, conquered Tunisia, had already undermined Italy's commitment to the alliance with Germany. It was clear that the Allies would press on to attack Italy. Moreover, by 1943, Anglo–American bombing had wrecked 60 per cent of Italy's industrial capacity and badly undermined Italian morale, encouraging the sense that Mussolini had failed. This belief contributed greatly to his overthrow, although the Allied invasion of Italy was more significant. Mussolini was arrested on 25 July 1943, and a non-Fascist government was formed by Field Marshal Pietro Badoglio, a former Commander-in-Chief. This government was backed by the army and excluded the Fascists.[66]

The king played a major role in ensuring Mussolini's fall, but was sufficiently linked to the regime to provide opportunities for the Left to press for republicanism. The king was obliged to surrender first his powers (1944) and then his throne (1946) to Crown Prince Umberto. However, a republic was to be the result of a postwar referendum in 1946, albeit one secured by the narrowest of margins.

In 1943, Badoglio sought to reach an agreement with the invading Allies while avoiding the need to acknowledge defeat. Meanwhile, the Germans built up their forces in Italy. An armistice with the Allies was signed by the new Italian government on 3 September 1943 and was announced on 8 September. However, the rapid German military response, and the pathetic failure of the new Italian government to organise effective opposition, left the Germans in control in central and northern Italy. The Germans also rapidly gained control of Italian-held parts of the Balkans and Aegean, including much of Albania. The flight from Rome of the king and the new government left the military, in both Italy and the occupied Balkan territories, without orders and disorganised, although much of the fleet was able to sail to Malta. Victor Emmanuel III, Badoglio, and the General Staff fled to Brindisi, which was already occupied by British forces, and they established a new government there. The army effectively disintegrated. Units were dissolved by their commanders, to avoid coming into conflict with the German army, or were disbanded by private initiative. The units of the regular army which continued officially remained with the King, but some joined the partisans or were arrested by the Germans. A large number of troops were taken to Germany and Poland to work, mostly in armament factories.[67]

In a daring airborne operation, the Germans, on 11 September 1943, rescued Mussolini from captivity. He was put in charge of a puppet state in northern Italy, the Italian Social Republic, or Salò Republic, established on

15 September. The following month, the Badoglio government declared war on Germany. Although that declaration made little difference to the course of the conflict, it eased Allied occupation issues.

In 1943–5, there was, at the same time, a patriotic war against the Germans, a civil war in Italy between Fascists and anti-Fascists, and a class war. The combination of these conflicts contributed to a disintegration of beliefs, and of faith in institutions, and resulted in violence that had profound effects in the postwar period.

The collapse of the German alliance system

The following year, 1944, Germany's other allies similarly abandoned her. Finland, which had been hit hard in a Soviet offensive in June, signed an armistice on 2 September. Moreover, the defeat of the German army in Moldavia that August exposed Romania to invasion and led to the overthrow of its dictator, Marshal Antonescu. Bound by misguided honour and unwilling to accept the degree of Romania's plight, he had refused to abandon his German allies or to accept the armistice terms which had been reached in negotiations with the Allies in April–June. Antonescu considered these terms unacceptable, and, as he was seen as the bar to an armistice, King Michael played a key role in his arrest on 23 August.

This coup led Romania to change sides. The subsequent Romanian attack on German and Hungarian forces provided Stalin with 16 additional divisions and led to Romania regaining Transylvania from Hungary in the eventual peace. In turn, invaded by Soviet forces on 8 September 1944 (three days after the Soviet Union declared war), Bulgaria declared war on Germany the same day, providing about 339,000 troops to fight alongside the Red Army.

In response to concerns about the loyalty of its government to Hitler, Hungary was occupied by German troops in March 1944, although Admiral Horthy, the head of the government (as Regent), was left in power, while the new Prime Minister, Döme Szótay, was acceptable to Horthy as well as the Germans. That summer, Jewish Hungarians were sent to Auschwitz, the last of the major national contingents to be slaughtered: over 400,000 were killed.

The Red Army overran much of eastern Hungary in October, but a pro-German coup by Hungarian Fascists on 15 October, supported by German special forces, blocked the attempt of the Hungarian government under Horthy to settle with the Soviets. Horthy had declared a unilateral armistice, but did not prepare to resist the Germans, in part because he wished to focus on opposing the Soviet advance until Anglo–American troops could enter the country. Under German pressure, Horthy withdrew the armistice and appointed Ferenc Szálasi, the leader of the Fascist Arrow

Cross Party, as Prime Minister. Hungary fought on and was conquered by Soviet forces.

Home Fronts and civilian morale

If the progress of the war directly affected the defeated, it was also of more general importance for the Home Fronts of all powers. For the political and military leaders of all the combatants, it became clear that a rapid victory in what was a war of unprecedented scale was unlikely, and that sustaining the conflict had serious social implications. This was true because of the needs of the war economies and due to the impact on many countries of sustained, large-scale bombing.[68]

Concern about the populace led, in many countries, to a social politics that put a greater emphasis than hitherto on social welfare, albeit within a context that frequently sustained pre-existing social alignments and assumptions.[69] Churchill declared in a speech at the private school he had attended, Harrow, delivered on 18 December 1940: 'When this war is won, as it surely will be, it must be one of our aims to establish a state of society where the advantages and privileges which hitherto have been enjoyed only by the few shall be more widely shared by the many'.

Concern about the populace also led to systematic attempts to report on, and categorise, the public. The Home Fronts were a major concern of combatant (and indeed neutral) governments. The Mass Observation surveying organisation was used in Britain to monitor responses to the war and its privations. Germany and the Soviet Union also closely monitored civil opinion, although in a more obvious way. Propaganda played a role, and reflected the sense, even among the totalitarian powers, that popular support had to be wooed. News-management was the case for all the powers. Thus, the BBC removed Conscientious Objectors from its staff in 1939 by declaring them superfluous to its needs. It got rid of pacifists the following year.[70]

The Nazi reading of World War One led to a great emphasis being placed on propaganda in Germany. First, it was argued that civilian society was more vulnerable than the military to war-weariness and the Home Front most fragile. Secondly, it was believed that British propaganda had been particularly effective in 1918. It was blamed in Germany for the November revolution that had led to the overthrow of Kaiser Wilhelm II and the end of the war. Thus, propaganda was a matter not only of maintaining the resolve of the German population, but also of waging war with Germany's opponents. Obedience was insufficient; there had to be positive mobilisation for the war effort. In *Mein Kampf*, Hitler wrote of wartime propaganda as a key weapon for the German people, so that 'all considerations of humanitarianism or aesthetics crumble into nothingness'. Reflecting his view of the people, Hitler also argued that propaganda should be aimed at the feelings as, he claimed, the majority of people were feminine by nature, and propaganda should be advanced at an intellectual level geared to those of limited intelligence.

Inter-war Nazi propagandising led towards wartime propaganda, and for the military as well as civilians. In 1943, National Socialist Leadership Officers, the equivalent of Soviet commissars (party officials responsible for ensuring obedience), were introduced, while, by 1944, soldiers were being used to spread favourable propaganda in German cities in 'word-of-mouth propaganda' campaigns. The incessant Nazi propaganda offensive was a matter of disseminating favourable opinions, as well as of monitoring the public and suppressing critical opinions. There were important modulations in the offensive, from victory propaganda to an emphasis on the need for fortitude, combined with warnings of the dire possible results of defeat.

The shift was most marked in the case of defeat at Stalingrad. For long, German public opinion was assured that victory there was imminent. However, about 110,000 men from the Sixth Army surrendered to the Soviets on 31 January–2 February 1943, despite Hitler's instructions that they fight to the last man. The army's commander, Friedrich Paulus, was promoted to Field Marshal on 30 January as Hitler knew that no German Field Marshal had surrendered, but Hitler was to be disappointed. The government reported that the troops had fought to the end; their self-sacrifice, that Germany might live, being held up to urge more dedication on the German public. News about surrendering troops was concealed, but distrust about the accuracy of the official line led rumours to enjoy great credibility, even though the public expression of doubt was suppressed.[71]

Subsequently, unrealistic hopes of a turn in the tide in favour of Hitler were conjured up by discussion of miracle weapons that would rescue the Reich, such as the V-missiles, and also by historical resonances, notably that of how Frederick the Great (II) of Prussia won through in the later stages of the Seven Years' War (1756–63), despite being attacked by France, Austria and Russia. The Nazis tapped into that tradition in the film *Kolberg* (1945), an account of stoical and eventually-successful endurance against Russian siege;[72] while, on 11 March 1945, Goebbels presented Hitler with an abridged translation of Thomas Carlyle's heroic 1858 biography of Frederick.[73]

Nazi propaganda also worked differently for various constituencies, but there was a general move, as the war went badly, from persuasion to intimidation. This was a move that reflected the changing politics of the Nazi regime, although violence and intimidation had very much been there from the outset.[74] A belief in 1944–5 that unconditional surrender to the Allies would mean annihilation for the Germans contributed to the impact of this intimidation. Goebbels combined fear and hatred, of the Soviets in particular, in bolstering attitudes.

At the same time, a reliance on intimidation in part reflected the weakness of government propaganda. This weakness arose not only as the war went badly for Germany but also because the news distributed by the media was no longer credible. Thus, rumour flourished in a public world where the authority of the regime was breaking down and where the public atmosphere was therefore becoming more febrile.[75]

The war saw the politics and culture of nationhood deployed to support the cause of particular regimes. Thus, while the state-sponsored annual Wagner Festival at Bayreuth served as a platform for Nazi racial mysticism, the Antonescu government in Romania presented the war in terms of a crusade against Bolshevism which was understood as a foreign and non-Christian movement. A Heroes' cult was deployed to commemorate the Romanian war dead, and war memorials sought to combine Orthodox religiosity with folk art, presenting a ruralist concept of a traditional national identity, the latter a theme also seen in Hungary. Jewish Romanians were brutally excluded from this identity. They were persecuted, while a large Heroes' Cemetery in Bucharest was planned on the site of a Jewish cemetery. In the event, Antonescu's overthrow in 1944 ended this scheme.[76]

For all the powers, propaganda was an aspect of a re-education of the public, a re-education, intended as intensive, that ranged from eating habits to political goals.[77] There was a functional as well as an ideological dimension to this re-education. As far as the first was concerned, domestic consumption and activity had to be reduced in order to free resources and labour for the war effort. This process challenged established assumptions about how society should be organised, assumptions that were a matter both of supposed entitlements and of the inherent nature of individual and family behaviour.

The results were often complex, as in Germany in 1943 when the closure of non-essential businesses led to anger as self-employed workers were obliged to become wage-labourers. In the event, opposition to the policy led the Propaganda Ministry to insist on it being shelved. The strength of established assumptions was demonstrated by the failure to draft women for military service even as Germany collapsed. The situation in the Soviet Union was very different, in large part because the Communists had had over two decades, starting with a bitter civil war in 1918–20, to terrorise and transform civil society.

Ideology was important for all the combatants, as it was deliberately fostered to encourage a sense of common destiny and of antagonism to the enemy. The results varied greatly, but the central theme was one of state direction. Thus, in Japan, the Ministry of Education approved a new university course in 1939 that was intended to make students even more conscious of national policy.[78] Such policies appeared particularly necessary to governments keen to ensure well-motivated conscripts. Direction by the state became a marked characteristic of Japan's increasingly authoritarian government. In October 1940, the Imperial Rule Assistance Association was established as a National Unity front headed by the Prime Minister, and the existing political parties were pressurised to dissolve themselves and to join the Association. Once Tōjō had come to power in October 1941, strict controls were imposed on opinion. 'Thought criminals' were arrested, and the Special Emergency Act of December 1942 considerably enhanced the government's power. The secret police became more active although not on the scale of the Gestapo or the NKVD. At the local level, neighbourhood associations were answerable to the Home Ministry in Japan.

Yet, alongside the emphasis on state pressure and ideology, it is important also to note the degree to which popular interest and commitment played an autonomous role for all the combatants, albeit to a very differing degree. For example, on 11 February 1941, an estimated crowd of 200,000 enthusiastic people welcomed the crew of HMAS *Sydney* when it marched through Sydney on its return from a tour of duty in the Mediterranean.

Resistance and collaboration: the case of France

A key aspect of politics, and one that particularly joins wartime activity to postwar contention, the subject of the second half of the book, was that of resistance to occupation. Resistance acted as a nexus linking Home Fronts to the alliance politics involved with governments in exile. The latter sought to direct and to represent the Resistance, while also to set the prospectus for postwar politics. This was a goal that proved especially divisive in the case of Poland.

Wartime resistance has proved a particularly contentious issue in France, where it has also been most extensively studied. In France, the Home Front was contested between the collaboratist conservative government based at Vichy and the Resistance, which itself was divided. Vichy presented the Third Republic, overthrown as a result of the Fall of France, and particularly its politics, as decadent and weak, and as in large part responsible for the defeat of 1940. Moreover, Vichy's account of the past still fought the 1790s: it was very much opposed to the French Revolution.[79] More generally, the focus was on a Catholic and conservative presentation of France, one that was anti-liberal, leading to particular hostility to Jews and Freemasons, as well as unsympathetic to cities, especially Paris. Vichy combined a longstanding opposition to the Third Republic's liberalism with the hostile conservative reaction to the Popular Front of the 1930s, and also drew on the French Fascist movement, the *Action Française*. Anti-British themes were also emphasized notably with a cult of Joan of Arc.

Yet, there was also considerable complexity within Vichy as a result of strong cross-currents. Thus, conservative nationalism led to a hostility to German penetration, a hostility seen both in the hunting down of spies operating for the Germans and in the determination to retain control of Empire and fleet, keeping Germany as well as Britain at a distance. Moreover, within the Vichy élite, there was only limited support for Fascism, as opposed to a more broadly-based conservative nationalism that was particularly open to Catholic activism. Vichy passed anti-Semitic laws and French authorities collaborated with the Holocaust, rounding up Jews for deportation; but most Vichy figures were not committed to the mass murder of French Jews, although they were far less sympathetic to Jewish refugees from other countries.[80] In 1941, Cardinal Baudrillart called for men to join the League of French Volunteers against Bolshevism, but most French bishops responded icily and Pius XII refused to declare the war in Russia a 'crusade'.

At the same time, the theme of eternal France as well as other aspects of Vichy ideology were in practice an excuse for collaboration as much as accommodation, and to a degree that would strike many impartial observers as treasonable. Many who had made their names under the Third Republic overthrown in 1940 proved all-too-willing to damn it, while benefiting from the misfortunes of others. Thus, the writer Jean-Paul Sartre accepted a teaching post that was vacant because its Jewish holder had been removed.

After the war, many French accommodators, and some collaborators, were able to pursue distinguished careers. Without suggesting any equivalence, the Vichy treatment of France's history was to be paralleled by contentious postwar accounts of the war years, and notably so in France. It is to those accounts that we will turn in chapter five.

CHAPTER FOUR

Explanations of Victory

The politics of war extend to the explanations of victory and defeat.[1] The mixture of 'realist' and 'idealist' factors advanced, from the number of tanks to morale, tells us much about assumptions, both as to why victory is won in war, any war as well as this war, and as to what reasons can most appropriately be offered. For World War Two, there is the additional factor provided by the sway of the conflict, so that the powers finally defeated in 1945 had earlier victories, indeed spectacularly so in 1939–41 for Germany and 1941–2 for Japan. Thus, the explanation of victory and defeat also entails an account of how circumstances changed for the respective powers. As a result, the military history of the war is in part an aspect of its politics with myths accordingly encoded.[2] This is true of specific campaigns or types of war, notably strategic bombing, but is also the case with the discussion of why the Allies won, and, in winning, overcame the consequences of earlier Axis success.

Resources to win?

A key issue is that of resources. Explanations of the Allied success in terms of the greater resources deployed from their 'global hinterland',[3] and thus of the productive strength of their economies and trading systems, provide accounts that can suggest that superior Axis fighting quality was therefore overborne, although that is not an inevitable conclusion of this approach. These explanations also imply that the Allied societies were more effective, notably in using their industrial base, employing technology, and mobilising women for the labour force.[4]

This effectiveness can then be discussed in terms of a more benign social ethos, notably in contrasting the USA and Britain with Germany and Japan. Without the same degree of credibility, the Soviet Union, a totalitarian state, can be presented as less harsh in its labour control than Germany. At any rate, the net impression is that a better society prevailed, and did so as an aspect of the conflation of total war with the varied characteristics of competing ideologies.

This interpretation has proved a prime instance of the 'War and Society' approach, a valuable approach to both military history and that of wartime society which enjoyed much favour in academic circles from the 1960s, and which remains highly influential today. This was an interpretation that, for World War Two, brought together Western democratic and Soviet Communist public myths. Like many public myths, the interpretation rested on a degree of accuracy, although it underplayed the cruelty of the highly authoritarian Soviet war economy. Nazi racism and Japanese oppression certainly made it difficult to derive the benefit that might have been anticipated from extensive conquests.

The 'War and Society' approach is conducive from the point of subsequent public commemoration as it provides a wider amplitude for the emphasis otherwise on the heroism of particular combatants and operations, for example the British stress on the Few (the pilots during the Battle of Britain) or the Dambusters, an élite air unit that destroyed German dams in a raid in May 1943. The 'War and Society' approach, however, risks underplaying the significant dimension of aggregate military activity, as well as of key related aspects, such as logistics. The aggregate military activity involved relates to issues such as fighting quality, unit cohesion, tactical skill, and operational ability. In each case, it is possible to point to an improvement on the Allied side, namely from poor performance in 1939–42 to improved outcomes from 1942.[5]

This improvement was, indeed, important to Allied success, but does not make for a good public memory as it entails an acceptance in the first instance that performance had been initially unsatisfactory. Conversely, this interpretation is also undesirable from the Axis perspective as it suggests that initial Axis successes owed much to Allied deficiencies, and that, subsequently, the Axis failed to maintain their capability advantage. Indeed, a stress on the campaigns in the war, especially on fighting qualities and command skills, ensures that there is due attention to the defeat of the Axis on land and sea, and in the air.

Post-mortems

The post-mortems carried out during the conflict were significant in subsequent accounts of the war. These post-mortems ranged from Divisional After-Action Reports to higher-level analyses. They were produced as combatants sought to rectify their own limitations and to understand how best to profit from their opponents' mistakes. Thus, in April 1940, soon after the end of the Winter War with Finland in which they had initially done very badly, the Soviets held a secret high-level analysis of the conflict. Its subsequent publication after the post-Communist opening of the archives contributed to the debate on the quality of the Red Army on the eve of the German attack in 1941.[6]

In 1940, in contrast, the British response to defeat in France was inadequate. Moreover, British generals manipulated the reporting of the conflict, releasing, through the press, their version of a 'stab in the back' myth. Failure was blamed on inter-war neglect, the inadequacies of the French high command, and the alleged failure of the French to fight.[7]

As the most significant recent conflict, the war also dominated military attention for several decades from 1945. A number of factors helped explain this situation. The officer corps, notably at the senior ranks, was for long composed of those who had fought in the war. Montgomery was to be Chief of the Imperial General Staff (1946–8) and Deputy Supreme Commander of North Atlantic Treaty Organisation (NATO) forces in Europe (1951–8). Conduct during the war was highly significant for subsequent reputation and promotion.

Moreover, the war appeared to have much to teach. The campaigns were carefully scrutinised for indications about how best to wage war in what appeared to be the imminent conflict between the Soviet Union and the non-Communist powers allied in 1949 in the NATO. When, in 1949, the Soviets developed a nuclear capability, the possibility that the threat of nuclear devastation would prevent either side from using it led to revived interest in conventional operations. Fascinated by the model of German *blitzkrieg*,[8] the Americans also took a close interest in the experience the Germans had acquired in fighting the Soviet Union. For example, in the 1950s, they persuaded *Luftwaffe* commanders to write a series of reports. In addition, General Franz Halder, head of the German army's General Staff in 1938–42, was employed by the American army's Historical Division for 14 years and in 1961 was given the Meritorious Civilian Service Award.

Both Soviet and, later, NATO forces came to focus on manoeuvre warfare, and there was great interest on both sides in the successful Soviet campaigns of 1943–5, especially the concept of 'deep operations'. A clear lesson learned from World War Two was that linear defences were vulnerable and that the retention of mobility offered the best form of defence. The consequences for air power were also a major lesson of the war. The doctrine of strategic air power was taken forward with the addition of the atom bomb. In addition, Air–Land concepts were a development of the war's campaigning, with a heavy emphasis on ground-support airpower.

The process of learning lessons was also seen with the war at sea, even if the parallels with current needs might appear more indirect. Thus, between 1946 and 1951, the British navy produced studies of the battles of the Coral Sea and Midway in order to provide texts for those studying maritime war.[9]

Aside from the functional approach to learning from the war, there was also the public, official and academic dissection of the conflict. Allied failures led to persistent controversy. This was true, for example, over the Japanese assault on Pearl Harbor, notably the lack of American preparation,[10] as well as the British loss of Malaya and Singapore. There were also controversies over the causes of Allied success and over whether more could have been achieved. These included the dispute over Allied strategy in 1944 in the Battle of Normandy and subsequently in the advance across France, and that over the wisdom of the American decision to invade the Philippines that year as part of the campaign against Japan: it was claimed that this invasion had been a costly diversion from the necessary focus on Japan itself.

The dominance by memoirs was a prominent feature of the published work in the postwar decades. A willingness to attribute blame to others saw campaigns fought out before an engaged and partisan readership, many of whom were keen to purchase books about their former commanders. Thus, the view of strategy in 1944 in Eisenhower's *Crusade in Europe* (1948) was different to that in Montgomery's *Memoirs* (1958). These disputes were particularly apparent in Britain, which, at least in this respect, was singularly undeferential. There were heated arguments over generalship in North Africa, especially over the respective importance of Auchinleck and Montgomery in causing the Axis defeat. The combative Dorman-Smith took his differences with Montgomery and Churchill to the legal battlefield, winning, in 1954, a libel case against the latter for statements in his *The Hinge of Fate* (1951). The controversies were further fuelled by critical scholarly engagement, notably Correlli Barnett's *Desert Generals* (1960). This caused great offence by offering an essentially civilian reading of military competence, and, in refuting what Barnett termed the 'Montgomery Myth', by castigating Montgomery in order to praise General Sir Claude Auchinleck, the Commander-in-Chief Middle East Command who stopped Rommel's advance on the Nile valley in the first El Alamein battle in July 1942.

The 1960s is not generally seen as a period fascinated with war, but, on 3 September 1969, the British comic weekly *Punch* put 'The War Industry' on its front cover, showing on it a book and film, television and theatre shots of war. World War Two was the focus of the war, notably thanks to the success of Purnell's *History of the Second World War*, the first issue of which appeared on 7 October 1966. The project was a gamble as there was little experience with part-work publishing, while the production cost was over £800,000.

This gamble was confronted with a major sales promotion campaign. Costing £95,000, and focusing on ABC men over 40 years old, this campaign included two 45-second television commercials as well as newspaper advertisements stressing the direct link with readers, such as 'If you can whistle Lili Marlene – this is your story', and special issue posters. The magazine-style layout of the weekly and the 3,000 illustrations in the 128 weekly issues helped, and by 1967 nearly 300,000 copies were being sold weekly.[11]

Foreign-language editions followed, including in Italy and France, and in November 1967 over 1,000,000 copies of the various editions were sold in Europe in one week. The average weekly sales in Britain of the 128 issues were 325,000 and the project made a pre-tax profit of £7 million.

Surviving correspondence indicates the pressures that moulded such a project, with scholarship and commercial appeal at variance, as in the response to the idea of 'featurettes'.[12] The publishers, Purnell, part of the British Printing Company, pressed Basil Liddell Hart, the Editor-in-Chief, to increase the number of American, Japanese and Soviet contributions in order to aid the chance of co-publication deals with foreign publishers, and they also wanted a book club style. In response, Liddell Hart argued that most Japanese and Soviet scholars wrote badly, while 'the basic difficulty about the American ones is that, while there are plenty of good academic ones, there are few of these who can write readably enough for a popular history such as ours', and that they would want too much money.[13]

Individual items led to controversy, Liddell Hart privately responding to complaints from two Polish generals, 'It seems to me that the Poles remain just as touchy and as inclined to overrate their importance as they were in 1939'.[14] There were also complaints about omission: Major General Moulton, in his review of the first volume in the *Glasgow Herald* of 18 February 1967, took exception to the lack of an adequate account of the British Expeditionary Force in action before the Dunkirk evacuation in 1940. Hugo Stafford-Northcote, however, replied to complaints about his article on the British invasion of Vichy-ruled Syria in June–July 1941 that, as the original piece had been ripped to pieces by sub-editors, he was not fully answerable, but also that: 'the relative importance of the Palmyra and Damour battles depends, I suppose, on whether the writer is Australian, British, Indian, Free or Vichy French – or even Syrian or Lebanese! ... Palmyra – viewed from Iraq, possibly loomed as large in the scheme of things as would Damour to observers at, say, Middle East Command H.Q. in Cairo!'[15] This was a more generally instructive remark: Palmyra was a target for the advance from the east and Damour from the south.

Alongside popular coverage, there was continuing scholarship. The major source of additional archival material in the 1970s for this scholarship came from the revelation of the role of signals intelligence, principally the British ULTRA system. This material produced a fresh bout of controversy, as decisions were refought in its light, for example the response to the German invasion of Crete in 1941. There were also revelations about the obtaining of information about Japanese plans by American signals intelligence.

Subsequently, the end of Communist rule in Eastern Europe and the Soviet Union in 1989–91 led to the release of far more documentary material. This freed scholars, there and elsewhere, from the shadow of the official histories and encouraged them to re-examine campaigns and issues. For example, it was shown that the official Albanian Communist view of the war was so politicised as to lessen greatly its value, not least because it underrated both the role of the early non-Communist resistance and initial German success.[16]

The opening up of Soviet material from 1992 permitted a major re-examination of the Eastern Front. Archives such as those of the Soviet Supreme High Command provided an opportunity for reconsidering both narrative and explanation, and this has not only been a matter of altering details. Instead, there has been a re-evaluation of entire campaigns. Moreover, operations that were hitherto obscure have been brought to the fore. Operation Mars, a disastrous Soviet attack in November 1942 on the central front west of Moscow, failed and was covered up, not least with a wholly inaccurate and incomplete account of the poor planning and execution of the operation, which may well have been revealed in advance to the Germans by a planted agent in order to detract attention from the offensive against German forces in the Stalingrad area. Operation Mars has now been rescued from neglect.[17]

Scholarship taking advantage of the opening of archives was not restricted to Eastern European topics. In his first-rate revisionist account of the Malaya campaign, somewhat misleadingly entitled *Singapore 1942*, Alan Warren noted that 'the case for a reconsideration of the Malayan campaign has been immeasurably increased by the release of new material by the British Public Record Office [now National Archives] and the Australian War Memorial during the 1990s'. As with many other studies of generalship, Warren offered a criticism of a lack of rapid responsiveness on the part of the commander. Attention was also drawn to the failure of subordinate commanders, to the wider problems of British military conduct, and to the Japanese skill in mobile warfare.[18]

The 1980s on also saw great interest in the operational dimension of war. Added to the strategic and tactical, this dimension, which drew heavily on the analysis of the Soviet offensives in 1944–5 against Germany and Japan, entailed a focus on campaigning methods and skills.[19] The after-echoes of World War Two remained strong during the last stages of the Cold War. Moreover, the American-led coalition defeat of Iraq in 1991 exemplified the success of military methods of manoeuvre and firepower honed during the Cold War on the basis of World War Two developments.

However, the influence of the war appeared of lesser relevance from the 1990s, not least with the argument that a Revolution in Military Affairs, or paradigm shift in capability and warmaking, had occurred. This emphasis on a new departure was taken forward, albeit in a different context, in the 2000s, as insurgency and counter-insurgency warfare came to the fore, most prominently in Afghanistan and Iraq, but also more generally. Indeed, in that context, the discussion shifted to the extent to which World War Two was definitely misleading. In addition, the frame of reference changed. That for American military activities in Iraq in 2003 moved from being the rapid success of the Gulf War of 1991 (and through that back to World War Two) to the intractable commitment of the Vietnam War.

The military after-echoes of World War Two therefore apparently ceased to have resonance, even as the political ones continued to be significant. There were references in military education, but the mass warfare and long-term fighting between conventional forces of World War Two no longer appeared relevant in very different circumstances.[20]

Military effectiveness

At the same time, public and academic interest in World War Two remained strong, and with significant contrasts between interpretations. On the German side, the widespread tendency to regard defeat as due to being beaten in 'the production battle in the factories'[21] leads to a frequent failure to engage with the extent to which the Germans were outfought. Linked to this, there is much material on German operations, especially corps- and division-level sources, that still requires critical evaluation. All too much of the work on the German side is based on postwar analyses of their own campaigns by German commanders and staff officers. This work places the responsibility for defeat on resource issues, the size and climate of the Soviet Union and, above all, Hitler's interventions. This German interpretation was present from the outset. Asked in June 1945 why the Germans had lost, a German interpreter who had seen action on the Eastern Front told a British officer 'Because our lines of communication were too long, and because, in spite of our killing thousands until we ran out of ammunition, they still came in hordes'.[22] In the public, 'the quasi-mythical level of excellence attributed to German operational and tactical planning' persists in the face of extensive archival evidence that highlights battlefield mistakes by German commanders.[23] Furthermore, the willingness to accept that the *Wehrmacht* was repeatedly involved in atrocities, indeed that large-scale violence against unarmed civilians was integral to its conduct, is contested.

As far as discussion of the fighting itself is concerned, the central thesis that needs to be displaced is that of the rise and fall of the Axis as their superior fighting quality was supposedly overcome by greater Allied resources. This account was, and is, one that was particularly conducive to the defeated powers, indeed matching that of other defeated parties, such as the Royalists and the Confederacy in the English (1642–6) and American Civil Wars (1861–5) respectively.

Thus, the reading of the military history of World War Two was, and is, an aspect of its politics, not least a reluctance to ask searching questions about failure. This reluctance is not the case for much of the academic scholarship, although there is still a failure of some of the work at that level. More serious is the argument at the public level as it suggests that the war would have had a different result, but for the resource dimension, and therefore almost should have had a different result. Heroism is generally seen in terms of fighting on against superior odds. Such an argument neglects the inherent flaws in Axis warmaking, for example the limitations of the *Blitzkrieg*.

The unusual aspect of the widespread approach, and its emphasis on resources, is that this neglect of Axis flaws is seen not only in Germany and Japan, but also in Britain and the USA. In part, this is because the German image of the war is one that has been assimilated even as the political message has been rejected. This image can be seen with the frequent use of German film-footage in anglophone television programmes. Accounts sympathetic to Germany were propagated from the 1940s, not least with the overly favourable postwar British treatment of the views of prominent Axis generals, especially Rommel and Manstein.

However, the improvement in the Allied ability to deliver success later in the war can be better understood if there is an understanding of the extent to which Germany and Japan's enemies made the mistakes Germany and Japan needed in the early stages in order to help them win. That the advantages derived from the poor strategic choices of opponents and their inadequate preparations, rather than from a totally different quality of conception and fighting, is now general to the scholarly literature. Moreover, there were significant deficiencies in German and Japanese warmaking.

At the same time, German warmaking rested for much of its effectiveness on a greater willingness than that of its opponents to centre operational planning on the tactics of combined arms, and joint (air–land) operations, the two joining to make manoeuvre warfare possible. This potential, which was enhanced by generally good tactical and (to a less-consistent standard) operational command, and by a high level of tactical skill did not, however, mean a certainty of success. For example, far from a pre-determined result, the Germans benefited in their somewhat improvised conquest of Denmark and Norway in April 1940 from comparative advantage: both less-flawed planning than the Allied forces that intervened in Norway, let alone the poorly-prepared Scandinavians, and a greater ability to respond, indeed improvise, under pressure.

In the case of the Western Front, the Germans launched their offensive on 10 May, pushed across the Meuse River on 13 May, reached the English Channel on 21 May, took the surrender of the Dutch on 14 May and of the Belgians on 27 May, entered Paris on 14 June, and dictated terms to the French on 22 June. For fewer than 30,000 of their own troops killed, Germany had transformed the situation in Western Europe and had ensured that the course and outcome of World War Two would be different, notably more global, than that of World War One.[24]

The success of the risky German strategy owed much to the deficiencies of French strategy and planning, deficiencies predicted in German war gaming in December 1939. The experience of the Polish campaign was also significant for the Germans, who would probably have been less successful had they attacked the French in 1938. In 1940, as with the Allies (but not, earlier in the year, German) in 1918, the attacking side won. The ability to take the initiative was a key point, as was the opponents' response. In 1918, the Allies had responded more effectively than they were to do in 1940 to German attack. Greater German mobility was an important factor in 1940, not least the triumph of an operational war of movement over position warfare, but it was not the only factor. Indeed, French strategic and operational inadequacies, rather than deficiencies in weaponry, ensured that inter-war German efforts at innovation, which had aimed at incremental improvement, produced, instead, a 'striking and temporarily asymmetrical operational revolution'.[25]

Nevertheless, the views of both victors and defeated combined to endow the German army with extraordinary strength and proficiency, not least overwhelming mechanised forces.[26] This helped boost German confidence and the sense of being at the cutting edge of progress. The reputation given the Germans also assisted the defeated in dispelling attention from issues relating to their own fighting quality, morale and command skills.

There is a parallel between the assessment of German effectiveness and the treatment of Japan. It is clear that Japan's attacks in 1941–2 benefited from poor Allied operational command, particularly in the Philippines, Malaya and Burma (Myanmar), but also from strategic inadequacies that in part stemmed from the range of British commitments. Concerned about the war with Germany, the British mistakenly hoped that the defence of Malaya and Singapore would benefit from the strength of the American fleet in the western Pacific, and also seriously mishandled their own naval units. At the same time, Soviet success in earlier clashes with Japan along the borders of Mongolia and Manchuria in 1938 and, more clearly, 1939, indicated deficiencies with Japanese war-making from the outset.

The resource issue certainly played a major role. For example, it can be profitably discussed with reference to the war at sea. Germany was at a clear disadvantage in the Battle of the Atlantic, both in warship numbers and as a result of Allied shipbuilding. Yet, a range of factors helped the Allies win, including effective anti-submarine tactics, by both convoy escorts and aircraft, and the use of signals intelligence. As a consequence, the number of submarines sunk per year was much greater than in World War One, while the percentage of Allied shipping lost was less. The strategic issue posed for the Germans by Allied shipbuilding interacted with the tactical and operational challenges offered by improved Allied proficiency in anti-submarine warfare. Contingency and chance were also important in battle.[27]

So also in the Pacific: alongside the availability of superior American resources, eventually greatly superior resources, the effective use of American air power, and the development not only of carrier tactics but of successful air–naval co-operation, was instrumental in the defeat of Japanese forces. The Japanese were less effective than the Americans at convoy protection and anti-submarine warfare, while the Americans achieved more with submarine warfare.

Relative effectiveness was also at issue in the air. Pursuing air dominance and air–land integration,[28] the *Luftwaffe* was designed to further operational warfare with a limited scope and range, which made it deadly in 1939, 1940 and 1941 against Poland, France and Yugoslavia. However, the *Luftwaffe* was unsuccessful in strategic warfare, such as the Battle of Britain in 1940, or war with the Soviet Union, or the ability to project itself into the Atlantic.

The inadequately prepared and poorly planned Germans were outfought in the sky when they attacked Britain in 1940. The Germans never deployed their full strength at any one time[29] while the RAF aircraft were equal to those in the Luftwaffe. Moreover, the British outproduced the Germans so that losses in fighters were quickly made good because of more efficient manufacture: whereas German manufacture was not maximised for war, Britain quickly developed an efficient system that drew on superior engineering and management. In addition, Britain benefited from an integrated air-defence system. Alongside the good fighters, there were effective sensors, notably radar, and the appropriate command and control mechanisms for controlling the firepower. Unable to defeat the RAF, the *Luftwaffe* did not gain the air superiority over English coastal waters necessary for *Operation Sealion*. This was the invasion that was projected, although with inadequate planning, preparation and resources.

The issue of fighting quality was much discussed in the scholarship produced in the 2000s and 2010s, scholarship that to a considerable extent supersedes earlier work, not least that of the official histories.[30] The most important development was the continued positive re-evaluation of Soviet fighting quality, notably as a result of the work of David Glantz and others on recently accessible archives. This work suggested that the German offensives in 1941, 1942 and 1943 had not primarily failed due to the factors cited by German generals and others – the size of the Soviet Union, disparities in resources, the harshness of the winter (which affected both sides), and maladroit command interventions by Hitler, important as they all were. Instead, the emphasis came to be on the quality of the Soviet defence; although, in addition, fresh insights were gained into German deficiencies.[31] In 1941, the Red Army learned to cope with both German tactics and German operational methods. Anti-tank guns proved crucial to weakening German tank attacks, while establishing defences in depth hindered the exploitation of German breakthroughs. To the surprise of Hitler, some Soviet forces fought well and effectively from the outset. As a result, German plans were derailed.[32]

So also with fresh German offensives on the Eastern Front in 1942 and 1943, for, despite America's entry into the war in December 1941, there was no deployment of American forces on the European mainland until the invasion of Italy in 1943 and none in major strength sufficient to threaten German hegemony until the invasion of Normandy in June 1944. As a result, the Germans, on land able to concentrate very heavily on the Soviets, had over two years to renew the offensive. They failed to do so successfully.

There is also a crucial political dimension. The stability of the Soviet regime was more significant in deciding the outcome of the 1941 campaign than the military issue of German operational failure in late 1941, and for reasons that highlight the importance of the political dimension in this and other wars. Over-confident of the prospects for a swift offensive, and completely failing to appreciate Soviet strength and resolve, the Germans suffered from a lack of consistency, with goals shifting over the emphasis between seizing territory or defeating Soviet forces, and also over the question of which axes of advance to concentrate on. The Germans also suffered from problems in sustaining the offensive, notably a shortage of oil, spare parts and, eventually, food, and from the difficulties posed by poor transport routes in the Soviet Union.

Their lack of consistency led to a delay in the central thrust on Moscow in September 1941, while forces, instead, were sent south to overrun Ukraine and to outmanoeuvre and destroy the Soviet forces there. Both these goals were accomplished, and very heavy casualties were inflicted on the Red Army, but the delay in the advance on Moscow hindered the Germans when they resumed it. In harsh winter conditions, the Red Army was able both to hold the assault eventually and to mount a major and successful counterattack in December 1941.

The standard focus in the discussion of the campaign is that of the possible consequences of an earlier German advance on Moscow, an approach that assumes that the seizure of the city would have been decisive.[33] Leaving aside the historical comparison with Napoleon's capture of Moscow in 1812, which, in the event, turned out to be the prelude to Alexander I's refusal to negotiate and to Napoleon's most deadly defeat, the key element in the unravelling of his empire, this approach makes the standard mistake in the discussion of military history: the assumption that output, in the shape of battlefield success, leads automatically to outcome, in the form of victory.

In contrast, for victory to be total and lasting, it requires that the defeated accept that they had lost, as both Germans and Japanese did in 1945, rather than attempting to fight on. There was scant sign of that in the case of the Soviet Union. Although the Soviet government was evacuated to Kuybyshev on the Volga, there was no military or political collapse comparable to that in France in 1940 or Yugoslavia in 1941 (or Italy at the hands of the Allies in 1943), no more than there had been with Alexander I in 1812. Neither the Soviet system nor the Red Army cracked.[34]

It is possible to play through the counterfactual of asking what would have happened had Japan also attacked the Soviet Union in 1941. The two were hostile, as well as neighbours on the Manchurian frontier, and Japan had both intervened in the Russian Civil War and clashed with the Soviets in 1938 and 1939. The Japanese had been defeated in the latter, and, as in 1904–5 when they had fought, there were serious transport and logistical challenges confronting any major Japanese advance, but such intervention would have had an impact by limiting the transfer of Soviet forces from the Far East to confront Germany. These were the units of the Red Army least affected by Stalin's damaging purges, and they were brought to the aid of Moscow against German attack at a critical point in late 1941. However, the German defeat was not simply a matter of the transfer of these forces, while the Soviet Union anyway had considerable strategic depth in the Far East and Siberia.

By late 1941, allowing for serious and persistent differences over strategy between army and navy, Japanese policymakers were more concerned about the USA. American pressure represented more of a threat to Japanese interests in China than Soviet strength, advancing south offered Japan the opportunity of increasing the pressure on China by cutting its external links, and the urgency of the resource issues confronting Japan encouraged this focus. Meanwhile, the non-aggression pact with the Soviet Union protected Japan's rear. Thus, the idea of joint military pressure on the Soviet Union was not really credible by late 1941 other than in the indirect sense that a Japanese attack on the USA and Britain made them less able to oppose Germany. In explaining Soviet success, it is necessary to mesh together military with political factors, and to look for the latter both within states and at the international level.

The recent scholarly emphasis on Soviet warmaking, rather than German failure, has continued with a discussion of Soviet successes on the offensive in 1942–5, and, again, the stress was on quality, rather than simply resources, and notably with the development of Soviet operational skill in 1944. By then, the nervous breakdown suffered by German troops was becoming an open subject.

Similar points could be made about improvements in Anglo–American fighting effectiveness against both Germany and Japan, from a low point in the early campaigns of 1939–42 (and, in the case of the Americans against the Germans at the Battle of the Kasserine Pass in Tunisia in February 1943), to more successful tactical and, crucially, operational art from late 1942 to 1945. With time, the problems posed by rapid expansion of the armies, the American for example from under 200,000 men in 1939 to nearly 7,000,000 in 1943, were overcome. This shift was fundamental to the flow of campaigning and cannot be reduced to the issue of resources. Training was a key element, as was the professionalism provided by prewar long-service officers.[35]

Command quality

Moreover, command skills had become more significant as the ability to articulate and integrate different arms, a long-established aspect of effectiveness, was made more important due to the greater range of available technology. Thus, it had become necessary to integrate infantry, artillery and armour successfully, as well as air and land, air and sea, and land and sea forces. This was necessary to achieve success not only in the attack, but also in defence. For example, the defensive effectiveness of anti-tank weaponry ensured that mixed or combined-arms formations were more effective than those that focused solely on tanks. In February 1945, Montgomery, then commander of the British 21st Army Group, argued that close co-operation with infantry was needed in order to overcome anti-tank guns: 'I cannot emphasise too strongly that victory in battle depends not on armoured action alone, but on the intimate co-operation of all arms; the tank by itself can achieve little'.[36]

One of the most impressive recent works on the war, John Buckley's *Monty's Men. The British Army and the Liberation of Europe, 1944–5* (2013), focuses on British success in finding a method of fighting through which the Germans could be defeated. Operational analysis has been significant in drawing attention to limitations in German campaigning other than in manoeuvring quickly, while the more full-spectrum operational effectiveness of the British has emerged, as has the particular strength of their artillery. The operational effectiveness included a superior logistical and transport capability. Montgomery's formula was to commit British troops to set-piece plans when they had guaranteed support in depth, a formula deviated from with the Arnhem operation in September 1944 with disastrous consequences.[37] This formula had similarities with that followed during World War One.

Command quality was a matter not only of integrating different military means and of ensuring operational effectiveness, but also of strategic insight. The Axis powers proved seriously deficient in this respect. Their political grasp was limited as was their strategic planning.[38] Hitler was a seriously flawed commander in attack, as seen in the poorly-coordinated pressure on Britain in 1940 and the inconsistently conceived and executed offensives against the Soviet Union in 1941 and 1942. He was also deficient in defence, due to his unwillingness to yield territory, and his consequent preference for the static, over the mobile, defence. In large part, this attitude was a reflection of Hitler's obsessions with willpower and with battle as a test of ideological and racial purity, as well as his suspicion about the determination of subordinates.

By concentrating decision-making, and being unable to match Stalin's ability to delegate operational questions, Hitler ensured that there was no alternative way to provide sound command decisions. By 1944, his diminished grasp on reality exacerbated the difficulties of German command and undermined support from within the senior ranks of the military. Generals who withdrew to escape encirclement, as Rundstedt did from Rostov in late 1941 and Kleist did across the Dniester in the spring of 1944, risked dismissal. No other major power faced a rebellion from within the military as Hitler did with the Bomb Plot in July 1944.

Yet Hitler's deficiencies were part of a more general failure of German warmaking, not least a dysfunctional system of civilian–military relations that echoed similar failures in the Wilhelmine period that closed in 1918. There was a misplaced emphasis on will. As with World War One, the will to win could not be a substitute for a failure to set sensible military and political goals, specifically the inability to make opposing states accept German assumptions.

Fighting quality

At the same time, there were cross-currents in the literature, notably a continued emphasis, especially in the popular literature, on German quality. Thus, Max Hastings, in *Armageddon: The Battle for Germany, 1945* (2004), argued that German and Soviet fighting quality in the last six months of the war in Europe was greater than that of the British and American. He traced this alleged difference in part to a contrast in fighting determination, and measured the latter in part in terms of a willingness to take casualties.[39] There were, however, serious problems with Hastings's methods. In particular, he made considerable play of complaints by Anglo–American commanders about the deficiencies of their troops. These complaints indeed existed, but their frequency, in large part, reflected the greater freedom of comment in British and American military cultures, a freedom that owed much to the desire for improvement through critical self-examination. Thus, after-action reports were reasonably objective, and some of the commentary, for example that by Auchinleck on the British army's performance in the Norway campaign of 1940 in which he had served,[40] was particularly harsh.

The contrast with most German and Soviet material is readily apparent, but there were obvious reasons why their commanders would not highlight deficiencies, for fear that they would be blamed on them. Moreover, the large number of troops punished, often executed, by the German and, even more, Soviet militaries scarcely suggested a confidence in fighting determination.

In part, the trading of national categories, indeed stereotypes, is unhelpful as it assumes that categorisation at the national scale is the most appropriate, and, indeed, argues the case for national ways of war.[41] In practice, there were significant differences between units within individual armies of the same nationality, some of which have attracted attention, for example contrasts in fighting determination between different British and different American units on D-Day.

There were also important variations between German, Soviet and Japanese units; as between the experienced motivated and ably-led SS divisions in Normandy in 1944 and some of the other German units.[42] In the Bulge offensive later that year, much of the German infantry displayed a lack of enthusiasm, tactical skill and training which shocked their own officers and contrasted with the fighting quality of the German armour.

In all armies, these differences were also seen within units. There was a range between those who had blood lust and others who were reluctant to fight. This reluctance was least apparent with the Japanese.

Variations within militaries deserve more attention, not least because they subvert the clear national stereotypes that have been employed. These stereotypes are overly crude as a means of military analysis, although they conform to the simplifications sought for in public memory.

Much hinges on rebutting the argument that troops from democratic societies were, and are, less willing to risk their lives than their totalitarian counterparts, an argument that is less than well-founded empirically. This argument is employed to suggest that democracies are somehow less effective in crises, an argument that joins the war years to modern irritation with the political process, or to the analysis that, for example, in some fashion a lack of domestic support on the American 'Home Front' was responsible for failure in Vietnam. In part, this approach reduces war to an exercise in will and determination and argues that these are best provided by top-down political systems.

Improving quality

Leaving aside the problematic nature of this analysis, there are also questions about the extent to which the relative freedom of a democratic society provides a greater opportunity for pursuing functionality without the complicating factor of totalitarian ideology.[43] This capability was demonstrated across a range of activities including the development, introduction and use of new weapons and weapons systems, and the ability to create joint forces with unified commands, notably integrating land, air and sea forces. Allied success in this contributed greatly to operational effectiveness.[44]

The use of information was a key element, with situational awareness a major factor in planning and in moulding, and responding, to circumstances. Notwithstanding the serious failure in 1940–2 to comprehend Japanese power and motivations, the Allies eventually proved better than the Axis at understanding the areas in which they campaigned and in planning accordingly. For example, an appreciation of the role of climate, notably for air operations and amphibious attacks, led to considerable efforts in accumulating and understanding meteorological information.

With the Allies, there was also a reasonably effective process of improving weaponry in response to flaws, limitations and the specifications of opposing weaponry. For example, the quality gap that favoured German against

American and British tanks was closed by late 1944 and 1945, as new Allied tanks appeared. Bigger guns came because of the need to penetrate thicker armour at long ranges. The Sherman was up-gunned with a higher-velocity 76 mm gun in mid-1944 and up-armoured to counter tanks such as the Tiger I and the Panther. Moreover, tank-destroyers fitted with a 90 mm gun were introduced: the first American M36 arrived in service in France in September 1944. Anti-tank and anti-aircraft guns were fitted to tank-destroyers, which were in effect lightly armoured or simpler tanks fitted with powerful guns. This stress on performance in tank combat reflected not only a response to the German tanks, but also the development of American doctrine away from the earlier emphasis on tanks that were fast and manoeuvrable, an emphasis that reflected the cavalry ethos and focus on manoeuvrability.

There were also major improvements in air conflict. Strategic bombing was made more feasible by four-engine bombers, such as the British Lancaster and the American B–29, as well as by heavier bombs and developments in navigational aids and training. British night bombing was improved by much electronic and radar equipment, which the Germans countered with developments of their own. The introduction of long-range fighter escorts for the bombers was important, especially the American P–38s (Lightnings), P–47s (Thunderbolts), and P–51s (Mustangs). Both of the latter used drop fuel tanks, which enabled fighters to reach German airspace and still engage in dogfights. The Mustangs, of which 14,000 were built, were able not only to provide necessary escorts, but also, in 1944, to seek out German fighters and thus win the air war above Germany.

This success contrasted with the *Luftwaffe*'s less well supported and unsuccessful offensive on Britain in 1940–1. The effectiveness and impact of the Combined Bomber Offensive became highly contentious after the war, and are in part discussed in the Germany section of Chapter Five. The impact was certainly seen across the German war effort. For example air raids caused delays and problems with the German development of jet aircraft, not least, as a result of the assault on German production facilities in the 'Oil War' of 1944, being responsible for a shortage of fuel. As a reminder of the multiplicity of factors involved, the raids exacerbated the serious difficulties in the German economy arising from poor organisation and the mismatch of goals, systems and resources.

In contrast to the Allied application of information, improvisation, always a central element in planning and military activity, particularly characterised Axis planning and responses. Hitler's emphasis was on the socio-economic and political conditions he wished to see, and not on those that occurred on the ground. In planning and campaigning, the Axis stress was often on the value of superior will, rather than on the realities of climate, terrain and logistics. The constraints posed by the last three were ignored; for example, in the totally unsuccessful Japanese offensive against the British on the India–Burma frontier in 1944.

Information was also necessary in assessing how best to produce the appropriate *matériel*, and when it was likely to become available, and thus in turning conception into possibility. Economists were employed by the American government to provide realistic production projections. These economists, notably Simon Kuznets, Robert Nathan and Stacy May, used statistics in an innovative fashion so as to understand and produce information on American national income. The resulting Gross National Product statistics clarified the viability of planning a massive rise in production for the military without needing to cut the consumer economy.[45]

A key instance of enhanced production came with the production of the atomic bomb which indicated not only the intellectual resources available to the USA, but also the nature and scale of activity possible for an advanced industrial society. This activity was the product of the application of science, and also of the powerful industrial and technological capability of the USA and its willingness to spend about $1.9 billion in rapidly creating a large new industry, a sum that is far larger in current values.[46] The electromagnets needed for isotope separation were particularly expensive and required 13,500 tons of silver. Major industrial concerns were able to apply their expertise, resources and manufacturing techniques to participate in the Manhatten Project to make the bombs, the chemical company DuPont producing the necessary plutonium. The American belief in the certainty of improvement through technological progress played a significant role in encouraging support.[47]

That Germany and Japan, each of which was interested in developing an atomic bomb, did not make comparable progress reflected more than resources. The *Uranverein*, the German plan, was not adequately pursued, in part because of the belief that it would take too long to develop and that the war would already be over. Hostility to what was termed 'Jewish physics' also played a role, as did the consequences of overestimating the amount of U–235 required to manufacture a bomb.[48]

Improvement in fighting quality were not only a matter of applying weaponry. There was also an engagement with the training requirements both of modern warfare and of particular environments. Training was supplemented by after-action analysis. This is clear not only from the institutional perspective, but also from that of individual accounts. For example, the diaries of Stanley Christopherson, an officer with the Sherwood Rangers, a regiment with the British army, indicates that a considerable amount of training and analysis occurred during wartime service, and notably after the regiment was mechanised and given a front-line role.[49]

Conclusions

The analysis of conditions relevant to the war was, and is, intensely political with, in each case, a fundamental divide opening up between the

democracies and the totalitarian states. Some democracies did not rise to
the challenge during World War Two, most obviously France in 1940, while
the Soviet Union showed that totalitarian regimes could be effective as well
as brutal. Yet, displacing attention from the excuse of relative resources
– namely that the Axis would have won but for the disparity in resources –
permits a focus on the deficiencies of totalitarian systems and the strength
of their democratic opponents. The extent to which this argument was of
more general applicability than World War Two is unclear, but it is even
more the case that a reading about the deficiencies of democracies should
not be offered from World War Two to the present.

This issue provides another instance of the extent to which politics plays
a continuing and varied role in the reading of the war, while the war itself
is important to key issues in modern political culture. This significance is
likely to decline, in part because of the apparently disposable character
of history with greater distance, and in part due to shifts in the relative
importance of countries with differing interests in, and accounts of, the
war. This decline, which can itself be seen as a political process, does not
preclude, however, a continued interaction between politics and the war at
present and for the foreseeable future. That interaction still plays a major
role in the historical imagination of the older generation in many (but
not all) states, and has also been institutionalised in terms of the publicly-
endorsed national myths of many, but not all, states. For an historian, this
is a situation of great fascination, but there is also a civic and professional
duty to engage with the accounts of the war in order to explain the contexts
of decisions,[50] and to try to limit the damage produced by toxic narratives.

CHAPTER FIVE

Recollection: The War in Europe

Retribution

Issues of responsibility and guilt linked the politics of the war years to what came later. War guilt and the treatment of war criminals played a role in thinking about the end of the conflict. To fix such guilt on the Axis, and to punish its leaders and their most prominent followers, accordingly became important Allied goals.[1] Indeed, ensuring these goals was a key aspect of the surrender in both Europe and Asia, and, alongside the occupation of the defeated powers, was designed to make certain that the sense of incompleteness left at the end of World War One was not repeated.

Nazi leaders were tried in 1945–6 by the International Military Tribunal in Nuremberg, which published a catalogue of Nazi crimes, and 12 of the most prominent leaders were sentenced to hang. Despite the grave hypocrisy, in light of Stalin's brutal regime, of Soviet membership of the tribunal, and despite the Nuremberg trials becoming 'one of the first fronts of the Cold War',[2] the tribunal was important in the development of international jurisprudence and of the concept of 'crimes against humanity', the fourth count or category designed for the indictments. The tribunal endorsed the principle of a higher law than national statutes, while the inmates in Spandau prison, most notably Hitler's deputy, Rudolf Hess, until his suicide in 1987, remained as a reminder of justice and retribution. There were also a large number of other trials of those involved in German war crimes.[3]

Although many Nazis and others, for example Croat *Ustašas*, escaped justice, other Nazis and collaborators were tried and many were executed, particularly in Eastern Europe. However, that remark conceals the extent to which those tried for war crimes included politicians who had held positions in states such as Hungary that had allied with Germany but who did not necessarily have Nazi sympathies. Thus, in Hungary, László Bardossy, who had been Prime Minister in 1941–2, was tried in 1946.

Whereas Hungary's wartime leader, Admiral Horthy, was allowed to go into comfortable exile in Portugal, Marshal Antonescu was executed in 1946 for leading Romania into the war and for crimes against humanity, a charge well-justified by the Romanian slaughter of Jews. The postwar purge of Fascists in Italy was also brutal. In contrast, Marshal Mannerheim, the commander of Finland's army, who became President in 1944 serving until 1946, retained public respect.

Few of the German senior commanders captured by the Western Allies were tried, in large part because of a failure to appreciate the extent of the German army's co-operation in the killing of civilians, as well as a degree of solidarity among senior officers.[4] Nevertheless, among these commanders, Field Marshal Erich von Manstein served four of the 18 years to which he was sentenced by a British military court in 1949 for war crimes in the Soviet Union, while Field Marshal Ewald von Kleist was handed over to the Yugoslavs, who convicted and imprisoned him for war crimes in 1946, before handing him over to the Soviet Union in 1948, which imprisoned him until he died in 1954.

At the same time, rivalry between the Allies, specifically, but not only, between the Soviet Union and the Western Allies, ensured that the issues of guilt and punishment were also politicised as a way to score points.[5] There were also differences among the Western Allies. In Britain, the Foreign Office pressed the case for trying Manstein, but the War Office was far more reluctant to see him imprisoned.

As a more lasting issue of postwar political grievance, the British and Americans handed over about 4.25 million people to the Soviets, in accordance with the agreement at the Yalta Conference of 1945 to return those captured who had been Soviet nationals before the Nazi–Soviet Pact of 1939. A large number were sent to the *gulags*, but many were killed at once, including the Cossack prisoners handed over by the British. The latter step caused much postwar criticism, notably against Harold Macmillan (Prime Minister from 1957 to 1963), who had served as Acting President of the Allied Council for Italy and had a relevant meeting at Klagenfurt with General Keightley, the local British commander. In practice, the action was in accordance with the spirit as well as the letter of the Yalta agreement.[6] Those who had not been Soviet nationals before the Pact, for example citizens of the Baltic Republics, were not handed over. The handing over of prisoners to the Soviets was encouraged by a need to ensure the return of the large number of British and American prisoners taken by the Germans and then in Soviet hands,[7] and by the huge problems facing Britain, France and the USA, especially with displaced persons in their own areas, as well as dire warnings of famine and deaths for the winter of 1945.

A similar distinction between Soviet territories before and after the Nazi–Soviet Pact was drawn on in the return of cultural property looted by the Germans. This and other aspects of restitution led to much bitterness involving claimants, notably by governments using this issue to advance their own agendas. Their grievances, as well as demands for compensation, have affected the work of the UNESCO Committee for Promoting the Return of Cultural Property to the Countries of Origin. Germany and Russia have taken opposing positions over this issue and it played a contentious role in their relations in 2013, notably when Chancellor Merkel met President Putin.[8]

Alongside governmental steps against those seen as collaborators, such as the establishment in Czechoslovakia of a network composed of a National Court, Extraordinary People's Courts and local judicial panels, which together took action against tens of thousands; there was also a widespread popular action against collaborators and those considered to be collaborators. This action had a particular gender dimension, with violence towards those who were accused of fraternisation.[9] In part, this process represented a purgative spasm of violence, the *épuration sauvage* in France, directed against those who had betrayed what were seen as communal links and norms, but, in part, it was also a reckoning with the weak and vulnerable, notably women who had had sexual relationships with Germans, the *collaboratrices horizontales*, the ultimate euphemism.

There was also a social dynamic in that the privileged tended to evade retribution. For example, the prominent French couturier Coco Chanel, who had advanced her interests by intimate links with the Germans and had sought to use the anti-Semitic laws to take control of the factory that manufactured her scents, was able to manage a postwar career in which, after self-imposed exile in Switzerland, she returned to profitable fame in France. In her case, as in that of many others, the collaboration was minimised or elided from the public record, notably in her biography by Edmonde Charles-Roux and in films such as *Chanel Solitaire* (1981), *Coco Avant Chanel* (2009), and *Coco Chanel and Igor Stravinsky* (2009).

The peace settlement

Postwar executions and other killings, as well as a range of activities including burials and reburials,[10] were traumatic. They could bring closure but were also aspects of the developing tensions of postwar politics. Specific political issues proved more significant in bridging the gap from wartime politics to postwar tension. This bridging became dramatically apparent in Greece in the winter of 1944–5 as the British committed troops in a successful effort to limit the attempt by the Communists to seize Athens. In some respects, World War Two in Greece was thus a stage in a struggle within Greece as the politics of the country were settled, a struggle that ended with Communist defeat in 1949. The same point can be made about China, with, again, a concluding date in 1949, although, this time, the conclusion was a Communist triumph.

Yet, such an account of the war as a stage in longer-term developments underplays the dramatically disruptive character of World War Two, and of the respective attacks of Germany and Japan. This point serves as a reminder of the degree to which academic revisionism can act to minimise what appear, with reason, to be clear-cut points, notably the greater blame that attaches to aggressive powers. In the case of Greece, for example, both country and state were more stable in 1940 than in 1945. Moreover, it is not helpful to suggest any sense of equivalence between civil war in 1944–9, and the politics or methods of German, Italian and Bulgarian wartime occupation in Greece.

The political rivalries that followed the Soviet advance into Eastern Europe, Manchuria and North Korea in 1944–5 led directly into the Cold War. In part, this advance was a resumption of the Soviet expansionism displayed in 1939–40 when Stalin was allied to Hitler. However, the context was different, notably as a result of the destruction of independent states, Poland and the Baltic Republics, in 1939–40. In 1944–5, in contrast, the Soviet Union was conquering the territories of the rival German and, then, Japanese empires. This process provided the opportunity for Soviet expansionism and preceded the process of new state-building. Thus, although much of the population was still in place, the slate seemed clean, an attitude that took precedence over prewar legalities, not that these were of great concern to Stalin.

From the Soviet perspective, the creation of new client states provided the opportunity to consolidate their military success, an entrenchment eased by the Soviet control over the local military forces, which might, otherwise, have been a focus of nationalist action. Thus, in March 1945, Stalin ordered the demobilisation of Romanian forces. As the situation in the Balkans, where existing states continued, showed, the Soviet determination to establish control was not simply a matter of drawing new territorial lines against a background of the destruction of the vicious German and Japanese empires.

Nevertheless, such a process was seen in the major redrawing of Poland's frontiers, and in the partition of East Prussia between the Soviet Union and Poland, while in the Baltic Republics there was a resumption, in 1944, of the opportunistic Soviet expansionism of 1940, once again accompanied by the large-scale deportation of local people to *gulags*. Such deportation, and the more general process of oppressive control, were designed to make the clean slate a reality. Moreover, in the Balkans, where the Soviets created a new indirect empire, their objectives took precedence over consideration of local political interests and wishes. Indeed, these were manipulated to serve Soviet interests.

Territorial changes, and those in political systems, were a major issue in Allied alliance politics in the last stage of the war. In 1944, as Britain responded to Soviet demands on Poland's frontiers, Anthony Eden, the Foreign Secretary who had been a critic of Chamberlain and had accordingly abstained in the Commons debate over the 1938 Munich agreement, asked 'If I give way over Lviv, shall I go down in the history books as an appeaser?' Soviet strength, in the shape of the advancing Red Army, indeed helped ensure that Lviv became part of the Soviet Union, but as part of what is now the independent state of Ukraine.

Indeed, the Ukrainian question was a key aspect of the postwar settlement of the Polish border, and one that saw a determination by the Soviet authorities to suppress Ukrainian nationalism. As the republics of the Soviet Union were then under firm central control, the extension of Ukraine into former Poland was not regarded as an aid to this nationalism.[11] So also with the annexation of part of Slovakia (prewar Czechoslovakia) to the Soviet Union and its allocation to Ukraine. Albeit in a very different context, this annexation throws instructive light on the positive remarks frequently made about opportunities for co-operation with Stalin both at the time of the Munich agreement and subsequently.

The fate of Poland, with much territory lost to the Soviet Union (alongside that gained from Germany) and with the country given over to Communist dictatorship, proved the most contentious and emotional issue in the new order. In part, this was because Britain and France had gone to war in 1939 to support Poland against German aggression. In part, the focus on Poland also reflected the extent to which it was not possible to muster much sympathy for states compromised by alliance with Hitler, notably Bulgaria, Romania and Hungary.

In the peace settlement, Germany lost its gains from 1938, Austria and the Sudetenland, and those from later, including much of Poland and Alsace-Lorraine. Germany also lost nearly a quarter of its earlier, post-1918 territory: Silesia, Eastern Pomerania and part of East Prussia to a Poland that Stalin could now rely on as a ductile client, and the remainder of East Prussia to the Soviet Union. Japan lost to the Soviet Union South Sakhalin and the Kuriles, and also to others Korea, Taiwan and the Pacific islands it had gained as a result of World War One. The territorial settlement of the war left both the USA and the Soviet Union with extensive spheres of control and influence, and the fundamentally satisfactory nature of the settlement to these two powers can be seen as helping ensure that the subsequent Cold War never became hot.[12]

Germany's defeat played a major role in discrediting hitherto powerful ideological currents, particularly racist formulations of identity, which became unacceptable, or, in practice, less acceptable. Ironically, however, the peace settlement entailed compulsory population transfers that rested on such formulations, although without a comparable ideology of ethnic hierarchy or a similar practice of large-scale murderous ethnic violence.[13] The expulsion of Germans from the territories lost, as well as from other parts of Eastern Europe, especially Czechoslovakia but also, for example, Romania and Yugoslavia, gave force to the territorial changes of the war.[14] The expulsions were deliberately designed to cut short any irridentist movements; but these expulsions remain contentious in German politics.

Indeed, this issue has been repeatedly raised by Germans, partly in order to suggest that they were not uniquely guilty of vile and murderous anti-societal behaviour, but also in a quest for compensation. In practice, it was the Nazi policies of ethnic categorisation, division and violence that encouraged the expression of an anti-German nationalism and led to it becoming policy, although this German violence was far more apparent in Poland than in Czechoslovakia, from which the Sudeten Germans were expelled. In Czechoslovakia, enforced participation by the Czechs in the German war economy had been accompanied by a *relatively* benign German treatment of those Czechs who were not Jews. After the war, the Czech government treated the Sudeten Germans as collectively guilty and they were expelled.[15]

Issues such as ethnic expulsion also serve the needs of present politics. This process of the politicised application of the war, a key element in public history and the politics of memory,[16] can be seen across the range of combatants and does not only affect the major powers. Moreover, this process is one that remains potent even more than 60 years after the war ended. Thus, in Denmark, the German occupation of 1940–5 has been used to serve and debate different political purposes, including to strengthen opposition to membership, and the terms of membership, in the European Union, or to justify Danish participation in the Iraq War of 2003.[17]

France

In all the countries occupied by the Axis powers, the extent of collaboration and resistance were key issues. This was notably so in France, where these questions were closely bound up in national politics, and, in addition, without an occupation by the victorious Allies to add a level of complexity but also a distancing from these politics. There was a postwar punishment by the French of collaborators, with possibly up to 10,000 killed and 40,000 detained. Those tried included Pétain, who was convicted of treason, although not executed, Pierre Laval, the Vichy Prime Minister, who was convicted and shot, and Weygand, who had briefly been Vichy Defence Minister, who was acquitted. As a reminder of the complexity of alignments, he was also an opponent of the Germans and as Delegate-General in French Africa in 1940–1 had helped the British and worked with the Americans.[18] Women who had had sex with Germans were publicly humiliated, notably by having all their hair cut off and then being paraded in public.

A huge, multi-volume, parliamentary *Rapport fait au nom de la commission charge d'enquêter sur les evenements survenus en France de 1933 à 1945* was published in 1951. There was a major rejection of the psychological grip of Vichy, and a particular shaping of the years from defeat to liberation in which Vichy was largely excised from the collective memory. De Gaulle declared that Vichy had 'always been null and void, and it never happened', while the prosecutor at the trial of Pétain stated that Vichy was 'four years to be stricken from our history'.[19] Vichy also instilled an anti-British shame: Churchill said of the Liberation of France: 'they will never forgive us for it', and such varied figures as de Gaulle and his long-term political opponent François Mitterrand were bitterly suspicious of Britain.

Instead of an emphasis on Vichy, an exemplary account of recent French history was produced and then actively propagated. While highly misleadingly, most of the French were said to have supported the Resistance. This was a necessary aspect of the emphasis on national honour. The process of myth-making, however, was also divisive, as Communist prominence in the Resistance was written out of the Gaullist myth – instead providing a separate Communist myth emphasising the role of the working class, the Communist Party, *le parti des fusillés*, and the Soviet Union in the Resistance. This contrast helped lead to rival, indeed harshly contested, commemorations of episodes and of heroes such as Jean Moulin, a major Gaullist Resistance figure. Captured by the Gestapo in 1943, he died after torture. His ashes were transferred to the *Panthéon* (the national site of the graves of the great) in 1964 in a key act of commemoration. Responsibility for his capture was bitterly contested amidst claims of betrayal.[20]

Alongside such clashes, there was a determination to present an exemplary account of the war and to suppress or limit alternative views. Thus, in Alain Resnais's documentary about the Holocaust, *Nuit et Brouillard* (1955), a film commissioned by the Comité d'histoire de la 2e Guerre mondiale, with the support of the Ministry of Veterans, the French licensing authorities censored a shot briefly showing the kepi of a French policeman among those guarding deportees. In fact, the French authorities, including the police, had played a major role in rounding up Jews who were deported to the extermination camps.

There was also controversy over the reasons for the collapse of France in 1940, controversy in which political divisions interacted with the impact, until the 1980s, of the closure of material in the archives. In echoes of the 1930s, the Left blamed proto-Fascists, and the Right the weaknesses of the Third Republic, while Gaullists presented de Gaulle as a prophet who had been neglected until the Fall of France.[21]

The sanitisation of the wartime years provided solace from a consideration of failure in 1940, and this sanitisation was given added force by the search for assurance and prestige that finally culminated in the formation of the Fifth Republic in 1958 and the presidency of Charles de Gaulle from 1958 to 1969. His refusal to collaborate during the war was presented as the quintessential origin and cause of the new France, and the fact that he was now President apparently vindicated the French of 1940–4 and, more generally, French history, as did the gross exaggeration of the popularity and effectiveness of the Resistance. The latter included an unwarranted stress on the role of the Free French in the Normandy landings of 1944 and in the subsequent capture of Paris. In practice, the former role was limited.[22] Moreover, it was the British (including Canadian) and, even more, American advances that established the context for the liberation of Paris and that of the rest of France.

The combination of an exemplary account of Resistance to the Occupation and of forgetting collaboration, notably, but not only, Vichy, proved a way to conceal what was unacceptable and also to respond to the marked diversity of experiences during the Occupation. Thus, a workable past was constructed, a collective account designed to encompass all.[23] Amnesty laws for wartime collaboration were passed in 1951 and 1953. The Memorial to the Deportation opened by de Gaulle in Paris in 1962 made no mention of Vichy.

This situation changed, however, in part because of developments specific to France itself, but also due to the greater weight that the Holocaust came to play in the collective Western consciousness, and to the less reverential approach to the past that was an aspect of the cultural changes of the 1960s, and was seen for example in Germany. Scholarship also played a role, notably Robert Paxton's *Vichy France: Old Guard and New Order, 1940–1944* (1972). In place of the presentation of Vichy and collaboration as something forced on France by the Germans, which was very much the dominant view at the time, Paxton, by extensively employing German archival material (the French archives were closed to him), argued (correctly) that the Vichy regime had been popular and was also keen to collaborate in order to win German support for a reconfiguration of French society that was to mark the triumph of an anti-liberal ideology. This approach, however, was unacceptable to many of those in academic authority in France, and there were difficulties in publishing a French translation of Paxton's book.

Similarly, *Le Chagrin et la Pitié* [*The Sorrow and the Pity*], a documentary by Marcel Ophuls, released in 1971, about the Occupation in Clermont-Ferrand, an industrial centre near Vichy, was not shown on French television for 12 years. Louis Malle's film *Lacombe Lucien* (1973) created considerable controversy because it made Fascism seem attractive and presented its protagonist as working voluntarily for the Gestapo.

From a political perspective, emphasising complicity and collaboration hit the nationalist historical account outlined for the Fourth and Fifth Republics; while tarnishing the Resistance, or questioning its popularity, seemed to serve the interests of those who looked back to Vichy, as well as to compromise the nationalist historical account. In response to mounting concern about France's wartime conduct, de Gaulle's successors, Georges Pompidou (President 1969–74) and Valéry Giscard d'Estaing (1974–81), pressed for reconciliation between the memories of Resistance and Vichy and, also, for moving forward away from a troubled past. The deportation of the Jews was largely neglected in the public account of the war.

Postwar views about laudatory wartime conduct continued to be expressed, as in François-Georges Dreyfus's *Histoire de Vichy* (1990), while individual Vichy figures, such as Weygand, attracted sympathetic coverage, in part on the grounds that they were not as bad as the rest.[24] Nevertheless, there was also a significant change. Growing interest in Vichy's complicity in the Holocaust, combined with the less deferential character of French society, especially after the traumatic political and student unrest of May 1968, to provide a more conducive atmosphere for the pursuit of the truth by journalists, scholars and others.

Politics also played a major part in other respects, as scores were settled with those who could be tainted for their role under Vichy. François Mitterrand, President from 1981 until 1995, was increasingly attacked for his misleading and self-serving account of his Vichy years, an account that underplayed his role in Vichy and that presented himself as playing a Resistance role without mentioning his continued ties to Vichy. As President, Mitterrand honoured the memory of Pétain. He was also criticised for his friendships with prominent Vichy figures, and for covering both individuals and the regime as a whole. One of Mitterrand's friends was René Bousquet, Chief of Police under Vichy, who was assassinated in Paris in 1993 just before he could be tried for his major role in rounding up Jewish children for deportation to slaughter in Germany.

Attention was also directed at the ambivalent role of the powerful French Communist Party during the Nazi–Soviet Pact of 1939–41, an issue relevant both for the compromised integrity of the Party and for the wider international situation. Moreover, prominent judicial proceedings further helped encourage interest and controversy, especially the trials in 1994 of Paul Touvier, head of the collaborationist *milice* in Lyons, and in 1997–8 of Maurice Papon, a former Secretary-General at the Préfecture of the Gironde. Papon had played a major role in the deportation of Bordeaux's Jews and later became a government minister. As an indication of the lack of zeal shown by Mitterrand, Papon's role had first been revealed in the press in 1981, the year in which Mitterrand was elected President, and yet he was tried only after Mitterrand's period in office had ended.

Nevertheless, the Vichy period was put under the spotlight, not least when a number of films were set there. The situation led to pressure for a new public memory,[25] and this need was grasped in 1995 when Mitterrand's political opponent and successor, Jacques Chirac, accepted national responsibility for the wartime treatment of Jews, responsibility that, by moving the focus from the Germans, represented a major condemnation of the Vichy regime, and a step that Mitterrand had refused to take in 1992. Similarly, in 1997, the French Catholic Church publicly sought forgiveness for having failed to come to the defence of the Jews. Thus, the Holocaust helped focus a more complex refashioning of the recent French past, creating a demand for the recognition of events and memories that had been ignored in the public account. The Holocaust also provided a clear basis for establishing a judgment of the integrity of French politicians.

Born in 1932, and first elected to the National Assembly in 1967, Chirac was from a very different generation than that of Mitterrand, for whom the relevant dates were 1916 and 1946. Chirac had no wartime record. Chirac also lay claim to the Gaullist tradition, whereas Mitterrand had been an opponent of de Gaulle and, indeed, had unsuccessfully stood against him for the Presidency. The relationship between Mitterrand's experiences of, and views on, Vichy and his conviction of the need for a close partnership with Germany within the European Union is unclear but suggestive. So, indeed, is the more general question of wartime politics and the creation of the European Economic Community, the origin of the European Union. Mitterrand certainly saw Britain as playing a marginal role in directing the European Union. Alongside domestic politics, Franco–German rapprochement was a key context for subsequent French governmental responses to the war.

In 2000, a national Holocaust day was instituted. The issue of French responsibility in the Holocaust continued to resonate, although it reached a form of resolution in 2009 when the *Conseil d'État* recognised the responsibility of the Vichy government in the deportation of Jews. This ruling established, for the first time, a legal recognition of France's role, as the *Conseil d'État* accepted (correctly) that France had acted independently, and not simply under pressure from the German authorities. At the same time, the *Conseil d'État* argued that postwar compensation was sufficient and that no more needed to be provided.

The ruling captured two of the major strands in the discussion of World War Two: recognition and compensation. Indeed, concern about the latter was often a factor affecting the former. Thus, at the same period as this issue was being considered in France, there was contention in Italy and Germany about the award by an Italian court of damages against Germany for a massacre of civilians carried out by German troops in 1944 in response to resistance activity. The issue also focused the relationship between local acts of violence and public, national recognition and (legal) retribution.

In France, World War Two continued to play a key role in the political struggle for appropriate historical references. The Gaullists argued that the National Front, their rival on the Right, looked back to Vichy. Indeed, the National Front did make such references, not least in the 2002 presidential election when the Vichy slogan 'Work, Family, Country' was deployed.[26] Jean-Marie Le Pen, who founded the National Front in 1972 in part by appealing for the support of those who had backed Vichy, became prominent when his party won 10 per cent of the national vote in the 1986 Assembly elections. In 1987, he was fined 1.2 million francs (£171,000) for declaring in a radio interview that the Holocaust was a detail of history. In 2009, Le Pen repeated the phrase in the European Parliament in Strasbourg: 'I just said that the gas chambers were a detail of Second World War history, which is clear'. The prospect that Le Pen would preside over the new chamber as the oldest Member of European Parliament led to successful action to block him.

Holocaust denial or diminishment had a varied, but extensive, audience in France. Marcel Lefebvre (1905–91), who had been Archbishop of Dakar, was suspended from the public exercise of his priestly and episcopal functions in 1976 for forming the 'Priestly Confraternity of Pius X' in 1970. This body represented a rejection of the reforms of the Second Vatican Council, reforms which included the abandonment of the Catholic Church's traditional anti-Semitic beliefs. Indeed, *Nostra Aetate*, the Declaration on the Relation of the Church with Non-Christian Religions, bluntly stated 'Whoever despises or persecutes this [Jewish] People does injury to the Catholic Church'. Moreover, Pope John Paul II was to call Jews the 'elder brothers' of the Christians. Although Lefebvre's major concern was not attitudes towards Jews, but the modernised liturgy and the definition of religious freedom as an inalienable human right, his following drew on a strand of French anti-Semitism that had been powerfully manifested in the Dreyfus affair and under Vichy. Moreover, the convent in 1989 where Paul Touvier was arrested belonged to this sect. Defying the suspension, Lefebvre ordained bishops without the mandate of the Pope, for which he was excommunicated by John Paul II in 1988. The four bishops he had ordained were also excommunicated, and in 2009 there was considerable controversy over the remission of these excommunications by Pope Benedict XVI, as one of the bishops, Richard Williamson, a Briton, claimed that fewer than 300,000 Jews died in the Holocaust, a wild underestimate of a figure that should be close to 6,000,000 killed.

The French government memorialised the Resistance with considerable zeal during the 2000s. In 2007, the new President, Nicolas Sarkozy, instructed schools to read to all classes a farewell letter written in October 1941 by the 17-year-old Guy Môquet on the eve of his execution by the Germans as part of a collective reprisal for the killing of the German military commandant in Nantes. Sarkozy presented this episode and lesson as an inspiring example of patriotic sacrifice, but opposition politicians and teachers objected to what they saw as the government's appropriation of Môquet, who had been a Communist.[27]

As a reminder of the complexity of the situation, there was also interest in France in the 2000s, in resistance from within Vichy (broadly put), including people who started out Vichy, but were sometimes not totally Vichy by a long shot, and who then moved into pure resistance by 1942 or later.[28]

The war provides an element in many issues in French politics and society, even if there is rarely a common thread. Thus, the service of North and West Africans in French forces during the war proved a key postwar issue, notably involving topics of pensions, residence rights and identity.[29] In practice, however ungenerous and racist the treatment of African veterans by France, there was no equivalent to the massacres of African soldiers by the Germans in France in 1940 (about 3,000 were murdered),[30] but the latter did not provide a prominent and contentious story comparable to French policy towards the veterans. The link between this issue with, say, Sarkozy's talk of an obligation to the USA stemming from the Liberation in 1944 was indirect, but the common theme was that the war provided a key way to engage attention and to elicit sympathy.

Germany

In Germany, there was initially a widespread lack of contrition over Nazism. This was unsurprising as Hitler had enjoyed much popularity across the country and its social groups. With time, the situation was to change. However, it was striking that in the western Erzgebirge, a part of Germany that was briefly unoccupied in 1945, the largely Communist antifascist 'action committees' that sought to tackle the postwar disorder encountered scant support from a population that still had many Nazi sympathies.[31]

At the national level, the chronology of adjustment was broadly similar to that in France. First, postwar occupation in Germany led to the punishment of many members of the wartime regime and to the dismantling of the Nazi state and its apparatus, although in East Germany a new totalitarian state was created at the behest of the Soviet Union. The absence of any movement comparable to the Resistance, and of any episode akin to the Liberation (of France), meant that punishment and dismantling were at the hands of the occupying powers. This situation helped ensure that, alongside a grounding of the new West Germany in democratic practices and the rule of law,[32] de-Nazification was less than complete, not least because it was abandoned in some areas due to what were seen as counter-productive responses. Aside from the serious inherent difficulties of the task, the Soviet occupiers and their Communist clients were more concerned in what became East Germany about rivals on the Left, notably Social Democrats and those Communists judged unacceptable.

In the Western Occupation Zones, in contrast, there was a desire on the part of both the occupation authorities and, even more, the local population to integrate what became West Germany into the West as the frontline against Communism,[33] as part of a focus on rebuilding and the future.[34] On the part of the occupation authorities, this focus became stronger as the Cold War began and developed. Whereas, in 1945–6, there was major concern to ascertain whether both Germans and Displaced Persons had taken part in the Nazi system, the emphasis changed later in the decade.[35]

Among West German politicians, there was a tendency to rebut claims of German guilt by stigmatising them as evidence of Marxist bias and support for East Germany.[36] The government of Konrad Adenaeur, Chancellor from 1949 to 1963, proved very reluctant to prosecute the crimes of the Nazi era. The German reluctance to accept collective responsibility and guilt[37] was a theme powerfully advanced in work by the American scholars Christopher Browning and Daniel Goldhagen.[38] Instead, the frequent German tendency was to focus on their own sufferings and to present themselves as victims both of the Nazi leaders and of the Allies.

At the same time, there was a reformulation of German nationalism, with pride in economic growth and the creation of a 'new' free Germany and, in particular, from 1955, a new German army designed for the defence of Western Europe. Such an objective produced a political need for an acceptable presentation of recent German political history. This presentation was characterised by a widespread desire to depict Nazism not as something inherent within Germanness, but rather as an aberration that had gained support and power due to the particular circumstances of the 1930s, especially the mass unemployment resulting from the 1929 Crash and the subsequent Depression.[39]

Others, therefore, could be described as bearing the burden of responsibility for the Nazis and, indeed, in part, this process involved a reiteration of criticism of the Allies in the 1920s and 1930s for the supposedly harsh peace terms after World War One. The whitewashing of the recent German past led to an emphasis on limited and/or misguided support for Hitler prior to his seizure of power in 1933, and to coerced support thereafter. Ordinary Germans were presented as separate from and, indeed, victims of the Nazi pathology. Among the first cases investigated by West German courts in the late 1940s and 1950s were the killings of ordinary German civilians in the last weeks of the war by hard-core Nazis, notably SS squads.

There was also a stress on resistance to Nazi policies, especially on the July 1944 Bomb Plot, as also on Catholic opponents of these policies, such as Archbishop Galen of Münster. There was much emphasis in theology on ecclesiastical figures who opposed the regime, notably Dietrich Bonhoeffer, a Lutheran theologian hanged at the concentration camp of Flossenbürg in 1945, and Martin Niemöller, another Lutheran pastor who spent the war in concentration camps for his public opposition to Hitler's government. Resistance to Hitler is memorialised at a number of sites in Berlin, including the Plötzensee prison and in the Bendlerblock, the army headquarters where the main July Bomb Plot conspirators were shot.

Whitewashing was pronounced in the business and finance community, which sought to shake off well-founded claims that it had played a major role in the Nazi rise to power, as well as the East German charge that capitalism and business had played a central role in the Nazi state. Individual companies, such as Siemens, produced favourable, and misleading, accounts of their activities.[40] Crucially, in the 1950s, relatively little attention was paid in Germany to the Holocaust, while the official response to the war on the Eastern Front was also limited. Discussion focused on the effort made to protect the West from the Soviet threat, and thus related it to Cold War calls about the need for West German rearmament.[41]

On the academic side, the denazification of the German historical profession was very incomplete, as was also the case of much else in West and, even, East Germany. The situation was important not only for the history produced but also for the training of the next generation of historians. In part, this situation reflected the drive to reintegrate Nazis into German society.

In East Germany, the war was presented by the Communists, who gained power under Soviet occupation, as an imposition by the Nazi regime on German worker-soldiers. There was an effort thereby to create an anti-Fascist unity, or at least friendship, with the Soviet Union, the target and vanquisher of the Nazis. It was hoped that this unity would bring legitimacy to the East German system which, in practice, rested on Soviet conquest and support.

As in France, the situation subsequently altered.[42] In part, this change was due to the pressures on the collective myth of general social and cultural changes. Key ones were the rise of a generation that did not feel responsibility for Nazism, and also the decline of deference towards the former generation, many of whom had participated in the Nazi state or had views on the Nazi years that condoned aspects of them. The 1960s proved a crucial period in this shift, not least with the use by student radicals of the Nazis as a comparator for the government's support for police action and emergency legislation. The Baader-Meinhof Gang (or Red Army Faction) sought to fight what it claimed was a 'resurgent Nazi state'.[43]

In part, the shift was due to a growing awareness of atrocities committed by the Nazi regime, notably due to the establishment in 1958 of the Central Office for the Investigation of National Socialist Crimes, in part to rebut East German propaganda. A series of episodes marked the great awareness,[44] including the 1958 Ulm *Einsatzkommando* Trial, the illustrations in Gerhard Schoenberner's book *Der gelbe Stern* (1960), and the Frankfurt Auschwitz trial of 1963–5. This awareness was matched by a markedly increased focus on the Holocaust from outside Germany, and by the widespread determination to treat it as the defining moment in public responsibility. The attempt to contain the effects on Germany's image by blaming the atrocities specifically on the Nazis was challenged, especially in a debate about the complicity of the army, which was indeed pronounced.

For long, the public coverage was an often heroic presentation of the experience of conflict. Veterans' associations expounded the idea that their conduct had been honorable and characterised by an exemplary comradeship. The latter notion was also advanced in literature, as in Lothar-Günther Buchheim's *Das Boot* (1973), about U-boats,[45] and also played a major role in American and British popular culture and scholarship, in part because of the absorption of German arguments and in part became of anti-Soviet attitudes.[46] Moreover, for long, most German commentators did not, or did not wish to, appreciate the extent to which the German army, as opposed to the SS, was involved in atrocities,[47] and, indeed, that military violence against unarmed civilians was not a matter of rogue commanders, but, instead, was integral to its conduct from the outset of the war. Ideological commitment was a factor in the conquest of Poland, not only with the brutality of the SS, but also with the harshness of army reprisals against armed resistance from Polish civilians.[48] In the Soviet Union, Jews were slaughtered by the German army on the bogus grounds that they were partisans. There was also the mass slaughter of Jews by the army in Serbia.

It was only in the 1980s that the West German government acknowledged the wartime crimes inflicted on the Soviet Union. Indeed, on 8 May 1945, President Richard von Weizsäcker felt able to declare 8 May 1945, the surrender date, as a day of liberation for Germany from Nazi rule. The criminally murderous policy of the army was underlined from the 1990s, although, in turn, this understanding was contested.[49] Many of Hitler's generals had proved willing to disregard international and common decency in framing and executing criminal measures.[50] Generals such as Guderian, Manstein and Rundstedt, also profited personally from German conquests in the shape of land and other loot, as well as receiving secret payments from Hitler. This bribery made a mockery of the so-called 'Honour Court' used against the military figures involved in the July 1944 Bomb Plot.[51]

This treatment of military conduct was a matter not simply of historical scholarship and popular impression, but also of justice, notably with cases brought in the 2000s, in both Germany and Rome, about wartime German massacres of Italians. In turn, the extent to which the Criminal Code made it difficult to pursue Germans guilty of war crimes, notably in such a case, proved the subject of Ferdinand von Schirach's powerful novel *Der Fall Collini. The Collini Case* (Munich, 2011; London, 2012). This well-received novel helped lead the Federal Minister of Justice, in 2012, to appoint a committee to assess the impact of the Nazi era on the Ministry.

Moreover, in place of the notion of the Germans as in some way victims of the Nazis came the realisation that they had collaborated and supported the regime. Whereas postwar trials had located blame on individual perpetrators,[52] there came to be a greater appreciation that 'ordinary' Germans, indeed Germans as a whole, were culpable. This was seen in the television treatment of the Holocaust, which for long had been depicted without due attention to the range of perpetrators, let alone bystanders. This situation changed from the early 1990s.[53] It was no longer felt necessary in the 1990s to subscribe to the defeated nations' denial of history in order to rehabilitate Germany and Japan as allies in the Cold War and to bolster France and Italy against Communism. Chancellor Köhl publicly referred to the suffering of Soviet civilians during the siege of Leningrad.

The view of Germans as victims had been, continued to be, and continues to be, pushed very hard, however, in Austria. There, the *Anschluss* was interpreted to present Austria as 'Hitler's first victim', a phrase widely-used from 1945. This approach entailed a dramatic underplaying of the enthusiastic role of many Austrians in the Third Reich, in the Nazi Party, the SS, the Holocaust, and the war-effort.[54] Furthermore, the combination of the acceptability to some of the Austrian public of Fascist or Fascistic views with the dynamics of coalition politics helped ensure that the Far Right played a role in Austrian government.

There were also different narratives about the war in Germany. These stressed the hardship experienced by Germans. During the Cold War, there was an emphasis on cruelties suffered at the hands of the Red Army, especially on widespread rape. Moreover, the last stages of World War Two were linked to the postwar to develop a national narrative of victimhood that drew much of its emotional charge from the large-scale postwar expulsion of Germans from Eastern Europe, an expulsion that involved much loss of life.[55] Much of this victimhood was a matter of agitation by refugee groups, but these groups, representing as they did large numbers, were also prominent in the political world, being closely linked to the Christian Democratic Union/Christian Social Union which dominated government for most of the Cold War years and thereafter. Moreover, there was a governmental presence, with a West German Ministry for Refugees and Expellees which advanced not only their claims, but also their historical narrative, notably by publishing *Documents on the Expulsion*. For much of the 1950s, the minister was Theodor Oberländer who, in fact, was greatly compromised by a Nazi past. However, the expellees became less significant politically from the late 1950s, in part because of a growing commitment to life in West Germany and a realisation that the refugees' homeland was now Polonised.[56]

Other states also saw complaints about the postwar expulsions. In Hungary after the Cold War, the Fidesz party won support from pressing for what it termed justice for the Hungarians deported from Czechoslovakia, Romania and Yugoslavia in 1945. Yet, in part, these expulsions of Hungarians, as well as expulsions of others, were a direct consequence of the wartime ethnic policies of the states whose citizens were now expelled, and notably of their support for enforced population exchange. Thus, having annexed Alsace-Lorraine in 1940, the Germans speedily evicted 200,000 French-speaking inhabitants.

Ironically, the postwar regimes were frequently more effective in moving peoples than the murderous Germans, although the latter's plans would have been brought to fruition after the war had ended. Whereas in 1942, Hitler planned the expulsion of the non-German population of the Crimea to make room for Germanisation by South Tyroleans displaced to satisfy Mussolini, only to be persuaded to shelve the plan due to the needs of military operations, Stalin, in 1944, deported the Crimean Tatars, as well as the Armenians, Bulgarians and Greeks, who lived in the Crimea. Yet, in the end, both the Germans and the Soviets failed in what Timothy Snyder has termed the 'borderlands' – Eastern Europe and the western, non-Russian, part of what was the Soviet Union. What had been an area of multi-ethnic states passed through a stage of oppressive imperial regimes and has now ended up as an area of nation states.[57]

In part, the postwar German stress on their refugees was an attempt to shift the focus of attention on atrocities, and, notably, to suggest that the Germans were not uniquely guilty of such atrocities.[58] For example, as a response to the discussion of the brutal conduct of the German army came attempts to argue that the Soviet army was as bad. While these attempts drew on a widespread pattern of Soviet atrocities, both killings and rapes,[59] they were disproportionate, neglected the consequences of Nazi victory,[60] and also ignored the extent to which the Soviet presence in Germany in 1945 was a direct consequence of the German invasion of the Soviet Union in 1941. These arguments, however, had scant resonance with those who stressed Soviet atrocities.

Instead, there were claims that those who focused on German atrocities were motivated by left-wing politics. An instance of a similar approach, albeit in a very different context, was provided by the argument of the historian Klaus Schmider when he wrote that the decision to remove the name of World War Two fighter ace, Werner Mölders, from the honorific title of a *Bundeswehr* unit, arose from a motion submitted in 2004 by 'a minority of Bundestag deputies belonging to the Green and Socialist (i.e. the former ruling party in East Germany) parties. The decision rested on the expert opinion of a member of the Historical Research Institute of the German Armed Forces, and he decided that Mölders was not representative of the Bundeswehr's spiritual core values. Schmider's smearing of this recommendation – 'the idea of a politically motivated hatchet job cannot be dismissed out of hand' – can be noted alongside his discussion of Dönitz, and the latter's sentencing for war crimes at Nuremberg to ten years in prison, without mentioning the admiral's vitriolic Nazism. Moreover, Schmider, who had very little in this article to say about Nazi sympathies among the *Luftwaffe*, sought, instead, to focus attention on the American shooting of parachuting German air crew.[61]

Blame-shifting also affected the positive response in some German circles to the misleading claim that, in attacking the Soviet Union, Hitler had in fact pre-empted a planned Soviet assault on Germany. This highly problematic thesis was pushed hard by Ernst Topitsch in *Stalin's War* (1985) and by Viktor Suvorov in *Ice-breaker: Who Started the Second World War* (1990).[62]

Greater traction was gained in Germany, especially by the 2000s, from attempts to argue that the Combined (Anglo–American) Bomber Offensive on Germany in some respects represented a war-crime, and one that levelled the playing-field in terms of German war-guilt and atrocities, and even offered some sort of comparison with the Holocaust. For example, Hermann Knell's *To Destroy a City: Strategic Bombing and Its Human Consequences in World War II* (2003) had a considerable impact in Germany with its account of the RAF's destruction of the city of Würzburg in March 1945. Knell, a survivor of air attacks, presented both German policies in the 1930s and the attack on the Soviet Union in 1941 as defensive and preventive, arguments that are completely inaccurate.

This literature proved very popular in Germany. Thus, appearing in 2002, Jörg Friedrich's *Der Brand: Deutschland in Bombenkrieg, 1940–1945* went into its thirteenth edition in 2003, and was published in English in 2007.[63] By 2007 it had sold 500,000 copies in Germany. Friedrich implied an equivalence between the Holocaust and the bombing, using terms employed to describe the first with reference to the second. He appeared to come close to suggesting that the Germans were right to defend Nazism.

In 2004, the issue of whether the British would apologise for their bombing campaign was stoked up in the mass-circulation German press prior to a visit by Elizabeth II. 'Sagt die Queen jetzt Sorry?' [Will the Queen say sorry?] asked *Bild*, the highest-circulation German newspaper on 28 October beside a picture of those killed at Dresden on 13–15 February 1945. Understandably, there was no such apology, and it is worthy of note that recent British work had emphasised the extent to which Dresden was a major centre in the German military–industrial complex, as well as a communications, especially railway, node seen as significant for German operations,[64] although the importance of the city has also been contested.[65] There has been controversy whether the Soviet Union sought the bombing of Dresden, with significant evidence that this was the case.[66] By visiting Dresden as well as the concentration camp of Buchenwald in June 2009 before commemorating the sixty-fifth anniversary of D-Day, President Obama risked suggesting some sort of parallel. The acknowledgment of German suffering risks challenging the issue of proportionality.

Dresden has served a number of politicised purposes. In 1945, Nazi propaganda made use of the devastation caused by the bombing, and this issue was also employed by the government of Communist East Germany in its propaganda against the West,[67] while David Irving, a discredited figure from the British Far Right, used Nazi propaganda as a basis for the highly exaggerated casualty figures given in his *The Destruction of Dresden* (1963).[68] The theme has been revived by the neo-Nazis of the National Democratic Party, whose parliamentary deputies referred in 2006 to 'a Holocaust of bombs'. In response, a civic declaration, outlining a 'framework for commemoration', acknowledged Dresden's role in the Nazi system and its crimes, including against the city's Jews. As ever in the modern world, television provides a way to present issues and seeks to do so in a digestible form. In 2006, the bombing of Dresden was the subject of a major German television programme. This included a fictional romance between a German nurse and a British airman, whereas, in practice, airmen shot down over Germany were sometimes lynched, a fate that also occurred elsewhere, for example in Bulgaria.

German pressure for apologies fails to recover the historical context of the bombing and its benefits to the Allies. There were expectations, from domestic opinion in Britain already heavily bombed by the Germans, from the USA, and from the Soviet Union, that major blows would be struck against Germany prior to the opening of the 'Second Front' by means of an Anglo–American invasion of France. The delay of this invasion, from first 1942 and then, far more, 1943, led to great pressure for alternative action. As such, it matched the pressure on the Western Allies in World War One to mount attacks in 1915 and 1916, in order to reduce the strain on Russia, pressure that led both to the Gallipoli operation of 1915 and to offensives on the Western Front. In 1942–3, the comparable pressure was encouraged by Allied concern about a possible separate peace between Germany and the Soviet Union.

The benefits of the bomber offensive included gravely weakening the *Luftwaffe*, and thus greatly helping the process of defeating German forces on the ground, notably in the Normandy campaign of 1944; although it is important to note that the *Luftwaffe* also lost heavily in conflict over the Fronts. The air battles over the Eastern Front in 1943 are particularly neglected. Those air battles over Kursk that July came at the climax to four months of sustained operations that in scale and intensity eclipsed the Battle of Britain, leading to the loss of over 1,000 German aircraft. Indeed, Soviet commentators have claimed that this success ensured the Allies' favourable position in the air over D-Day.[69] While overstated, and indeed underplaying the major role of the Anglo–American Combined Bomber Offensive in diverting German aircraft from the Eastern Front, this argument captures the degree of relationship between the Fronts, one that gave considerable force to the politics and strategy of the war, notably the attempts to secure concerted operations.

The interrelationship of action was also indicated by the impact of air attack on German land operations. For example, close to a third of German artillery production was devoted to anti-aircraft guns, which gravely affected German battlefield strength, notably on the defensive. The opportunity costs inflicted on the German war effort by the bombing were very heavy. Thus, the Germans expended intellectual effort, research facilities, weapons production, construction labour, steel and cement, on resisting air attack and the prospect of air attack.

The Anglo–American bombers' success in hitting German industrial production is also of note, as are the strategic goals of the Allied offensive. Attacks on German rail links and on the production of synthetic oil in 1944 were especially important to the disruption of the German war economy. The crucial drive for increased German economic output to fuel Hitler's determination to break through to world-power status from a limited base underlines the value of this air assault.[70] In particular, hitting marshalling yards, rail bridges and barge traffic crippled the movement of coal and oil.[71] Moreover, the bombing was responsible for a serious decline in civilian morale, in labour discipline and in the self-confidence of the Nazi party.[72]

Pressure for apologies also underplays or neglects the earlier and deliberate use of area (or terror) bombing by the Germans in 1939–41, notably, but not only, of Warsaw, Rotterdam, London, Belgrade and Soviet cities.[73] Furthermore, at the time of the Combined Bomber Offensive, the Germans launched V1 and V2 rocket attacks, on London and other targets, that, by the nature of their guidance systems, were very much intended to hit civilian targets. Postwar German self-presentation as victims of bombing revealed a complete lack of proportionality, although it also testified to a determination to express and make sense of personal experience. This included family loss as well as the extent to which bombing hit the German state of health, notably with a rise in stress-related conditions.[74]

Within Britain and the USA, there has been criticism of the Combined Bomber Offensive in ahistorical terms, alongside the more measured discussion of alternative strategies. There was particular debate in 2012 when the Bomber Command Memorial was erected in London after a major fundraising campaign supported by the *Daily Telegraph*, the leading conservative newspaper. When the memorial was opened, poppies were released by a Lancaster bomber, a veteran of the war. Criticism as well as support of the bombing has varied in content and tone. Rather than focusing on such practical issues as to whether better use could have been made of air assets (a case well-made by military specialists who argued, with reason, that, as a result, tactical air support at land and sea received insufficient backing), the moralists attacked bombing itself. Thus, Nicholson Baker, a sometime American novelist, in his much-reviewed *Human Smoke: The Beginnings of World War II and the End of Civilization* (2008), provided a pacifist theme and offered continually reiterated criticism of Britain alongside Germany. For example, Baker condemned British bombing in 1939–41 as if it was equivalent to German action (which was not the case), and directed much criticism against both Churchill and Britain's treatment of Jews.[75]

Intentionality is a key issue when considering the bombing. Thus, M. R. D. Foot, a British wartime intelligence officer who became an academic, compared the bombing offensive with the Holocaust in a passage that totally failed to capture this point:

> To days – day after day, regularly as clockwork – on which Himmler killed ten thousand Jews, nights followed, night after night, on which Harris killed a thousand Germans: both of them killing indirectly, as is the fashion with modern commanders. Sometimes Harris's body-count outreached Himmler's. What differences Saint Michael will see on the day of judgement between burning a baby to death in Dresden, and gassing a baby to death at Birkenau, is a question rather for the

theologian than for the historian; but one difference at least is obvious: Germany's cities were heavily defended, so that the aircrew who attacked them put their own lives at risk; very few such resources were available to the victims of concentration camps.[76]

Foot's argument, however, neglected the degree to which the intention at Birkenau – to kill all Jewish babies – was very different to that at Dresden. Similarly, the claim by the popular historian Antony Beevor that the Allied bombing of northern France in 1944 was 'close to a war crime' was somewhat weak on context.[77] It also underplays Churchill's great concern about the matter.

Moreover, these are questions for the historian as much as the theologian.[78] Indeed, the latter cannot operate appropriately in this context without the information and insights supplied by the former, a point also true for those discussing the theology of the Holocaust. Historians abdicate their civic and moral responsibilities if they shelve such issues by handing them over to theologians.

Among German academics, the currents of historical argument were different to those in popular argument, although there was an important relationship to popular discussion, not least because the German quality press gave copious space to the academic debates. A major controversy focused on the relationship between the Nazis and longer-term trends in German history. This controversy had a direct relevance to attempts to legitimate the West German political system. Some of the relevant literature did not relate directly to World War Two, but much of it had a political resonance that was relevant.

A key work was Fritz Fischer's *Griff nach der Weltmacht: Die Kriegszielpolitik des kaiserlichen Deutschlands, 1914–1918* (1961), a book translated into English as *Germany's Aims in the First World War*. Fischer focused on the primacy of domestic policy, particularly the response by the conservative élite to rising socialism. Condemning conservatism and capitalism, Fischer sought to undermine the attempt to present Wilhelmine Germany as a model for post-1945 West Germany, and the Nazis as an aberration. Fischer, instead, argued that there was an essential continuity from Wilhelmine Germany through to the Hitlerian regime. Naming battleships *Bismarck* and *Tirpitz* was indicative of more than simply claiming a legacy, although Bismarck proved a difficult legacy for Hitler, not least because he did not favour union with Austria or war with Russia.[79]

The Fischer controversy was linked to the challenge to the dominant conservative (and gerontocratic) character of postwar West German historical scholarship, as well as to the extent to which a misleading and self-interested account of German scholarly impartiality during the Nazi years was propagated. The reality was far bleaker. Numerous academics had profited personally and knowingly from the removal of Jewish colleagues, while many were involved in work that contributed directly to the regime's propaganda and planning, as well as to other activities.[80] These academics went on to profit in the postwar order. Thus, Hermann Albin (1885–1969), who was a key figure in work on the 'German East' that looked towards large-scale racial slaughter, was to become Chairman of the Association of German Historians and President of the Historical Commission of the Bavarian Academy of Sciences. Politics played a major and continuing role, because senior academic appointments were very much under the control of the government, and because academic debates were seen as playing a role in the validation of competing voices in the Federal Republic. Albin was given the title of adviser by Franz-Josef Strauss, the conservative head of the Bavarian Christian Social Union from 1961.

Subsequently, the *Historikerstreit* (controversy among German historians) of 1986–7, which linked discussion of the Holocaust to the question of how best to present national history, was played out in a very public fashion with many articles appearing in prominent newspapers. In part, this controversy was a product of the attempt by historians close to Chancellor Helmut Kohl, the leader of the conservative Christian Democratic Party which gained power in 1982, to 'normalise' German history, which was taken to mean make it more acceptable, in order both to ground national identity and to reject the criticisms of the 1968 generation. Kohl saw this process as a necessary basis for patriotism, national pride and spiritual renewal, a theme taken up more generally on the German Right. The controversy was also closely related to the attempt to create a favourable climate of opinion as a background to the federal elections of January 1987, elections won by Kohl.

In the controversy, the degree to which the Holocaust arose from specific German characteristics was debated, as was the extent to which the German state had a historical mission, specifically to resist advances from the east (the Soviet Union), an approach pushed by German conservatives such as Andreas Hilgruber. This argument, which in some respects echoed the wartime use of failure at Stalingrad in 1942 as an instance of an exemplary sacrifice, led to the claim that Nazi iniquities had to be considered against this background. However, justifying the German generals in the final stage of the war as if they were in some way defending civilisation was self-serving and, indeed, ignored the extent to which they mounted a fierce resistance to Anglo–American forces as well as the Soviets; while fighting on of course provided more time for the Holocaust. As a related instance of the concern with historical appearances, German officials in the 1980s perceived the establishment of the United States Holocaust Memorial Museum in Washington as 'anti-German' and unsuccessfully attempted to change its contents by including references to the anti-Nazi resistance and to postwar German history.[81]

Separately from, but related to, debates among historians, the controversial nature of the recent German past had a direct impact on German domestic and, possibly, foreign policy. This impact was seen in 2003 when a controversy arose over a speech by Martin Hohmann, a backbencher from the then opposition Christian Democratic Party, declaring that Germans should not, as a result of their support for Hitler, be treated as a 'guilty people'. Hohmann's comparison, indeed, was designed to deflect criticism onto those whose brutal treatment under Hitler formed the prime charge, the Jews, because he claimed that they were themselves guilty of a prominent role in Communist atrocities, a grossly misleading claim also made on behalf of anti-Semitic nationalists in Eastern Europe. After a fortnight's controversy, Hohmann was expelled from the Christian Democratic Party. Concerns that his attitude was related to, and might encourage, anti-Semitism were linked to claims that anti-Semitism was related to growing opposition to Israel's policies towards the Palestinians.

This was not an isolated episode. In Nuremberg, criticism of the granting in 1997 by the city council of honorary citizenship to Karl Diehl, a local industrialist who had, like many industrialists, used concentration camp workers, led to a bitter controversy, in which the majority of the council supported Diehl.[82] This was an instance of the extent to which the 'critical memory culture' could be resisted at the local level by those who did not accept a critical local remembrance.[83]

At the same time, compensation for Holocaust suffering was extended, with payments from 1997 for unpaid work carried out in the ghettos, which was followed, under the ZRBG (so-called 'ghetto pension') indemnity law of 2002, by allowing former residents of any ghetto incorporated into the German Reich to qualify. In part, as also with belated Swiss interest in the wartime role of Swiss banks, fears of legal action in and outside Germany, and notably in the USA, played a role in this compensation, which was not awarded to most of those who had been used to provide forced labour under the Germans.

Memorials and cemeteries were important sites for contestation as well as commemoration. The pressure from the Federation of the Expelled for a centre to commemorate the Germans driven from Eastern Europe at the close of the war led to controversy. More prominently, President Ronald Reagan caused a stir on a state visit to West Germany in 1985 when, joining Chancellor Kohl, he visited the military cemetery at Bitburg, the stir arising because the cemetery contained, among others, the graves of 49 members of the SS. The Waffen-SS was a vicious organisation, as well as a criminal one in clear breach of international law. Reagan then compounded the outrage by describing the soldiers as as much victims of the Nazis as those who had suffered in concentration camps – a bizarre equivalence.[84] In part, the symbolism of the visit was designed to counter German anger at not being asked to participate that year in fortieth commemorative anniversaries for the end of the war.

Print and, even more, the visual media came to offer an insistent coverage of the war. In 2004, there was controversy, inside and outside Germany, over the coverage of Hitler's last days in the film Der Untergang [The

Downfall] financed by the German state television network ARD. Released in 2004, the film, which showed Hitler as popular with his staff in order to demonstrate his humanity, minimised the evil of his policies. In an interview that year, the producer, Bernd Eichinger, further accentuated concern by referring to the German *Volk* [people], a term beloved by the Nazis. The year 2004 saw a highpoint in public interest in Hitler in Germany, with numerous articles in the mass-circulation press, especially the *Bild* and the magazine *Der Spiegel*. More positively, Gerhard Schröder, the German Chancellor, a Social Democrat, attended the annual commemoration of the 1944 Warsaw uprising and apologised for its brutal suppression.

The background to his action was a marked deterioration in public relations about the war due in part to claims on behalf of Germans expelled from Eastern Europe at and after the close of the war. These included 3,000,000 driven from Poland, and in 2004 the Polish Parliament pressed the German government to 'stop encouraging its citizens to bring lawsuits against Poland' (the Schröder government had not in fact done so), and called on the Polish government to press its German counterpart to resist such claims. Schröder's opponent in the previous German election (that of 2002), Edmund Stoiber, a Bavarian whose wife came from a Sudeten refugee family, made much of the refugee issue. German pressure for compensation entrenched differences and led the Czech Parliament in 2003 to pass a resolution applauding Edvard Beneš who, as President from 1945 to 1948, was in large part responsible for the postwar policy. These moves, in turn, further harmed Czech–German relations.

Discussion in Germany of how best to commemorate the refugees caused problems. Such a *Zentrum gegen Vertreibung*, for which Chancellor Angela Merkel gave the go-ahead in 2007, entailed controversy both within Germany and among the Czechs and Poles, who, understandably, remain reluctant to see the refugees as victims. A German tendency to present themselves as victims continues to be readily apparent over this issue, not least with the inaccurate argument by some that the Nazi period provided Poland and Czechoslovakia with an opportunity to implement long-standing plans for expansionism.[85]

In 2008–9, there was another highpoint in public interest in Hitler, with extensive controversy over *Walküre* (*Valkyrie*), a film devoted to the July 1944 bomb plot. In part, the issues raised were extraneous to the more general question of the commemoration of the war. This was notably so with complaints over the depiction of Claus von Stauffenburg, the leading plotter, by Tom Cruise, as he is a prominent Scientologist, and there is longstanding German political disquiet in Germany about Scientologists in part because they are seen as anti-Christian and in part as they are presented as conspiratorial. The film also gave rise to a debate in Germany about the nature of heroism.

Yet, as instances of the variety and extent of echoes of the war in contemporary German culture, there was acute sensitivity in 2009 when Pope

Benedict XVI, the German-born Joseph Ratzinger, lifted the excommunication of Richard Williamson, a British-born bishop who, it transpired, had greatly minimised the extent of the Holocaust. Chancellor Merkel was unusually forthright in demanding an unambiguous clarification from the Pope that there could be no Holocaust denial. The controversy led to a renewed airing of long-standing contention over the wartime conduct of the Papacy. Moreover, the particular issue of Pope Benedict's membership of the Hitler Youth was brought forward. Less attention was devoted to his account of the Third Reich, an account that, in presenting the Germans as victims, neglected the role of complicity. At Auschwitz in 2006, Pope Benedict announced:

> I come here as a son of that people over whom a ring of criminals rose to power by false promises of future greatness and the recovery of the nation's honour, prominence and property, but also through terror and intimidation, with the result that our people was used and abused as an instrument of their thirst for destruction and power.

His attitude was contrasted with that of his Polish predecessor, John Paul II, who was more willing to address the questions of anti-Semitism and Catholic complicity.[86] Before Pope Benedict visited the Yad Vashem Holocaust memorial in Israel in 2009, he was pressed by its head, Avner Shalev, to include in his speech a reference to the memory of the Holocaust in the present as well as in the future. The Pope himself laid a wreath at Yad Vashem on a stone covering the ashes of people killed in the Holocaust, and also met Holocaust survivors. On the visit, the Pope made a powerful denunciation of the Holocaust, stating that this act by the 'godless' Nazi regime would never be forgotten or denied; but he indicated that he did not wish to visit the museum exhibit accusing Pope Pius XII (1939–58) of failing to act to save Jews from genocide. The caption there declared 'When the Jews were deported from Rome to Auschwitz, the Pope did not intervene'. The Vatican has lobbied to have the caption changed, as it claims that Pius followed behind-the-scenes diplomacy to save Jews. However, Pius was certainly no hero or martyr,[87] and Pope Benedict's support for the beatification of Pius was controversial.

Pope Benedict's membership of the Hitler Youth was a minor instance (minor because his wartime role was inconsequential[88]) of the repeated issue of conduct during the war, an issue used not only in the pursuit of justice and a sense of justice, but also in political contention. The evidence of direct involvement in the process of mass-murder was sometimes absent, but individual culpability could frequently be established. Guilt by association played a major role in the usage of individual acts, as did accusations of cover-ups, which indeed occurred frequently.

In the case of Austria, the key figure was Kurt Waldheim, a wartime member of the intelligence staff of Army Group E, which had been involved in anti-partisan atrocities as well as in the deportation of Greek and Yugoslav Jews to slaughter. Despite criticism, Waldheim became President of Austria from 1986 to 1992. He also sought to avoid taking any personal responsibility for his actions. In response to criticism, Waldheim publicly claimed that Jews were trying to ruin the reputation of his generation. Taking up earlier Nazi themes, Waldheim linked this to a purported international conspiracy, with Jewish pressure against him being presented as centred in the USA, where Waldheim, the former Secretary-General of the United Nations (1972–81), was treated in the late 1980s as if an undesirable alien.

In Germany, most of the relevant individuals whose wartime role was highlighted were on the Right, although not all. For example, in 1996, Hans Schwerte, a prominent Social Democrat, was disgraced when he was revealed to be a former SS officer. Hans Filbinger (1913–2007) was a more typical figure. Minister-President of Baden-Württemberg from 1966 and a critic of the Left, Filbinger was correctly named in a newspaper article in 1978 as a wartime military judge who had sentenced German deserters to death. Such a career was common in the 1950s, as the 1959 exhibit of the International League for Human Rights, *Nazi Justice Not Atoned For*, made clear.[89] But, by 1978, the situation was different. Filbinger responded by denial, suing for libel and claiming that 'what was lawful then cannot be unlawful now'. In the face of public criticism, however, Filbinger was forced to resign in 1978, and his rehabilitation in the 2000s was contentious. After his death in 2007, controversy continued, notably over a funeral eulogy by Günther Oettinger, a later Minister-President. This eulogy led to pressure for an apology from Oettinger that was ultimately successful. The dispute was not simply about the past, but also part of the struggle over the future of the Christian Democratic Party: Merkel, who demanded an apology, was a centrist whose views were very different to those of Filbinger and Oettinger.

Not only politicians were involved. In 2006, Günther Grass revealed in his autobiography that he had spent several months in 1944 in the Waffen-SS. This revelation was notable and controversial because Grass was a major novelist who had made himself the conscience of Germany. Grass had pressed for an honest appraisal of the German role in the war without revealing his own part.

At a very different level, in 2009, the trial for the blackmail of Suzanne Klatten, Germany's wealthiest woman, by a gigolo, Helg Sgarbi, provided an opportunity to discuss the extent to which leading German companies had been implicated in the Nazi regime. Klatten, the owner of much of BMW and Altana, is granddaughter of Günther Quandt, a key figure in the armaments industry and a member of the Nazi inner circle. The Quandt factories used concentration camp labour and treated it atrociously. After the war, the Quandts refused interviews and denied historians access to their wartime archives. A German television documentary of 2007, 'The

Silence of the Quandts', provided evidence of the use of slave labour. As a twist to the particular case involving Sgarbi, it was suggested that, far from being Italo-Swiss, as he claimed, he was the son of a Polish Jew forced to work as a slave labourer in a BMW factory, and was therefore seeking retribution.

Such episodes were far from matters simply of individual concern, as their discussion provided an opportunity for the reiteration and redefinition of current mores. Although there was an increased interest in revisionist perspectives – notably those that sought to relativise German guilt, generally misleadingly – the key context was that of a Germany that sought to exercise peaceful power, and to lead Europe through persuasion supported by economic and fiscal strength; and, in particular, of a country that had renounced the militarism that had been the counterpart of the far more toxic revisionism after World War One.[90] Moreover, from the end of the Cold War, the German government proved more willing to address the issue of Nazi criminality and to make restitution.

At the same time, alongside and overlapping with the revisionism, is a commitment to neo-Nazism by a percentage of the population. The neo-Nazis are particularly strong in the former East Germany, where they benefit from the high rates of unemployment. Neo-Nazi support there is an instructive comment on the failure of East German political culture and indoctrination, although many neo-Nazis grew to awareness after East Germany was brought to a close as a separate state by the end of the Cold War. Moreover, the strength of Far Right sympathies in the Austrian province of Carinthia reflected in part the weakness of denazification during the British occupation,[91] although much else is involved.

In modern Germany, there is a governmental response, as in 2009, when the Interior Ministry banned the group Homeland-Faithful German Youth on the grounds that it organised apparently harmless activities in order to promote racist and Nazi views among the young. However, other groups were able to continue operating. Yet, the extent of neo-Nazi sentiment and, crucially, activity, also encouraged the government to emphasise the culpability of the Nazi regime, a process that was not taken as far in Austria. Sensitivity about neo-Nazi support led to uneasiness in 2009 when the satirical musical *The Producers* was staged in Berlin. The question of whether it was acceptable to make Hitler a figure of fun proved to be a difficult one.

The present situation sees a number of cross-currents. There is a continuing tendency, in Austria as in Germany, to focus on the travails of veterans and of those expelled from further east at, and after, the close of the war, and to ignore the enthusiasm with which, both from these groups and among their compatriots, many participated in the numerous crimes of the Third Reich. Yet, there is also a major effort to remember those crimes.[92]

Italy

In contrast to Germany, in Italy, even more than in France, it was possible for a positive approach to the wartime regime to enter the public domain. Moreover, the contest over the reputation of Mussolini, and not least over the degree of popularity of his Salò Republic in northern Italy in 1943–5, was directly linked to the legitimacy of political groupings across the spectrum – from Communists to neo-Fascists. These groupings looked back to the 1940s and earlier for evidence of their probity and of the iniquity of their opponents. As a result, the reputation of Mussolini had (and has) a greater resonance in Italian politics than that of Hitler or Tōjō in those of Germany or Japan.

There was also a distinctive chronology in Italy. The Left sought a praiseworthy origin in terms of its hostility to Mussolini, but, more generally, the emphasis in postwar Italian public culture was not on alliance with Germany in 1940–3, but rather on opposition in 1943–5. Thus, the focus was on a war of liberation, with the Resistance presented in a heroic light, not least as a redemption from Fascism. This provided an appropriate lineage for the postwar republican democracy established in 1948, directing attention away from widespread support for Mussolini. The focus on the Resistance also shifted attention from the major Italian imperial role, both prewar in Libya and Ethiopia, and in Greece and Yugoslavia in 1941–3. In all of these cases, opposition had been harshly treated, and ignoring this helped the Italians in their self-presentation as victims of the war. Indeed, Italian troops were frequently contrasted by Italian commentators with their German allies and were seen as *brava gente* who had not been involved in war crimes, and this contrast was more generally applied by Italians to occupation by the two powers.

Yet, as in France, there were also competing attempts by the different political parties to annex the positive reputation of the Resistance to their benefit: thus, the Christian Democrats challenged the Communists' effort to present the Resistance as their movement. In turn, the radicals of the 1968 generation criticised the Christian Democrats' usage of the Resistance by arguing that the true radicalism of the Resistance was thus neglected as was the extent to which the postwar government, although dominated by the Christian Democrats, owed much to the practice of Fascist government. This argument was taken to vindicate radical opposition to the existing system.

From another direction, the widespread positive re-evaluation of Mussolini and Italian Fascism, beginning with the work of the historian Renzo De Felice in the 1960s,[93] appeared to provide academic credibility for the interest in Mussolini. He was treated as a far more benign figure than Hitler, and it was claimed that, in a self-sacrificing fashion, he had agreed to head the Salò Republic in order to protect northern Italy from harsh German rule, a claim that research in the German archives has failed to substantiate. This re-evaluation of Mussolini was linked to a blame for the surrender of 1943 on the Allies and the Left, and, indeed, that it reflected longer-term weaknesses in the Italian state, an approach resonant of Mussolini's criticism of earlier liberal governments. There was also the argument that certain initiatives and organisations started during the Fascist period were positive and had functioned reasonably well long after the end of Fascism.

The decline in the reputation of the Italian Communists was also a factor in the positive re-evaluation of Mussolini, and one that gathered pace following the end of the Cold War, with Italy sharing in what was a general change in Europe. In part, as a result of this decline, there was a reduced stress on the role of the Resistance in Italy. Moreover, the Resistance itself was called into question by arguing that part of it had been compromised by its Communism.

Most people in northern Italy had to accept both German occupation and the Salò Republic, but that did not mean that they approved of either. People and activities were divided into the following categories: anti-Fascist; Fascist, but opposed to the Salò Republic; left-wing supporters of Salò; supporters of Salò but opposed to German interference; and co-operation with Salò and the Germans because of conviction in or as a means of survival, often in order not to be transported to Germany. Most industrialists were forced to keep on working for the Germans, and, for the local economies, this was preferable to the closure of factories. Large numbers of Italians had supported the Salò Republic and fought the Resistance in a low-level counter-insurgency conflict in 1943–5, and their history came to be more favourably treated from the 1990s. Already, during the Cold War, the pressures of Italian politics and the anti-Communist position of the Italian state had ensured a degree of acceptance for the Salò Republic.

These changes in reputation were also related more directly to political developments in Italian politics, not least the restructuring of the Right linked to the decline of the Christian Democrats. The Italian Social Movement (MSI), the Fascist Party, had itself broken with its past in order to move from the political margins, both within Italy and in the European Union where support for Fascism was regarded as particularly unwelcome. As late as 1992, the extremist section of the MSI marked the seventieth anniversary of Mussolini's seizure of power by donning black shirts and giving the Fascist salute, but, in 1994–5, the leader, Gianfranco Fini, as part of a reconstitution of the Right, changed the MSI into the more moderate *Alleanza Nazionale* (National Alliance). The latter kept some aspects of Fascist social thinking, but sought acceptance, not least by a rejection of anti-Semitism, a direction Mussolini had taken in 1938. Distancing himself from the Party's legacy, Fini, who made repeated trips to Israel, declared, in 1996, that the verdict on Mussolini was 'best left to the historians'. This was a rejection of his 1994 claim that Mussolini was 'the greatest statesman of the twentieth century, on which he commented in 2009, 'If I still took that view I would be a schizophrenic, given every-thing I have done in the past fifteen years'. Also, in 2009, Fini (from 2008 to 2013, President of the Chamber of Deputies) declared, 'We have come to terms with our past, we have said clear words of condemnation on Italian history between the two wars'.

Yet, an unwillingness to let well alone was shown by Silvio Berlusconi, the erratic head of *Forza Italia*, the leader of the Italian Right in the 2000s and early 2010s, and the Prime Minister in 1994–5, 2001–6 and 2008–11, as he sometimes sought to defend the Fascist era from attacks. Equally, this defence indicated the degree to which totems had changed in Italian politics, with Mussolini now more broadly semi-acceptable to a wide current in Italian opinion. In 2009, *Forza Italia* and the *Alleanza Nationale* were merged into the new People of Freedom movement under the leadership of Berlusconi.

Berlusconi's relationship with Mussolini is indirect at best, but it is easy to understand why links and parallels have been asserted. In part, it is a matter of Berlusconi's willingness to embrace aspects of the Mussolini legacy. Aside from defending the Fascist era from attack, Berlusconi supported legislation in 2009 that would have given a new national honour to those who fought in the war, whether for the Resistance or for the Salò Republic. The proposal was not approved. More particularly, as far as the past providing a resonance for the present was concerned, Berlusconi, as Prime Minister, displayed scant time for the legislature or the judiciary. His authoritarianism was defended on the grounds that checks and balances make Italy ungovernable, but they were erected to block the chance of another dictator like Mussolini. Thus, the defence of the latter proves a way to justify Berlusconi's interest in changing the constitution, but, looked at differently, reference to Mussolini helps make such change more difficult.

Compensation was offered to Libya, an Italian colony from 1911 to 1942, in large part because the Berlusconi government wished for good relations with oil-rich Libya. However, this government generally displayed the tendency on the Far Right to underplay or ignore Italian atrocities abroad, while also calling for acknowledgement of those that Italians had suffered. This was an argument focused not on the Anglo–American armies, who, indeed, had acted well as they advanced up Italy, but, rather, on the Yugoslavs. Thus, in 2004, Italian television addressed the brutal treatment by advancing Communist Yugoslav forces of Italian civilians in Istria in 1945, as the Yugoslavs sought to secure control of a region that Italy itself had gained from the Austro-Hungarian empire after World War One. This slaughter, with many thrown to their death into the *foibe*, limestone chasms, was a key aspect of the memorialisation by Istrian exiles whose view became influential in the 2000s.[94]

The events in Istria in 1945 were an episode of 'ethnic cleansing' that had hitherto largely escaped the public eye, in part because the victim-culture approach to World War Two was less pronounced in Italy than in Germany and, thanks to the atomic bombs, Japan. Readier than its predecessors to express or channel xenophobic sentiments, the Berlusconi government, however, was more prepared to advance the issue. In 2005, a new national day of remembrance was introduced for Italians slaughtered in Istria. In 2009, Fini, by then President of the Chamber of Deputies, declared in a speech in Trieste, the nearest Italian city, 'Istria was Roman and then Venetian, which means it is Italian'. This overlooked the long period in which Trieste had been ruled by the Habsburgs. Emphasis on the events in 1945 was deployed to support the claim, and was linked to a denigration of the Slovene role in the war, with attacks on war memorials commemorating their loss, as well as the daubing of swastikas, presumably by unreconstructed neo-Fascists.

As a reminder, however, of the variety of Italian approaches, in both past and present, there has also been scholarship since the 1990s on the brutality of Italian occupation policy in the Balkans, a brutality, drawing on Fascist ideology, imperial expansionism and racialism, that included war crimes.[95] Moreover, the Italian forces on the Eastern Front slaughtered Jews and treated other civilians harshly.

Recent scholarship has also emphasised Italian culpability in the Holocaust, notably in the shape of the Salò Republic which was encouraged, but did not need to be coerced, into arresting and deporting Jews to slaughter in the extermination camps. This work challenges the attempt by Renzo De Felice and others to blame the German occupation and to exculpate Mussolini, Salò and the Italians.[96] In the former ghetto in Venice, the list of names of the many Jews deported and killed is a poignant memorial.

Eastern Europe

A similar process of change occurred in Eastern Europe with the collapse of Communist rule in 1989–91. A Communist orthodoxy had been dominant in the postwar years, with other historical accounts ignored or suppressed. Thus, as part of the Kafkaesque quality of life in Eastern Europe, other narratives of developments during the war years were prevalent, but in the private worlds of memory and conversation. These narratives played very little or, more commonly, no role in the state accounts. Instead, during the Communist years, these state accounts were very much stage-managed to provide an exemplary past that could be linked to claims of legitimacy in the present.[97]

For example, in Bulgaria, the emphasis was on resistance to the wartime regime, rather than on the pro-German character of the regime itself. There was also a stress there, and in Romania, on liberation in

1944, and on subsequent participation in Soviet operations in Yugoslavia and Hungary. In Czechoslovakia, there was an emphasis on the Slovak uprising in 1944 against the Germans and their Slovak allies, but this rising was presented as an aspect of a wider struggle in which the Red Army played a key role. The Battle of the Dukla Pass that September, when Soviet and Czech troops failed to break through to assist the insurgents, was treated in an heroic light. In Eastern Europe, the large-scale ethnic cleansing of postwar years was neglected, as were wartime territorial expansions that were subsequently ended, for example those by Bulgaria, Croatia, Hungary and Romania.

In Yugoslavia, the Tito regime disguised the complexities of the war, not least the prevalence of ethnic violence, in order to facilitate peaceful cohabitation, 'but also to enable continued one-party rule based on the one-sided, single-track and simplified version of the Peoples' Liberation War which was its founding myth'.[98] The key element was that this was the all-Yugoslav Peoples' Liberation struggle, rather than a struggle that was preponderantly linked to the people of one of the constituent republics, notably Serbia. There was also a failure to note negotiations in 1943 between the partisans and the Germans.

The state accounts were seriously flawed as an account of military operations, let alone of the politics of the war. For example, the Soviet account of the Great Fatherland Patriotic War exaggerated the role of the Communist Party and emphasised heroism and resolution not grief and uncertainty.[99] The role of the Soviet partisans was also minimised because Stalin distrusted the autonomy they had displaced.[100] Communist regimes stigmatised their opponents, both domestic and emigré, by referring to them as neo-Nazis. Indeed, a binary account of politics was central to the historical and contemporary vision of these states.

Across Eastern Europe, memorialisation was very much focused on the officially-sanctioned account of the war. This tended to mean the Soviet contribution,[101] although there was also room for the role of local Communists. Breaks with the Soviet Union, notably those of Yugoslavia in 1948 and Albania in 1960, led to very different accounts of the war. In one respect, these breaks prefigured the situation with the fall of the Communist regimes in 1989–91, but there was the important difference that the earlier breaks only led to new state-controlled historical accounts; simply ones that devoted less attention to the Soviet role.

Romania provides an instructive instance of this shift, albeit one that was less stark than the cases of Yugoslavia and Albania. In Romania, the key war memorials constructed after the fall of the Antonescu government in 1944 were monuments to the Red Army. Obelisks topped with a Communist star were constructed in all the major cities and also in many villages. The key monument in Bucharest was a large statue erected on a tall column in 1947 in the centre of Victory Square. However, in the 1950s, the emphasis shifted to the construction of memorials for Romanians, albeit only for the soldiers who had fought alongside the Red Army in 1944–5. In practice, in some instances, the soldiers buried were also those killed fighting against the Soviets in 1941–4, but this point was ignored in the inscriptions.

In the 1960s, there was another twist in Romania, with a new interest in honouring civilians, including an emphasis on civilian resistance to the war effort. This emphasis was an attempt to construct a notion of widespread pro-Soviet Romanian nationalism, and thus to create a benign inheritance for Communist rule. Nationalist themes were also pursued, notably with monuments in Transylvania to those killed for supporting opposition to Hungarian wartime occupation, a theme designed to underline the anti-Romanian nature of Hungarian links. The nationalism of the Ceauşescu regime, and particularly its distancing from the 1960s from the Soviet Union, also led to the removal of the Soviet statue from Victory Square in the capital, Bucharest, and its allocation to an obscure setting.[102]

From 1989–91, in contrast, explicit attacks on the historical role of the Soviet Union and of Communism were freely ventilated across Eastern Europe, contributing to a situation in which scholars and opinion, both there and then in the West, had to confront the question of whether Hitler was worse than Stalin, an issue largely measured in terms of their violence against civilians.[103] The Soviet Union in 1944–5 no longer appeared as a liberator, as it had done in Communist Party propaganda. Instead, there was a focus on atrocities by the advancing Red Army in 1944–5, not least the large-scale rape of women not only in Germany and Austria, but also across Eastern Europe. The statues of Soviet soldiers in Vienna, Vilnius and elsewhere were popularly referred to as the 'Unknown Rapist'.

The Russians were very sensitive to the fate of the statues. In 2007, the removal of the Bronze Soldier, a monument erected in Tallinn, the capital of Estonia, in 1947 to Red Army casualties and to the Soviet liberation of Estonia from German control in 1944, was denounced by the Russian government as an act of 'neo-fascism' and as 'blasphemous'. To most Estonians, the monument was a symbol of Soviet occupation in 1940–1 and from 1944, but ethnic Russians living there, a quarter of the Estonian population, had a very different view and rioted in Tallinn.

In an attempt to assuage tensions, the Estonian Prime Minister, Andrus Ansip, paid his respects at the monument, which had been moved to a military cemetery, but the Russian Ambassador refused to accept this gesture by attending, while Vladimir Putin, Russia's President, criticised Estonian policy. An attempt at even-handedness was provided when Ansip also attended ceremonies at a Holocaust memorial and at a cemetery commemorating soldiers who had died in Estonia fighting not only for the Soviet Union but also for the Germans. Ansip and President Toomas Ilves issued a joint statement calling on Estonians to maintain 'dignity towards oneself and others', adding 'For many, the end of the World War Two means the victory of freedom over tyranny, and for many it means that one violent regime was replaced by another'. This was an assessment that represented a fundamental rejection of the politics of World War Two taught, from 1945, in Eastern Europe and, in large part also, elsewhere.

This rejection of the war's politics was, from the 1990s, reflected in some popular works in Western Europe, although often presented there as a revelation. Thus, Lawrence Rees, a BBC history guru, produced in 2008 a radio series on the war that was very critical of Stalin and that became a book. In it, he rejected 'the central popular myth that surrounds the war, a kind of Hollywood version of the history ... that this is a simple story of an alliance of good people who fought an alliance of bad people'.[104]

Such a rewriting is totally unacceptable to the current Russian government, not least because the 'Great Patriotic War' continues to strike a deep resonance in individual and collective memories.[105] On Victory Day, 9 May 2007, the annual commemoration of the defeat of Germany (but to the Balts marking the years of Soviet occupation), Putin condemned those who 'are desecrating monuments to war heroes, and ... sowing enmity and a new distrust between nations and peoples'. The Soviet role in defeating Nazi Germany remained a key theme in the post-Soviet years, and provided a background for demanding influence in Eastern Europe and for rallying Russia against the USA. In his speech on 9 May 2007, Putin presented the American challenge as if akin to that from Nazi Germany. Such attitudes played a role in his response to the Ukraine crisis in 2013–14.

Putin's emphasis on the Soviet role provided an opportunity to vindicate Stalin. Indeed, teachers' manuals issued in Russia in 2007 described him as 'the most successful Soviet leader ever', and one who had to use force to mobilise the country; and, at a conference held at his presidential dacha that year, Putin referred to Stalin's purges as terrible but also compared them to the American bombing of Hiroshima as a necessary step.

Putin's argument was not intended to argue an equivalence between all horrors, the route taken or implied by German and Japanese revisionists, because he continued by saying 'in other countries even worse things happened. We had no other black pages, such as Nazism, for instance'. Yet, his comparison of the purges to the use of the atomic bombs was not one that would have commanded much confidence in areas that suffered Soviet occupation, notably Eastern Europe, and also confused a key element of domestic policy (the purges) with a strategic tool of war. Putin's argument, that internal control and violence was crucial to success in war, was one in keeping with Soviet ideology and Communist practice.

Across Eastern Europe after the fall of the Iron Curtain, the emphasis on Soviet misconduct was an aspect of a self-portrayal as victims, a tendency in which all sought to share, not least by emphasising different aspects of the wartime years. In part, as a result, right-wing leaders from the war years were favourably proclaimed as anti-Soviet nationalists, an account that was often less than frank about their willingness to brutalise fellow-citizens (notably, but not only, Jews), to pursue territorial expansion, and to serve German interests. In Slovakia, Josef Tiso, a priest who had headed the pro-Nazi and anti-Semitic wartime regime and been executed after the war, was, following the end of Communist rule, publicly proclaimed by right-wingers as a patriot. Furthermore, right-wing nationalists celebrated the gaining of Slovak independence in 1939, which had been a direct consequence of Hitler's invasion of Bohemia and Moravia. This stance was linked to their campaign for the renewed dissolution of Czechoslovakia – the separation of Slovakia from Bohemia and Moravia, eventually achieved in 1993. In 2000, there was considerable contention in Slovakia over proposals to establish a memorial to Tiso.

Ion Antonescu, dictator of Romania from 1940 until 1944, and an ally of Hitler, had been executed for war crimes in 1946. In the 1990s, however, Romanian cities rushed to name streets after him. In turn, the appropriation of Antonescu was complicated by the international sensitivity of his brutal persecution of Jews, notably, but not only, in areas conquered from the Soviet Union in 1941, such as the city of Odessa where tens of thousands of Jews were killed.[106] This persecution was a key instance of the extent to which the Holocaust was not simply a German project, but, instead, part of a wider murderous anti-Semitism. Throughout Eastern Europe, both during the Cold War and subsequently, there was a reluctance or failure to acknowledge the degree of local complicity in the Holocaust.

The positive treatment of those displaced by the Communists in the mid-1940s ensured that in Bulgaria, Croatia, Hungary, Romania and Slovakia, regimes that had collaborated with Hitler were presented more favourably than in the past. In Hungary, for example, there was a revival of commitment to the Christian nationalism associated with the Horthy regime, a Christian nationalism that had failed to protect over 400,000 Hungarians from the Holocaust.[107]

Conversely, there was less sympathetic support for the wartime partisan resistance to the collaborative regimes, and indeed to the Germans. Moreover, as wartime resistance to Germany and its allies was re-examined, the Communist role in it was downplayed or criticised. Thus, in the castle museum at Bled, the display on Slovene history includes the passage, 'The excessive desires for absolute power among members of the Communist Party of Slovenia caused the original, unsullied idea of united resistance to Nazism and Fascism to disintegrate'.

The praise for anti-Communist nationalists extended to those who had collaborated with the Germans in the absence of a regime allied with Hitler. Thus, in Lithuania, occupied by the Soviets in 1940 and then conquered by the Germans in 1941, some nationalists had supported the Germans even though they did not re-establish an independent Lithuania. As a result, in the 1990s, the process of exonerating anti-Communists extended to include celebrations of 'heroes' who fought with the SS. Indeed, there was large-scale local co-operation in the slaughter of Jews, notably in Lithuania; although the major killers were the Germans, they instigated the killing, and their responsibility was central.[108] Those who fought in the SS included the Latvian Legion, two Latvian divisions, formed in 1943.

Without praising collaborators, scholarship and public history moved in similar directions as far as challenging Communist-era accounts were concerned, although there were significant differences in other respects. For example, in Estonia, Latvia and Lithuania, it was possible after the end of the Cold War to probe the earlier period of independence ended by Soviet occupation in 1940, an occupation that ended these states' ability to manage their future. It was also possible after the Cold War to work on the harsh aspects of Sovietization, in 1940–1 and from 1944, and to discuss both the many victims and those who resisted.[109] These issues led to a focus on the Nazi–Soviet Pact of 1939 under which the annexations had taken place. This was a pact that the Soviets had done their best to ignore and to sweep from the historical record, because it apparently equated the legitimacy and goals of their regime with that of Nazi Germany.

The Nazi–Soviet Pact was not the sole occasion in debate, nor was it the only episode that the Russian government did not like recalled. For example, there were complaints about the annual commemorative march of Latvian veterans who had fought for the Germans, while the Lithuanian sponsorship in 2000 of an International Public Tribunal on the Crimes of Communism also caused anger. More generally, the tendency to criticise the Soviet Union led to a failure to devote due attention to Jewish victims of Nazi rule.

In Ukraine, the destructiveness of Soviet wartime policy, both during the retreat in 1941 in the face of the German advance, and with the re-conquest in 1943–4, was emphasised. In the former case, there was the execution of many imprisoned Ukrainian nationalists, as well as the destruction of Ukrainian symbols, notably buildings and documents.[110] From 1943, there was both a brutal suppression of Ukrainian nationalists, in which counter-insurgency was interpreted in the widest of terms, and the driving of Poles from western Ukraine. The NKVD also turned its savage attention to the Polish resistance. The rear-area campaign waged by the NKVD required the deployment of thousands of troops. A stress on Soviet brutality served in the 1990s and 2000s as a rallying call in the bitterly divided world of Ukranian politics for those who emphasised opposition to closer ties with Russia. At the same time, there was a tendency to evade mention of the murderous wartime treatment of Ukranian Jews by the Germans and by some Ukranian collaborators.[111]

The wartime role of Ukranian nationalists became controversial in 2014 in the crisis over Russo–Ukranian relations. Svoboda and Right Sector parties with ultra-nationalist roots were particularly active in the overthrow of the pro-Russian government. The Russian media brought up echoes of World War Two, and, on 3 March 2014, the Russian Foreign Ministry referred to 'the West's allies' in Ukraine as 'outright neo-Nazis'.

Similarly, in Poland it became possible after the fall of Communism to assess episodes in recent history that had previously been openly considered only by émigré historians, for example the Nazi–Soviet Pact of 1939 and what followed: the Soviet invasion of 17 September 1939, and the subsequent large-scale Soviet killing of Poles. The Home Army, the non-Communist Polish resistance, which, under Communist rule, had been condemned as reactionary and pro-Western, if not worse, was reinterpreted as a patriotic organisation. Indeed, the Soviet failure to come to the relief of the Warsaw Rising in 1944 became a major issue in Polish political culture, just as in Czechoslovakia, although to a lesser extent, the Soviets were suspected of duplicity in failing to fight through the Dukla Pass to aid the Slovak insurgents in 1944. The question of aid to the Warsaw Rising was also directed at Britain and the USA, with the claim that they could have done more to provide support for the Rising. The latter was far less plausible than the criticism of Soviet policy, not least because the argument failed adequately to consider the range and intensity of Anglo–American commitments at that juncture, as well as the problems facing air operations over Warsaw.

At the same time, it was clear that the Home Army had been unwise in rebelling prior to the German defeat, as this rebellion, clearly intended to show that Warsaw owed its liberty to Polish actions, did not match the reality on the ground. De Gaulle had a similar goal in the case of Paris. An excellent Museum of the Warsaw Rising opened in 2004.

Since the fall of Communism, there has also been more attention paid to the Holocaust, both within Poland and from outside.[112] Particular controversy focuses on Polish anti-Semitism. It was certainly a factor in the fate of the Polish Jews across the 1940s,[113] but scarcely on the scale, or with the deliberation, of the slaughter and destruction caused by the Germans.

The rewriting of the Communist years in Poland was not restricted to the war years, but much of it overlapped with it, as in accounts of the cruelties of Stalin's government. The *Glasnost* or openness of the last years of the Soviet regime, under Mikhail Gorbachev, permitted a greater openness about events such as the Katyn massacre of about 22,000 Polish officers by the Soviets in 1940, an episode they had earlier blamed on the Nazis, in part as a counter to the Nazi use of their discovery of the graves in April 1943 in order to score political points about the massacres. At the time, the Katyn case had put strain on the British governmental response to Soviet policy towards Poland, and gave the Soviets an opportunity to break off relations with the Polish government-in-exile in London and, instead, to move towards creating a government in exile under Soviet influence.

Given that senior British ministers believed that the Soviets had massacred the officers, the British government was involved in deception as it did not wish to see the issue damage Anglo–Soviet relations.[114] After the war, the case was regarded as a key cover-up, and one used to criticise Britain as well as the Soviet Union. Thus, Katyn played a central role in Robert Harris's novel *Enigma* (1995), which was subsequently filmed. In 1990, the Soviet Union acknowledged responsibility for the Katyn massacre.

Katyn was only one of a number of Soviet atrocities, but most did not receive attention until after the fall of Communism. In Belarus, the remains in mass graves at Kuropaty, where the NKVD had slaughtered at least 100,000 people between 1937 and 1941, were exhumed from 1988.

As far as military operations were concerned, the opening up of Soviet material from 1992 permitted a re-examination of World War Two on the Eastern Front. Indeed, a key aspect of the politics of World War Two is the extent to which political changes have affected access to archival material. Such material was not made accessible by the Soviet state, in part because information was seen as a weapon. The situation radically altered with the fall of Communism. Archives such as those of the Soviet Supreme High Command provide an opportunity for re-considering both narrative and explanation. Moreover, this has not only been a matter of altering details. Thus, the use of Soviet archives has clarified the extent to which Stalin received accurate information on German preparations to attack. This throws critical light on Stalin's failure to take appropriate measures,[115] as well as on his contemporary popularity with the Putin circle. The operational history of the war was also concealed under Stalin. The opening of the archives provides information on Soviet effectiveness, for example in the Winter War with Finland in 1939–40, and failures.[116] Since the fall of the Soviet Union, there has also been Russian work on Allied military assistance.[117]

Within Yugoslavia, once the Tito regime's public myth had broken down, there was an emphasis on collective and communal memories,[118] and with those written from a Communist perspective becoming less heroic.[119] The end of the Communist rule and the collapse of Yugoslavia in 1991 led to a major rewriting of the historical account, not least with very different versions in the new states created out of Yugoslavia. In Slovenia, for example, returning right-wing émigrés, especially from Argentina, sought to rehabilitate the reputation of the Home Guard which had fought in support of the Germans. This goal led them to criticise the wartime partisans and also Britain which, in 1945, handed over to the partisans those of the Home Guard who had surrendered in German uniforms to British forces in Austria; they were then killed.

In Serbia, there was a more understandable attempt to rehabilitate the Chetniks, the largely Serb nationalist royalists who had fought both the German occupiers and the Communists, although, increasingly, the latter rather than the former. Subsequently, during the Communist ascendancy, the disparaging of the Chetniks was a means to make the Communist triumph appear necessary and inevitable. The Chetnik leader, Draza Mihailović, executed by the postwar Communist government in 1946, was, in turn, honoured in the 1990s.[120]

In the 1990s, the politics of the moment infused and was infused by the recollection of the war, which was linked to the struggle between

Yugoslavia's constituent parts. The role of Croatia was particularly contentious, as Croatian units in the Yugoslav army had mounted only limited resistance to German conquest in 1941. Moreover, subsequently, under the *Ustaša* regime, many Croats had supported Hitler. Franjo Tudjman, a former general who had set himself up in the 1960s as a revisionist historian, became President of Croatia in 1990. Tudjman used his history to support his virulent Croatian nationalism, attacking the Yugoslav public myth associated with Tito. Instead, Tudjman argued that the Croat role in the resistance to the Nazis had been minimised by Tito, and himself played down the iniquities of the *Ustaša* regime. In his book *Bespuća povijesne zbiljnosti* [*The Wastelands of Historic Reality*, 1989], Tudjman greatly minimised the numbers killed in Jasenovac, the concentration camp in which large numbers of Serbs were slaughtered during World War Two. As President, Tudjman considered bringing back to Croatia for an official state funeral the body of Ante Pavelic, the head of the wartime regime. Tudjman also adopted the *sahovnica*, the medieval red-and-white checkerboard emblem of the Croats which is associated in Serb minds with the *Ustaša* regime. Croat and Serb nationalists looked back to the 1940s in redefining geographical regions as historical ethnic territories and then using that as a justification for genocidal attacks.[121]

The treatment of the war in the textbooks produced in the newly-independent states varied greatly. The Slovene textbooks were reasonably objective, although, unsurprisingly, there was a narrative that linked exemplary wartime conduct to the cause of Slovene independence. The emphasis was on resistance organised by the partisans, whose role was presented as very positive, while the old political élites were discussed in a less positive light. The Slovene partisans were seen as leading to the liberation of the whole of the Slovene ethnic territory and the formation of a Slovene republic (with, crucially, a right to secession) within Yugoslav federalism.[122] Thus, the account of the war years was important to the issue of postwar legitimacy.

The situation was less positive in Croatian textbooks published in 1998–2000. There was criticism of the *Ustaša*, but praise for the Croatian Home Guard. The common theme was that Hitler and Mussolini exploited the Croatian desire for a state. The cruel Chetnik treatment of the Croats was emphasised, and the textbooks sought to point out the complex character of the anti-Fascist movement, with the *Ustaša* regime seen as giving rise to resistance. Yet, more space was given to repression where Croats were victims than to the ethnic dimension of much of the *Ustaša*'s killing.[123]

In the Serbian textbooks published in 1992–6, the defeat of Yugoslavia in 1941 was presented as the result of betrayal by others, especially Croats, while the Serbs were seen as always in the right. As an obvious means to decry the Croats, the harsh treatment of detainees in Jasenovac was described in detail, as was brutalisation by Kosovars (Muslims from

Kosovo who were aligned with the Germans) and by occupying Bulgarian troops. The textbooks were critical of the Chetniks, although less so than in the Communist period.[124]

In parts of Eastern Europe, the changing borders of the war years were also used as subsequent justifications for territorial claims. Thus, from 1989, Belarussian activists revived their claims to the Lithuanian capital of Vilnius, claims that had been pushed earlier in the century, especially with Soviet success in 1939 and 1945.[125] Nevertheless, as after decolonisation in Africa, there was only limited interest after the Cold War in territorial change, and the stabilisation of the postwar boundaries was taken further with the entrenchment of the existing order seen as necessary for membership of NATO, the EU and the United Nations.

If, initially, most of the new politics of the war in Eastern Europe was directed against the Soviet Union and its allies, the situation rapidly became more complex. As a counterpoint to a process of joining a European Union seen, with some reason, as German-dominated, as well as of responding to German economic and fiscal dominance of Eastern Europe, there was an assertion of national identity through historical complaint focused on German conduct in World War Two. In 2004, 320 MPs in the Polish Parliament passed a motion instructing the government to demand compensation from Germany for its actions in 1939–45, in order to right the wrong of 'the enormous material and spiritual destruction caused by German aggression, occupation and genocide'. President Kwasniewski pressed the MPs not to vote in favour of the resolution, as he claimed it could harm relations with Germany for years. Also in 2004, the Mayor of Warsaw, Lech Kaczynski, announced that he had appointed a group of statisticians and economists to calculate, building by building, the heavy damage done to Warsaw by the Germans so that, if necessary, they could be presented with a bill. He indeed demanded reparations.

As President from 2005 to 2010, Lech Kaczynski, whose father had fought in the unsuccessful and harshly suppressed 1944 Warsaw uprising, was highly critical of German policy, and notably of the co-operation between Gerhard Schröder, Chancellor of Germany from 1998 to 2005, and the Russian leader, Vladimir Putin. Kaczynski's brother, Jarosław, the Prime Minister from 2006 to 2007, who was also critical of Germany, argued in 2007 that the proposed voting formula for the European Union based on population was unacceptable because of Poland's heavy losses at German hands in the war. Roman Giertych, the Deputy Prime Minister, attacked the threat by Schröder's successor, Angela Merkel, to press ahead with the treaty even if Poland would not compromise, and claimed that she was forcing Poles to put their hands up, a reference to the German occupation.

Netherlands

Immediately after the war, there were arrests and trials of traitors as well as enquiries into the behaviour of Dutch companies in order to establish the degree of collaboration. Although public interest in these matters faded after the conclusion of those trials in 1948, the tone was set when interest in the wartime experience was revived during the 1960s, mainly due to the publication of the 14-volume *Het Koninkrijk der Nederlanden in de Tweede Wereldoorlog* (1969–91) by Lou de Jong, the Director of the *Rijksinstituut voor Oorlogsdocumentatie*, who had been trained as a radio presenter by the BBC in England during the war. De Jong provided a view of all that had happened during these years, based on eye-witness reports and original written sources. The focus of this work was on fact-finding, but there was a latent moral bias, as if De Jong wanted to establish, for once and for all, who had been right and who wrong during those years. This element was even more apparent in the television series *De Bezetting* (1960–5) made under De Jong's supervision and presented by him in 21 episodes. The agony and moral despair of the participants, and their effort to find the justification for their deeds, was tangible in these broadcasts.

This element was criticised during the 1980s by a new generation of historians, most notably Hans Blom and Jan Bank, who deemed the projection of moral categories on the behaviour of past generations to be unscientific. This view was enthusiastically adopted by commentators whose parents had been Fascists, such as Chris van der Heyden, who argued, notably in *Grijs Verleden* (2001), that such categories never had any real meaning at all. This relativistic perspective was adopted without much reflection in the film *Zwartboek* (2006) by Paul Verhoeven, in which Jews and resistance fighters appeared to change sides at will.

There has also been criticism of the dominant account that the Dutch did not collaborate, with, in its place, some discussion of co-operation with the Germans. This was true of collaboration with the deportation of Jews,[126] and also of participation in the SS, for which the Dutch, per capita, provided more volunteers than the French or Belgians. It is instructive, therefore, that the Dutch have not shared in a popular opprobrium for wartime conduct comparable to that of the French. Instead, the dockers' strike in Amsterdam on behalf of their fellow Jews gave the Netherlands a reputation for resistance to German demands which survived the true facts of collaboration until fairly recent times.

Some historians, for example Joseph Michman and Jaap Meyer, have argued that the non-Jewish Dutch population was latently hostile to Jews, or, at least, indifferent. In *Om erger te voorkomen* (1997), Nanda van der Zee stressed the cowardice of Dutch officials and their willingness to please the Germans. She also criticised Queen Wilhelmina for mentioning the Jewish deportations only once in her radio speeches from London. This book was welcomed on the Left, for example in the weekly *De Groene Amsterdammer*, but attacked by Wilhelmina's biographer who argued that the Queen knew little about what was happening on the Continent and could not have known about the atrocities in the concentration camps.[127] Feelings of guilt may have played a role in Dutch support for Israel in the Arab–Israeli wars of 1967 and 1973, and were cited as a reason by Bram Stemerdink, the Minister of Defence in 1973, who decided to send missiles to Israel on his own authority.

There has also been a controversy over the Dutch resistance to German invasion in 1940, controversy similar to that about Norway earlier that spring. Scholarship has played a role, notably the publication in 1990 of what became the standard work, *May 1940. The Battle on Dutch Soil*, edited by Piet Kamphuis and H. Amersfoort, two leading military historians. This book, produced, like many, in accordance with a commemorative timetable, in this case the 50th anniversary of the invasion, showed how the oral and written accounts of the campaign had varied over the years and provided a critical appraisal of the existing explanations of the rapid Dutch defeat. The book did well, both critically and commercially, but also met with resistance and became the object of sometimes heated debate. In 2000, a veteran, aided by a number of veteran organisations and the major Dutch newspaper, brought a lawsuit against the editors, and their employer, the Minister of Defence, with the intention of forcing them to alter certain passages that displeased them. The court rejected their demand, and in 2005 an updated version of the book appeared. In practice, there is only limited room for controversies over the Dutch defeat, as it is difficult to deny the lack of courage shown by Dutch politicians and the poor state of the Dutch defences.

The war also had a major impact on public policy. The Netherlands had been a neutral country for a century prior to the conflict, and there had been a strong belief that it could remain so. In 1935, the government was warned by General Reynders, the Chief of Staff, that a German surprise attack was likely in the event of war between Germany and France in order to circumvent the Maginot Line. At the time, this claim fell on deaf ears. However, after the war, the Dutch had learned their lesson and joined the anti-Soviet NATO when it was founded in 1949, with the full support of all political parties bar the Communists. In contrast, before the war, neutrality was defended by both the Right and the Left, with the Left arguing for total disarmament as well. This shift of policy took place without public controversy. Looking back to the war, there were few points to be scored by Socialists, who had argued for total disarmament, but nor for Christian Democrats and Liberals, who had been in charge for most of the 1920s and 1930s, advocating neutrality, while neglecting Dutch defences.

Other aspects of the war inspired political controversy. Symbolism and substance each played a role. In 1966, Crown Princess Beatrix married Claus von Amsberg, a German diplomat who, for a short period, had served in the *Wehrmacht*, albeit without taking part in any atrocities. This marriage was heavily criticised, and photographs of the Prince Consort in *Wehrmacht* uniform added to the public indignation. The latter culminated in riots in Amsterdam where smoke bombs were thrown at a gilded carriage containing the Princess and her newly-wedded husband.

In 1970, a Dutch government effort to organise a census was frustrated by the unwillingness of a large section of the population to co-operate. In large part, this arose from a press campaign pointing out the abuse by the Germans during the Occupation of publicly-stored information about individuals such as their religious beliefs. Later, during the 1980s, the efforts by the government to introduce compulsory identity cards were criticised on the basis that the German occupiers had introduced similar cards. This caused much delay and in 1994, when compulsory identification was introduced, it was only for foreigners, as well as for Dutch citizens found on public transport without a ticket. In contrast, as a sign that the memory of the occupation was finally fading away, an Act of 2005 stipulated that everyone had to carry their identification at all times.[128] The rise in the 2000s of criticism of large-scale Turkish and Moroccan immigration played a role in this shift on identity cards. The Holocaust references bound up in accusations of xenophobia, initially led to caution about how to express opposition about immigration, but this opposition became a major theme from the 2000s.

Britain

In Britain, World War Two has not been subject to revisionism as brutal as that affecting Britain's role in World War One, possibly because the character of fighting, nature of command, and political rationale of the latter conflict provides the focus for such revisionism. The contrast in public treatment between two conflicts, from both of which Britain emerged victorious, with indeed the British playing a greater role in the success of World War One, is notable. World War One attracted anti-war sentiment to a far greater extent than World War Two, in part because Hitler was (correctly) seen as much more malevolent than Wilhelm II.

The extent to which World War Two was presented as a 'People's War', a description in practice as much justified for its predecessor, was also important for the positive account of the later conflict, while the claim that Britain 'stood alone' against Germany in 1940–1 was important to the heroic presentation of the war, as were what were presented as the key episodes of that period, the Battle of Britain and the Blitz. This claim can be seen as ignoring the fundamental contribution of the Empire in 1940–1, but 'standing alone' was taken to mean Britain and the Empire,[129] although, in most war films, the British war effort was usually depicted with scant, if any, imperial component.

The period after the war was one of the portrayal of heroism. The sacrifice made by Britain and its Empire to defeat the Axis seemed a culmination, justification and even a destiny for both. Numerous books and films provided accounts of the major military episodes on land, sea and air, as well as of fictional episodes, with a sense of stiff-upper-lip comradeship, understated heroics and emotional restraint[130] being the dominant impression.

This approach was encouraged by the government. Thus, the BBC series 'War in the Air' was deliberately developed to counteract the American 'War at Sea' series. A patriotic account, 'War in the Air' stressed the role of the 'Few' in the Battle of Britain, and also the valour of the RAF.[131] This account took forward the wartime stress on the role of the RAF, rather than the Royal Navy, whereas, in practice, the strength of the latter proved the prime deterrent to German invasion.[132] In part, this stress reflected the sense that the RAF was particularly attractive to the USA.[133] It was instructive to see the emotion aroused in 2006 when there was an attempt to shift the emphasis more towards the role of the Royal Navy in thwarting German invasion plans.[134] There was a strong strand of prison camp accounts seen in books, television and films, notably with *The Great Escape* and *Colditz*.

There were also heroic accounts of the Resistance, such as *Carve Her Name with Pride*, which was devoted to Violette Szabó, while the resistance in France and Belgium was popularised in the 1970s by the television series *The Secret Army*. At the younger level, male interest in the war was incessantly inculcated by boys' magazines, such as *Lion*, *Valiant* and *Commando*, and by popular fiction, such as the Biggles and Gimlet stories of W. E. Johns.[135] Many popular films drew on their themes, for example *Where Eagles Dare* (1969). Public interest led to a widespread readership for serious works on the war, although they also led to controversy.

British hopes of a better postwar Britain (and world) were tarnished and then overthrown by the successive crises of the late 1960s and 1970s. However, the war was not treated as critically by the 1960s generation as World War One, although there was a decline then in public interest among the young. Yet, over the following decades, the media became readier to run with critiques of aspects of British policy during World War Two, notably the strategic bombing campaign, and also to highlight particular failures and to discuss them in terms of incompetence and cover-ups. In addition, the revelation of the existence and extent of ULTRA after 1975 with the publication of *The Ultra Secret: The Inside Story of Operation Ultra, Bletchley Park and Enigma* (by Group Captain F. W. Winterbotham) encouraged interest in the secret history of the war, or, rather, in uncovering supposed secrets and in debating failures to use secret material, as in the defence of Crete in 1941 and the Arnhem operation in 1944.

At times, the coverage of the British war-effort was particularly critical of the war, and notably of Churchill,[136] while left-wing British writers tend to be overly favourable to Stalin.[137] This is in contrast to the continued popularity of the RAF's role in the Battle of Britain,[138] a popularity seen in 2009 when there was discussion of putting a Hurricane or Spitfire or their designers on the empty plinth in Trafalgar Square; nevertheless, the Combined Bomber Offensive was also the target of considerable obloquy, much of it somewhat ahistorical.[139] As a consequence, there was criticism in 1992 when the Queen Mother unveiled a statue to Sir Arthur Harris, the head of the Bomber Command, who had, conspicuously, not been given a peerage after the war. In contrast, the Dambusters' Raid of 1943 was applauded, not least with the 1951 book and 1954 film, as an instance of exemplary skill and derring-do. Ironically, the main controversy in 2009 as a remake of the film was prepared was over the name of the hero's dog, Nigger, which was felt inappropriate for modern sensitivities.

Criticism of the war could reach the point that there was public concern over the alleged debunking carried out by the media. Thus, in late 2003, there was controversy about a forthcoming BBC series on the evacuation from the Dunkirk beaches, specifically whether the BBC was intent on 'debunking the myth of the heroic little ships'.[140] In practice, the Royal Navy evacuated more troops, but the role of the 'little ships' was both impressive at the time and an important boost to morale. It also helped distract attention from the striking failure of the land campaign. A different instance of controversy over the respective role of participants arose from the claim that the Royal Navy played the key part in deterring the Germans from invading in 1940, and that that of the RAF had been deliberately exaggerated at the time for propaganda reasons.[141] The author received abuse for this argument which was based on his doctoral thesis.

Anniversaries continued to provide an opportunity for contention, notably over the degree to which the state was overlooking the conflict. Thus, in 2009, the Prince of Wales and Gordon Brown, the Prime Minister, went to Normandy to attend the 65th anniversary commemorations of D-Day after the original decision for no official commemoration until the centenary led to complaint.

The balance in assessment was largely that struck in the fictional television series *Foyle's War*, about a Detective Inspector of Police based in Hastings: alongside a full account of individual failings, including neo-Fascists in 1940, profiteering, thieving ARP wardens, a rapacious air force officer, and incompetence, there was bravery, pluck and determination in an honorable cause. *Foyle's War* was therefore a far darker version of the comic triumph of *Dad's Army* (1968–77), the fictional account of the Home Guard that enjoyed particular success not only in the 1970s, but also in subsequent revivals.[142] The humour of *Dad's Army*, like that of the popular 1980s sitcom *'Allo 'Allo*, a comedy set in Occupied France, reflected the fact that Britain was not occupied.

The reiterated appearance of reminiscences of those involved in the war contributed to a relatively favourable impression of the war, a situation also seen in Britain's former Dominions, such as New Zealand and Australia. Most of these works were autobiographical or biographical and many were self-published or vanity publications, but public sponsorship also played a role, notably in the encouragement of the production of accounts based on oral history. Thus, the New Zealand Ministry of Culture and Heritage sponsored the publication of oral histories of the war.[143] Most campaign accounts emphasised the quality of the Allied soldiers,[144] even if they were sometimes less favourable to their commanders.

Aside from the favourable accounts of participants, the use of World War Two in Britain was not particularly political in terms of the contentions of the present. This situation, however, was qualified in the run-up to the Suez Crisis of 1956 and the Iraq War of 2003, with those critical of the conflicts accused, in each case, of Appeasement, a charge that could be employed by both Left and Right. Thus, both Conservative and Labour politicians made reference to Appeasement when calling for action against the Argentinean invasion of the Falkland Islands in 1982. Churchill had used the argument in his *The Gathering Storm* (1948), a book about Appeasement clearly designed also to warn about the Soviet Union. Ironically, rather as Chamberlain had also sought peace, Churchill, as Prime Minister from 1951 to 1955, was to try to negotiate an end to the Cold War, although he tried to do so from the position of an alliance prepared for war. In calling for action against modern 'tyrants', notably Prime Minister Ahmadinejad of Iran, the journalist Daniel Johnson argued in 2009 that Mrs Thatcher had played a key role in encouraging Western opposition to the Soviet Union, before concluding 'Just as in the two world wars, Britain proved that it could make a difference; indeed, all the difference'.[145]

The range of possible reference to the war was captured the same month when Ian Watson, a Church of Scotland minister opposed to moves within that Church to accept homosexual clergymen, delivered a sermon (subsequently posted on his blog) in which he compared the campaign against homosexual clergy to resistance to Hitler's expansionism. In particular, he focused on the failure to resist the German remilitarisation of the Rhineland in 1936: '[Hitler] guessed correctly that the French had no stomach for a fight. If only they had, then the tragedy of a Second World War might have been avoided ... have we learned nothing from history? Remember Hitler and the retaking of the Rhineland. He got away with it. No one stopped him. So next it was Austria [1938], then Czechoslovakia [1938], and then Poland [1939] and only then world war.'

Whereas Appeasement had long been prominent to the British account of the war, the Holocaust became increasingly important, both to the public account, for example that on television, and to the academic one. Thus, Michael Burleigh, a historian writing for the popular market, argued, in his *The Third Reich* (2000), that 'the Holocaust' was 'the central revealed truth' about the Nazi regime and that 'there is no "normal" history somehow adjacent to, or detached from, the fact of the Holocaust ... certainly not the military history of the war'.[146]

Yet, in Britain, there was also pressure from the would-be relativisers and diminishers. This pressure was seen with the film *The Reader* (based on a book by Bernard Schenk), in which there was an underplaying of the degree of personal responsibility of SS guards (2009), notably of the SS guard 'Schmitz', the role entrusted to Kate Winslet. This invented character was linked to Hermine Braunsteiner, a sadistic murderess at the extermination camp at Majdanek. There was first-rate press criticism of the apparent message of the film and its screen-writer David Hare, and notably of the attempt to argue a moral relativism that extenuated some of the guilt of the participants and, more generally, of wartime Germans.[147] This criticism was an aspect of a more general debate about how best to represent the Holocaust on screen,[148] with, for example, filmmaker Jean-Luc Godard denouncing Steven Spielberg's *Schindler's List* (1993) for presenting too affirmative an account and for demanding no action from the spectator.[149]

The Holocaust was also used elsewhere as a way to approach wartime conduct. Thus, Ian Kennedy Martin, an Irish writer, in his play *Berlin Hanover Express* (2009), employed knowledge of the truth about the concentration camp at Belsen in order to criticise the wartime neutrality of Eire (Ireland), a neutrality that, despite the honourable conduct of many Irish individuals, was in large part sympathetic, if not supportive, to the German cause.

Elsewhere in Europe

It was not only in formerly Communist states that the end of the Cold War signalled a change in public history about World War Two. For example, in Finland it became possible, with the end of the Soviet Union, to make explicit reference to an account that was unfavourable to the latter. It became more acceptable to mention the close to 500,000 refugees who had fled Karelia when it was annexed by the Soviet Union in 1940: it is still part of Russia. Moreover, the *Lotta Svärd*, a women's movement that had provided food and nurses for the army, and had taken part also in plane-spotting during the wars with the Soviet Union in 1939–40 and 1941–4, had been banned subsequently as a result of Soviet pressure. After the Cold War, in contrast, the movement was revived, received a medal from the President, and was celebrated in a museum. In neighbouring Norway, there was academic and political controversy over the conduct of the Norwegian government before and during the German invasion in 1940.

Neutrals came to confront the collaboration, or at least co-operation, often involved in their neutrality. In part, this process was a matter of responding to criticism, which was the case in particular with Switzerland[150] and the Papal States. Switzerland was financially complicit not only in the Third Reich but also in the Holocaust. The activities of individuals and institutions proved subjects for contention: most prominently Pope Pius XII's failure to condemn German or Italian anti-Semitism more markedly than in his Christmas message of 1942,[151] as well as the postwar role of the Papacy in providing a route to Argentina for killers such as Adolf Eichmann, Josef Mengele and the Croatian leader Ante Pavelić.[152] Alongside criticisms of Pius, notably Rolf Hochhuth's play *Der Stellvertreter* (*The Representative*) (1963) and books by John Cornwell (*Hitler's Pope*, 1999) and Gerard Noel (*Pius XII: The Hound of Hitler*, 2008), have come claims that the Pope has been misrepresented, that many Jews were sheltered by the Church in Rome, and that, in response to Pius's criticisms, Hitler considered the arrest of the Pope and of senior cardinals.[153]

To take another case, the reputation of Count Folke Bernadotte, who led a Swedish Red Cross relief expedition to Germany, proved highly contentious. He was assassinated in 1948 while United Nation's mediator in Palestine, and his role in 1945 was subsequently criticised. Interestingly, Bernadotte's account of his mission involved accounts of discussions with Himmler and Ribbentrop. These detailed their wish for peace with Britain and the USA while fighting on with the Soviet Union, but also a conversation about bombing. Himmler asserted 'that bombing was not started by the Germans, but I reminded him of Warsaw, in 1939, and Rotterdam, in 1940'.[154]

In Spain, the equivalent to the end of the Cold War was the death of Franco in 1975 and Spain's transition to democracy. This shift permitted a questioning of the Francoist myth that Spanish neutrality during the war was a result of Franco's brave and adept rejection of Hitler's pressure. In fact, as scholarship in Spain, Britain and the USA since 1975 has shown, Franco actively collaborated, for example refuelling U-boats, providing bases for German reconnaissance planes, facilitating German espionage and propaganda, exporting raw materials, sending troops to the Eastern Front, and offering to join in the war. To Franco, a firm opponent of democracy, and a sharer in Hitler's belief that Judaism, Communism and cosmpolitanism were allies and threats, Hitler was bound to win, and this likelihood provided an opportunity to gain control of Gibraltar, Morocco and even Portugal, a traditional ally of Britain.

Franco's commitment was increased when Hitler declared war on the Soviet Union, and he sent the volunteer Blue Division to help on that Front. About 47,000 Spaniards fought in the division.[155] Moreover, within Spain there was widespread support for Franco, while those opposed to his Catholic-nationalist totalitarianism were repressed, and many were imprisoned. Exhausted by the Civil War, others accepted the stability that was anyway enforced with considerable brutality. There had been a large-scale shooting of Republicans in 1939 when Franco triumphed.

However, to Hitler, Spain was largely inconsequential, a source of minor advantages that were not worth major effort, not least due to the weakness of the Spanish economy. Indeed, Spain was dependent on the Allies for fuel and food. The multiple problems posed by alliance with Mussolini discouraged Hitler from taking on Franco, and the latter was believed to offer little bar distraction from the goal of war with the Soviet Union. In turn, when the war started to go very badly for Germany, the Franco regime became more accommodating to the Allies and also tried to make itself look less Fascist. This process prepared the way for the postwar myth of neutrality, a myth that facilitated Franco's military co-operation with the USA during the Cold War.[156]

The rewriting of World War Two since 1975 has been relatively easy because modern Spain is based on a rejection of the Franco years. In this, public ideology and popular views are reasonably in concert, although there is a contrary Francoist strand in popular memory. Thus, in Spain, discussion of, and contention about, World War Two has been clearly linked to political trends, and is subordinate to dissension over the Civil War.

The USA

Parallels between World War Two and contemporary politics were more strongly drawn in the USA than in Britain, in part because the war has played a key role in defining American greatness and also the greatness of Americans. Thus, the 'Greatest Generation' who fought 'The Good War' have served as a base and standard against which what followed has been measured and has sought to measure itself, a theme that has linked politics and culture.[157] In practice, much of the popular account of American policy and conduct in World War Two has been misleading, not least in underplaying American isolationism prior to Pearl Harbor,[158] as well as the fundamental role in the war of other powers, notably the Soviet Union and its massive casualties; but this is scarcely a problem restricted to the USA, and, indeed, is more than matched in the Soviet Union.

The sway of the war in American public culture was seen in the discussion of subsequent conflicts. In seeing Iraq as a latter-day Nazi Germany, President George W. Bush employed the term 'Axis of Evil' in his State of the Union speech in 2002, a deliberate reference to the wartime Axis. Saddam Hussein was presented as a latter-day Hitler and, in 2003, misleading comparisons were drawn over Iraq with the Werewolves (the Nazi resistance), the Nuremberg trial of Nazi leaders, and the Marshall Aid Plan. It was also argued that the USA had to live up to its World War Two role and to spread democracy. Many commentators assumed an Iraqi response to 'liberation' from Saddam Hussein comparable to that of many Europeans, notably the French, in 1944–5, as the Americans advanced in 2003. There was a location of the subsequent occupation in terms of the successful occupations of Germany and Japan from 1945.

In turn, once the conquest of Iraq was followed by an insurrection, the theme of persisting in Iraq drew on the memorialisation of World War Two, with the 60th anniversary of D-Day, and the inauguration of the memorial for that war on the National Mall serving in 2004 to affirm the value of struggle. Earlier, World War Two had served as an encouragement for action in the Korean and Vietnam wars.

A demand for action was as one with the view that not enough had been done by the USA in World War Two, in large part because policymakers had allegedly failed then. In particular, President George W. Bush argued that a war that left the Soviets as successful conquerors of Eastern Europe was an incomplete triumph (a theme already voiced by President Truman); while, in 2008, at the Holocaust Memorial in Jerusalem, he stated that the Allies had failed in their response to Auschwitz: 'We should have bombed it'.

In turn, historians and their publishers used World War Two and Iraq as interchangeable reference points. Thus, the jacket cover for the American edition of William Hitchcock's *The Bitter Road to Freedom. A New History of the Liberation of Europe* (2008) ended 'Today, with American soldiers once again waging wars of liberation in faraway lands, this book serves as a timely and sharp reminder of the terrible human toll exacted by even the most righteous of wars'. The preface to the third edition of Bruce Pauley's *Hitler, Stalin and Mussolini* (2000) included a reference to Saddam Hussein.[159]

Looking at World War Two from the perspective of the present, and vice versa, were scarcely new processes. Indeed, immediately after the war, the Americans joined their allies in sanitising the history of the conflict, not least the devastation involved in the Liberation and such ambiguities as reconciliation with unashamed Germans. This 'American myopia' has been seen as particularly oblivious to the European experience of liberation, just as the European myths underplayed collaboration and exaggerated resistance.[160] Reconciliation with the Germans was in part an aspect of an anti-Communist Cold War narrative that affected the understanding of wartime policy, notably of links with the Soviet Union as well as policy towards China. Careers were affected as policies for present and future were assessed in light of a perception of the past, and vice versa.[161]

Moreover, the war was used for specific political purposes, as in the forewords of 1940 and 1961 to the editions of J. F. Kennedy's *Why England Slept*, an authorship that was powerfully ironic given the isolationist stance of his father, Joe Kennedy. The forewords were written by Henry Luce, a key Republican publisher and proponent of American power. Like the earlier, the later foreword was a striking call to action. Warning Americans of the 'grim possibilities of destruction and surrender', Luce asked whether Kennedy, by then President, and the modern Americans, would do better than Chamberlain and his British counterparts, and warned of the enemy of weakness within. Readers were told that 'The '30s marked the high tide of the "revolt of the masses" in the West. The revolt was expressed in many

ways – in fascism, in communism, in cynicism, in the intellectual repudi-
ation of the great Liberal Tradition of the West … Western Democracy
came near to perishing as much from its own inner betrayal as from
outward aggression'. Luce continued by locating the Cold War in terms of
the legacy of World War Two: 'The world-wide menace of Communism is
no less evil than the menace of Hitlerism'.[162]

At the same time, the war and Holocaust consciousness led in a variety
of directions, not least towards a commitment by some Americans to
Liberalism.[163] In the USA, as elsewhere, political narratives of the war based
on the needs of the present overlapped with more academic readings, but
the relationship between the two could be distant, in large part because they
arose from autonomous spheres of activity. There could also be a divergence reflecting the political sense and requirement that history was past.
Thus, American governmental concern for good relations with Germany
and Japan encouraged a willingness to share commemorative occasions,
for example the 60th anniversary of D-Day, whereas American academics
became more willing to emphasise the complicity of Germans in the Nazi
regime and eventually the idea that most Germans were willing to imbibe
Nazi ideas.

Conclusion

The availability of more evidence about the war, notably, but not only,
both the nature of alliances and, separately, the Holocaust, and the
presence of a critical distance, now permit the development of a more
complex history of the conflict.[164] It is possible that a ready reading of
political messages for the present may well continue to be preferred by
many commentators. Nevertheless, a further element of complexity is
provided by the number of states in which accounts of the war are offered.

In addition, there is the role of World War Two in developing and
debating the identity and ethos of Europe and, more specifically, of the
European Union. The established narrative was that European unification
was a reaction against the horrors of the war, and that this factor motivated
a determination to ensure that there were no other wars.[165] That narrative
led to a downplaying of the extent and impact of wartime co-operation
within the new German empire, notably between Germany and Vichy
France but also with elements in the Benelux countries.

Moreover, other themes of European co-operation looked back to
older twentieth-century movements, notably anti-Communism, especially
Catholic anti-Communism. From this perspective, the war was simply a
stage, albeit an increasingly important one in the development of understandings and practices of European identity. This stage cleared a path
for a new practice and vocabulary of Europe, notably by discrediting

the parties of the Right and by ending German imperialism. However, in advancing Soviet power to the Elbe, the war ensured that anti-Communism became even more significant to European identity, while strengthening the Communist versus Catholic axis in Eastern Europe, especially in Poland and Hungary.

Timing was also significant to the identifying and memorialisation of the war. The Holocaust was relatively insignificant in the European discussion of the war in the two decades after 1945, both west and east of the Iron Curtain. Moreover, there was a reluctance to insert the Holocaust in the historical analysis. Instead, Holocaust memory was confronted mainly by adapting the old frameworks of anti-Fascism and anti-totalitarianism.[166] As a result of the change from the late 1960s, the memorialisation of the Holocaust came to play a major role in the identity of the new Europe, at times almost crowding out other narratives. This became less clearly the case from the 2000s as the European Union expanded eastwards and the demand grew to give greater weight to Communist barbarities.

CHAPTER SIX

Recollection: The War in Asia

This chapter is shorter than the previous one because fewer countries are discussed. Nevertheless, the continuing significance of the war for acrimony between China and Japan ensures that the topic is of great significance. Recollection of the war within Asia has been dominated, and continues to be dominated, by the vexed relationship between China and Japan, although a host of other narratives have also played a role. Outside of Asia, recollection has centred on wartime relations between Japan and the USA, not least because one side of the discussion was readily accessible in English. Indeed, the focus has been on American views of the war, rather than those of Japan. The sensitivity of the latter was apparent only to the (relatively) smaller number who visited Japan and/or read Japanese works.

China and Japan

Definitions, dates and nomenclature continue to play a role in the controversies focused on the war, and these definitions, dates and nomenclature have varied for all the combatants. For example, the conflict is not known as World War Two in Japan. Instead, critical left-wing historians, seeking to emphasise Japanese aggression, referred to the Fifteen Years War of 1931–45, beginning with the Japanese invasion of Manchuria. Conservatives, however, referred to the Great East Asia War of 1937–45 that began when large-scale, but undeclared, war with China commenced: in China, this conflict is known as the War of Resistance.

Another Japanese viewpoint, one encouraged by Douglas MacArthur when Supreme Commander of Allied occupation forces in Japan (1945–50), referred to the Pacific War of 1941–5. The rationale for the Japanese attack on America, Britain and Dutch possessions in Asia and the Pacific in 1941 in practice largely stemmed from the intractable nature of the ongoing Japanese military intervention in China, and, specifically, the extent to which the Japanese military could see no acceptable alternative beyond that of pressing on in China. However, a focus on war with the USA enabled some Japanese commentators to downplay the issue of responsibility for the war, its conduct and its outcome, because the USA was portrayed as following a provocatively interventionist policy against Japanese expansion in 1940–1, while the American use of atomic bombs in 1945 was employed by the Japanese to diffuse the question of guilt over launching the Pacific War and over atrocities.

For China, the period 1931–45 is the key issue in its negotiations with Japan about the past, an issue that has become more prominent over the last two decades, although, at the level of personal loss, conflict was on a far greater scale from the spread of direct hostilities in 1937. At present, new grievances are fed into the discussion in China. These grievances have ranged from evidence of Japanese government concealment or indifference about the past to more episodic occasions, such as the alleged 'orgy' held by Japanese businessmen in Zhuhai on 18 September 2003, the anniversary of the Manchurian Crisis.

The Japanese were not the only villains to the Chinese, nor the sole issue. Long before 1931, China had been riven by civil war between the Kuomintang Nationalists (KMT) and the Communists. Within China, the role of the Communists in opposition to Japanese conquest and occupation was emphasised from the 1940s, as the Communists became more prominent, and notably from 1949 when the Communists finally won control of China. The war had certainly been good for the Communists, enabling them to enhance their position within China, from control of a small area with a population of fewer than two million in 1937, to that of much of north China outside Japanese hands and a population of over 100 million in 1945.[1] Mao is said to have told a visiting left-wing Japanese politician after the war that the Communists owed their success to the Japanese invasion.

Moreover, paralleling the treatment of the Chetniks during the years of Communist rule in Yugoslavia, the role of the rival Kuomintang Nationalists in opposing Japan was minimised; as indeed was that of Communists who fought at a distance from Mao Zedong's zone of control. However, because the focus in mainland Chinese recollection was on continuing rivalry with the Nationalists, who still ruled Taiwan, there was, for a while, more emphasis on the renewed Chinese Civil War of 1946–9 than on the earlier war with Japan.[2]

The different Communist and Kuomintang narratives of the war rested on longer-term accounts of China's decline and revival. These accounts provided different explanations of China's decline, and thus of the placing of Japanese aggression.[3] Yet, from the 1970s, and, even more, the 1980s, there was a shift in approach in China, with an emphasis on a new, more specifically targeted (rather than generally anti-capitalist and anti-imperialist) nationalism designed to help counter the strains created by economic and social transformation, as well as the political challenge posed by American-led pressure on human rights. Commemoration of the Sino–Japanese War, as an acute form of the imperialist aggression in China that was repeatedly condemned by the Communists, played a major role in this Chinese nationalism.

This condemnation linked the critique of nineteenth- and early-twentieth-century Western and Japanese exploitation of China with a defensive hostility towards Japan's strong and persisting postwar alliance with the USA and to greater conservative nationalist activism in Japan from the 1970s. Partly as a consequence, there came to be stronger emphasis in China on the scale and brutality of the Nanjing Massacre of 1937 carried out by Japanese troops after they had captured the city.

The eventual Chinese Communist wooing of Taiwan in the 1990s in pursuit of unification also played a role in this greater stress on wartime Japanese aggression and brutality, not least in encouraging a more favourable portrayal of the Kuomintang war effort; although 'even now, the space to remember and to grieve is constrained by the demands of contemporary ideology'.[4] As a result of the emphasis on Chinese nationalism from the 1980s, the war with Japan ultimately came to loom larger than the 1946–9 Civil War in Chinese consciousness.[5] Nanjing itself was the Kuomintang capital at the time and so was of no direct consequence to Communist positions in the 1930s.

The war is currently used to unite people within China and to present the nation as a co-operative rather than confrontational actor in world history, with the term 'anti-fascist war' serving to depict China as playing a key role in collective resistance to the Axis.[6] A focus on Japan, past and present, underlines the extent to which Chinese survival against Japanese attack in 1931–45 opened the way for China to offer a new nationalist agenda, one that went beyond Chinese divisions then and subsequently.[7] Reconciling Taiwan to Chinese Communist control was not going to come from any stress on Communism.

A focus on the state alone, however, was and is insufficient. It is also necessary to appreciate the degree of public interest, notably by the 2010s on the Chinese internet, which contrasted with the limited media opportunities earlier available. In the early 2010s, much of the Chinese press, which, due to its dependency, generally very much reflects the Communist Party line, as well as much of the content on the Chinese internet, linked the crisis with Japan over the East China Sea to China's historical losses, and, in particular, to the war of conquest launched by Japan in 1937. This line was also very much taken by Chinese diplomats, notably in the winter of 2013–14. This approach was similar to that taken by the Communist bloc when discussing West Germany, and, notably, its rearmament in the mid-1950s. The militaristic Japanese expansionism of the 1870s–1940s was taken by China as a descriptive model for the very different constitutional system, political culture and foreign policy of modern Japan. Past aggression is used by China to pressure Japan into publicly renouncing any intention of reverting to an interventionist military posture.[8] Historical grievance provided a way to mobilise identity and to expound policy. For example, anti-Japanese programmes became very common on Chinese television in the early 2010s, many produced by Hengdian World Studios. The popularity of the stories of war with a villainous Japan in 1931–45 ensured their production.

In Japan, the brutal wartime conduct of its forces was actively contested in public memorialisation. As a reminder of the danger of assuming a unitary view, a reminder that is also pertinent for other countries, including totalitarian ones, there are a variety of Japanese views. Nationalists, Marxists and liberals were each able to define different and competing interpretations of the national past.[9] Silenced during the war years, left-wing scholars were very influential in the early postwar decades. Their approach was broadly Marxist in terms of seeing a conspiracy, prior to 1945, between the military and big business, supported by conservative governments and the newly-created urban bourgeoisie, both to repress the masses at home and to exploit surrounding nations. The most common terms in this historiography were *gunkoku-shugi* (militarism, though taken to mean a mix of Fascism and militarism) and *tennō-sei* (the Emperor system: a system of repression using the symbol of the monarchy in education and propaganda to keep the masses docile).

From the late 1960s, the now dogmatic Marxist critiques of aggression by Japanese élites were accompanied by a greater range of scholarly writing. Indeed, conservative Japanese historians, particularly from the 1960s era of economic resurgence and the global respect accruing from the Tokyo Olympics of 1964, tried to defend aspects of the authoritarian and bellicose Japan of the 1930s and early 1940s, especially in terms of Japan's ideology of pan-Asian liberation. This they did with greater commitment than their German counterparts. The contrast between the fate of the wartime leaderships is important, with Emperor Hirohito continuing to reign until his death in 1989, albeit as a constitutional monarch who had renounced his divinity (enshrined in the earlier Japanese constitution of 1889); whereas Hitler had a very different fate. There is a scholarly view in Japan which blames the Allies for 'letting off' Hirohito, and also blames Hirohito for allowing himself to evade responsibility for the war.

Japanese views remain divided. The Textbook 'Reform' Society is opposed by the Center for Research and Documentation on Japan's War Responsibility. The *Peace Osaka* exhibition showed the hardship inflicted by Japan on its conquered subjects as well as the suffering of the Japanese. Politics plays a major role, with the nationalist revisionists opposed by the powerful left-wing Japan Teachers' Union. The Socialist Party supported an official apology to China and Korea, the Japan–China Friendship Association was highly critical of wartime policy and supported research on it, and the Japan Association for Memorialising Student-Soldiers Fallen in Battle used the war as a basis for advocating pacifism.[10] When, in 1980, a monument to Tōjō and the other executed war criminals was erected on the sites of the executions in the former Sugano prison, there was criticism as well as praise. Similarly, contrasting responses in 1989 to the death of the Emperor Hirohito, the wartime monarch, made these differences readily apparent.

In contrast to the general German willingness among scholars and public to accept responsibility for the war, there was and is, however, a widespread reluctance, in both government and public in Japan, to highlight Japan's role in beginning the conflict with both China and the Western allies, as well as to take primary responsibility for what had happened during the war, notably atrocities towards Western and Asian civilians and the mistreatment of prisoners. For example, the photograph in the Australian War Memorial of an Australian prisoner about to be beheaded is a revelation to most Japanese visitors, and one that (understandably) leaves them uncomfortable.

Instead, there was an increasing determination from the 1960s by some Japanese politicians and commentators to accept nothing that might compromise both nationalist pride and, more charitably, the creation of a modern patriotic citizenry. This tendency was accentuated by conservative activists who sought to emphasise Japanese heroism, idealism and sacrifice during the war, when, in practice, the Japanese military reacted to the impasse in China, particularly the impossibility of controlling such a vast territory and the persistence of opposition which made Japanese intervention an intractable commitment, by becoming more brutal, most notoriously with the Nanjing Massacre.

This large-scale, if unplanned, slaughter of civilians was the culmination of barbarous Japanese conduct during their advance up the Yangtse Valley. The violence testified to an increasing brutalisation in war (long before the German invasion of the Soviet Union in 1941 which some have seen as a turning-point in wartime brutality) that was given official Japanese sanction in the 'kill all, loot all, burn all' campaign launched in 1942, a campaign whose inhuman methods simply strengthened Chinese resistance.[11] In 1942, the Japanese killed at least 250,000 Chinese in a savage offensive that included the use of biological warfare. In this campaign, the Japanese employed cholera, dysentery, typhoid, anthrax, plague and paratyphoid germs. While not genocide, the mass-slaughter displayed aspects of genocidal conduct.

From the 1960s, high school textbooks dealing with Japanese atrocities in China were a *cause célèbre* in Japan and then more widely. Cases brought in the Tokyo District Court in 1965, 1967 and 1984 pitted the Ministry of Education against the historian Ienaga Saburō. The descriptions, in Ienaga's projected high school textbook *Shin Nihon shi* [*New History of Japan*], of the Nanjing Massacre in 1937 and of biological warfare experiments in China by the Japanese army's Unit 731, had attracted the attention of the ministry's censors. The ministry won cases in 1989 and 1993, but, in 1997, Ienaga narrowly gained a favourable decision from the Supreme Court. In 2013, much of the Japanese Cabinet wanted school textbooks rewritten so as further to minimise Japanese aggression.

From the 1980s, particular controversy focused on the Nanjing Massacre, which, by this time, had become a key point in differing recollections of the war between China and Japan, and also within Japan itself. There were heated arguments over both the number of Chinese civilians killed, which was in fact very large, and the extent to which massacre was an integral aspect of Japanese warmaking in China. The postwar Tokyo War Crimes Trials had treated Nanjing as a serious atrocity, and Hirota Kōki, Japan's Foreign Minister, was convicted and executed for his inaction when informed about the war crimes at Nanjing, establishing that a civilian could have responsibility even though not in the military chain of command.

Japanese nationalists, however, became more open in rejecting responsibility for the Nanjing Massacre (some even claiming that it had never taken place), and indeed for Japanese policy as a whole. In the 1980s, there was an infamous case (exposed by the *Asahi* newspaper) of a Japanese writer who took the army's record of the death toll, and, in his published version of it, crossed out a nought on every figure. The *New History of Japan* (2001), produced by the Society for History Textbook Reform, adopted a crudely apologist, if not jingoistic, account that led to formal protests from both China and South Korea. Rumours that the 2005 edition of *The New History Textbook* would not even refer to the Nanjing Massacre resulted in demonstrations in China, while there were also boycotts of Japanese goods.

The contrast with Germany is instructive. There are indeed many revisionists there, and they offer an account of the war designed to shift responsibility and blame onto Germany's opponents, but views comparable in their selectiveness or distortion to those in Japan enjoy only slight purchase in German government or, even, politics, and are generally treated as embarrassing.

This contrast may appear under challenge, notably given the situation discussed in the previous chapter: the disproportionate and unwarranted responses in Germany to the recent coverage of the Allied bombing and of the cruelties perpetrated by the advancing Red Army in 1944–5, especially large-scale rape. Nevertheless, scholarly historical judgments generally involve gradations, not the binary divides of some public discussion, and, if these gradations entail a degree of well-informed subjective assessment, that is an aspect of scholarship. The view here is that German revisionism is not yet as widespread or publicly supported as Japanese denial, and is highly likely to become so.

Underlining the issue of gradations and judgment, it is also important to contrast Japan with China. Ambivalence by the Japanese government about the war has reflected the strength of nationalist currents and the difficulties of taking responsibility for actions and of rejecting the appeal of the past. Yet, in China, where it is difficult to debate openly many aspects of the Communist years, and especially of the years that led to the seizure of power, the government remains actively involved in shaping an historical memory of Japanese aggression against China that shuts out most ambiguities. In particular, the many Chinese who co-operated with Japanese rule, and indeed fought for the Japanese, are neglected,[12] as are the entanglements and implications of the three-way struggle between Japan, the Communists and the Nationalists.

This situation provides a context within which to interpret Chinese governmental views, but it does not vitiate their point. China has proved critical not only of the Japanese nationalists, but also of signs of official tolerance of their views. Thus, in 2002, the Chinese Foreign Minister protested when the Japanese Supreme Court refused to consider any appeal by Azuma Shirō, a veteran who had been found guilty of libel in 1996 by the Tokyo District Court for allegedly attributing an atrocity to his platoon in the journal about Nanjing he had published in 1987. In 2007, ultra-nationalist Japanese MPs claimed that only 20,000 people had been killed at Nanjing, a figure that is far too low, only to meet with a response from the Chinese Foreign Ministry of 300,000, a total, in contrast, at the highest end of the range of suggested figures.

The visual media also entered the fray, and again with governmental encouragement and interference, and to a degree not seen in Europe since the close of the Cold War. In 2007, the Chinese Foreign Ministry responded critically when Satoru Mizushima, a nationalist Japanese film-maker, proposed to make a documentary, *The Truth about Nanjing*, that was intended to deny claims of Japanese atrocities, not least by challenging the evidence. This documentary was intended to counter the Chinese film *Nanjing 1937* (1995), which had provoked nationalist demonstrations in Japan. In turn, in 2007, an American film that had received permission to film from the Chinese government, underlined the extent of the atrocities.

City of Life and Death (2009), a Chinese film about the Nanjing Massacre, was on the whole well received and took $10 million in its first week, although the response was also complicated by the favourable portrayal of an individual Japanese soldier, an unexpected approach in a Chinese film. As a result, the director, Lu Chang, had to put up with death threats and with claims that he served the cause of Japanese revisionism. The same year, *John Rabe*, a co-produced German–Chinese film, focused on the activities of a German businessman in Nanjing who sheltered about 650 refugees. In 2012, Zhang Yimou's film *Flowers of War* returned to the topic of Nanjing.

Meanwhile, the diminishment of the Nanjing massacre continued in Japan. In February 2014, Naoki Hyakuta, a right-wing novelist who had been appointed by Abe Shinzō in 2013 to be one of the 12 governors of NHK, the public broadcaster, reportedly declared in Tokyo while campaigning on behalf of another revisionist standing for the governorship of Tokyo that the massacre was mere propaganda and never happened. The Chinese Foreign Ministry rejected these remarks as a 'barefaced challenge to international justice and human conscience'.

Academic scholarship also plays a role. There have been numerous conferences bringing together Chinese and Japanese historians to discuss the legacy of the Sino-Japanese War. If the situation outside the world of scholarship is less positive, Japanese students and the public, nevertheless, for all the experience of reactionary nationalism in Japan, are readily able to explore alternative readings of national history, and the most active critical participants in the debate about Japanese actions are Japanese. Moreover, the media has confronted difficult issues, as in the special programme, including testimony by participants on the Nanjing Massacre broadcast by TV Asahi, a leading network, on 15 August 2002, the anniversary of Japan's surrender. For Japan, this is the key commemorative anniversary for World War Two, as it is for Korea, as Japan's surrender brought about its immediate release from colonialism.

In Japan, where the Ienaga case shows that the Japanese government is also actively involved in shaping the historical consciousness, the role of national honour, and its international sensitivity, were repeatedly under-lined by the controversial visits by Japanese politicians to Yasukuni. This shrine to the war dead in Tokyo has, from 1978, included memorials to 14 convicted and executed Class-A war criminals from World War Two, notably General Hideki Tōjō, the bellicose Prime Minister from 1941 to 1944. In the shrine, the war dead are supposed to be rewarded for their sacrifice with a role as deities, and the shrine's place in national memori-alisation has long been an issue in Japanese politics. An attempt in 1963 to make Yasukuni a state shrine, which would have clearly breached the postwar division of church and state and reversed the separation seen when the Emperor renounced his divine status, failed, but political identification with Yasukuni became more prominent from the mid-1980s.

The six visits by Koizumi Junichirō, Prime Minister from 2001 to 2006, were seen in Japan and in Asia as particularly provocative. Koizumi's successor, Abe Shinzō, avoided further provocation by refraining from visits to Yasukuni while Prime Minister in 2006–7, although he had visited the shrine before becoming Prime Minister. Abe's grandfather, Nobusuke Kishi, had played a key role in the economic development of occupied Manchuria in the 1930s and was imprisoned by the Americans as a suspected Class A war criminal. In 2009, Taro Aso, the Prime Minister, donated a potted plant to the shrine, and although he did not visit it, this gift angered Chinese commentators.

Abe Shinzō did not visit Yasukuni initially when he became Prime Minister again in 2013, but some of his Cabinet ministers did, and Abe finally did so that December. Aside from the issue of honouring the dead, this visit was seen as important in strengthening Abe's position as he sought to push through his domestic agenda.[13]

However, there was criticism of the visit from other powers, including Singapore and the USA, which had asked him not to go, and fierce complaints from China and South Korea. Seeking a wider global resonance, Chinese government spokesmen referred to the war criminals remembered at Yasukuni as 'the Nazis of Asia'. Writing in the *Daily Telegraph* on 1 January 2014, Liu Xiaoming, China's ambassador in London, argued that 'visits to the shrine by Japanese leaders cannot simply be an internal affair' as they raised 'serious questions about attitudes in Japan and its record of militarism, aggression and colonial rule'. Moreover, this issue was linked to the crisis over competing territorial claims in the East China Sea by claiming that Abe's visit amounted to beautifying aggression. According to Liu, Abe posed a 'serious threat to global peace' by 'rekindling' Japan's militaristic spirit. He added that as China and Britain were 'wartime allies', they 'should join together both to uphold the UN Charter and to safeguard regional stability and world peace'. China's envoys wrote similar pieces in the newspapers of over 30 countries.

The issue of Yasukuni is compounded because the shrine's adjacent museum is uncritical about Japan's military past, indeed depicting it in terms of honour and glory, and presents Japanese imperialism favourably. The contrast with the state-sponsored Holocaust Memorial in Berlin is particularly stark. Yasukuni plays a role, or at least receives a prominent mention, in much of the contention surrounding the war, in part because the shrine is readily understood in these terms. Thus, in 2007, Tōjō Yūko, a granddaughter of General Tōjō, claimed that prime ministerial visits were a matter of duty. She also ran for election to the Upper House in order to realise the general's last wish before he was executed, the establishment of an official memorial day for the country's war dead. Her campaign talk linked nationalism with conservatism. Tōjō Yūko claimed that 'school-teachers who refuse to stand up for the playing of the national anthem or the raising of the flag are not even fit to be teachers', and she rejected the postwar constitution, written by an American team (without Japanese input) during the Occupation, on the grounds that it had 'forced Japan to lose its spirit as an independent country. We have lost pride and confidence and it must now be revived'.

Such talk plugged into a powerful Japanese strand which made frequent reference to World War Two, with no other historical period resonating so insistently. Museums and commemorations illustrated this theme and were designed to guide it. Thus, the Hall of Shōwa, which opened in 1999, displaying everyday life during World War Two, was entrusted to the Japan Association of War-Bereaved Families, a nationalist body that, like other such bodies, was far from critical of Japanese wartime policy. Two years later, a Tokyo banquet attended by prominent figures, including a former Prime Minister, commemorated the death of the progenitor of the kamikaze attacks, Admiral Ōnishi Takijiro, who killed himself a day after the Japanese surrender in 1945. At the banquet, youths dressed as kamikaze pilots sang war songs from the stage before the general singing of a patriotic song. There was no reference to the extent to which many pilots, while volunteers, were pressurised into giving their lives.[14]

There is a continuing pride in Japan's early military success in 1941–2 and pride in the endurance and/or self-sacrifice of many ordinary people, though not pride in the leadership. Indeed, Tōjō is still largely regarded with contempt, especially for his delayed and botched attempt at suicide, although a Japanese film called *Pride* presented him with new respect. The tradition of pride in the war, as well as a reluctance, or refusal, to accept war guilt or responsibility, goes back to the immediate aftermath of the conflict, with the rejection then by most of Japanese opinion of the Tokyo war crimes trials. They were regarded as unfair and as 'victors' justice', a phrase still employed by critics today. In practice, the trials did establish that aggressive war was a crime under international law (and one for which you could be punished if you lost) and also provided much evidence of Japanese war crimes against civilians and captured Allied military personnel. The use by nationalists of a mythical reading of the trials again indicated an unwillingness to come to terms with Japan's role in the war.[15]

In 2007, Wen Jiabao, the Prime Minister of China, raised the issue of memorialisation on an official visit to Japan, telling the Diet (Parliament) that the Japanese government should act in accordance with its official regret and apology for its wartime conduct. This remark was understood to mean that Japanese prime ministers should not visit Yasukuni. Wen noted that the invasion of China had been the cause of 'indescribable pain and wounds in the heart of the Chinese people', although he took a conciliatory view by claiming that the Japanese themselves had suffered 'enormous suffering and pain' and had been the victims of a 'handful of militarists', an approach intended to deny the linkage of past and present advanced by the Japanese nationalists. Wen's interpretation probably represents the mainstream of Japanese popular thinking: in other words, Japan caused great suffering in Asia, but also suffered greatly, especially as victims of nuclear attack.

This approach was in line with that of post-occupation Japanese governments. They depicted the 1930s and early 1940s as a disastrous interlude, in one Japanese phrase 'the dark valley', that could be forgotten in favour of a focus on a more exemplary history. Unfortunately, this approach not only neglected widespread contemporary support for the militant nationalism of the period, but also posed an acute problem for other countries in dealing with Japanese accounts of the past.

The mistreatment of the 'comfort women', enforced prostitutes for Japanese troops, sex slaves in effect, notably, but not only, in China and Korea, was also a controversial issue, and remains so, indeed increasingly so given greater awareness of this gender dimension of violence. There are no reliable statistics for the numbers used to staff the brothels for the Japanese military opened from 1938, but they are estimated at over

100,000, mostly Koreans and many quite young.[16] In 1993, Kōno Yōhei, the Chief Cabinet Secretary, admitted and apologised for the military's role in coercing women into prostitution. Moreover, in 1995, the Asian Women's Fund was established in Japan to provide financial compensation.

In 2007, however, Abe Shinzō, the Prime Minister, tried to introduce qualifications by arguing that there was no proof that women were coerced. The controversy that resulted was not restricted to principals. Notably, the American House of Representatives pressed for a full apology for the wartime coercion and for adequate compensation, and Abe offered a form of apology to President George W. Bush. The South Korean press angrily returned to the issue on a number of occasions, notably in early 2013. On 25 January 2014, Katsuto Momii, the Director-General of NHK (the public broadcaster), an appointment made by Abe, declared at his first news broadcast that the use of 'comfort women' had been common practice in the past 'everywhere in Europe', a claim which was rubbish. He retracted the comment when called before the Diet, but his views were regarded as symptomatic of Abe's circle.

Other issues include individual attempts to seek compensation for wartime forced labour, which was frequently murderous. This labour was mostly Chinese and Korean. In 2007, these attempts were rejected by the High Court in Sapporo. The Japanese record in responding to criticism over this issue in this matter is worse than that of Germany. Japanese companies, such as Mitsubishi, as well as the Japanese government, have done their best to deny responsibility and, in doing so, have seriously distorted the historical record.

Aside from presenting a largely uncritical account of what the Japanese had termed the 'China Incident', nationalist activists also sought to put a favourable gloss on the war with the Western powers. This gloss involved emphasising the role of Japan in challenging and gravely weakening the colonial rule of Western powers and thus, by bringing forward the demise of this rule, being on the side of progress. Such a process was presented as occurring both directly and indirectly, in the former case with the postwar failure to sustain the revival of Western power in colonies conquered and/ or occupied by the Japanese during the war, notably Burma, Indonesia and Vietnam. This process was also discerned indirectly in China, where Western, particularly British, economic and political interests were largely destroyed during the Japanese attack. Japanese forces in the 1940s deliberately paraded Western civilian and military captives in public in Asia in order to destroy the myth of Western superiority, as in Singapore in February 1942. In Burma and Indonesia, there is considerable acceptance of the idea that the Japanese (whatever their own intentions) did help to destroy Western colonialism.

These points were correct, but the political spin was far more problematic. The Japanese nationalists stressed their support for Asian nationalism, for example the nominal independence granted conquered Burma in August

1943 (a Central Burmese government was created the previous year), but ignored the reality of Japan's war record there: aside from a devastating air attack on Rangoon on 23 December 1941, there was economic exploitation and also the use of secret police to hunt down opponents of their quisling government. More generally, Japanese nationalists did not discuss Japan's harsh direction of conquered colonies. Although there were popular policies in such spheres as education and religion, for example in Indonesia, Japanese occupation policies could be cruel, particularly the control of labour and the allocation of resources. Maybe two and a half million Javanese alone died in 1942–5 as a result. At the time, Java was administered by the Japanese army. Similarly, rice consumption in Korea and the Philippines was pushed down in order to feed the Japanese, again hitting the local population. Agricultural production and food consumption were both hit hard in Burma.

The harshness of Japanese rule was exacerbated as the Japanese military situation deteriorated, a deterioration that, in turn, greatly compromised support. Thus, in the Philippines, resistance by American and Filipino troops who had not been captured in 1942 was supported by civilians alienated by Japanese occupation practice.[17] Outside China, this was the most prominent guerrilla movement against the Japanese, although the British-backed guerrillas in the Karen Hills of Burma proved an important aid in the closing stage of the war,[18] which was subsequently cited (without success) as a reason why Britain was honour-bound to provide them with support against the brutality of the Burmese government.

In large part, the contrast between limited opposition to Japanese occupation of European colonies and the situation in China reflected the absence of any equivalent to the governments-in-exile and popular resistance movements seen in Europe. In particular, the colonial powers enjoyed only limited popular support, and resistance in the colonies conquered by the Japanese did not match the situation in China within areas nominally under Japanese control. One reason for this may be that Asian nationalists were waiting to see how events unfolded during the war.

Civilian deaths in China as a result of Japanese action from 1931 to 1945, through massacre, forced labour, starvation, germ and chemical warfare, brutality and other actions, have been estimated as 20 million,[19] although figures are difficult to assess and there is the issue of competition with Russian war dead. There was no equivalent harshness towards the local population within the Western empires, and no equivalent intentionality in causing suffering. However, a massive famine in eastern India in 1943–4 did lead to a high death rate, of about three million, for which the British administration has received part of the blame, in part without understanding the logistical constraints on the British war effort and the consequences of Japan's control of Burma, a major prewar source of rice.

The harshness, and often murderous cruelties, of Japanese rule and, even more, conquest and occupation also provides another perspective on the use of atomic bombs to ensure a speedy Japanese surrender in 1945. This point significantly moves attention in this issue from a focus solely on the USA and Japan. Such a shift in concern is necessary as well as instructive. The use of the atomic bombs thus brought an end to a brutal and unsuccessful empire.

As a reminder of the possibility of holding different views, the deliberate nature of Japanese military violence can be set alongside the appeal, in Japan and in other parts of Asia, of the idea of pan-Asian liberation from Western rule. Such ideas of pan-Asianism had an attraction in parts of Asia from the 1890s on. Moreover, the violence of 1937–45 became more deliberate as Japanese resources and control were under pressure, and, in part therefore, were a reflection of unintended weakness rather than simple cruelty or viciousness, although both the latter were amply present. This point is also pertinent for the very different case of the treatment of Allied prisoners of war and civilians.

Nevertheless, the harshness of Japanese rule was such that reference to it provides a historical rallying point that can be used against modern Japan, and not only in China. As a result, those seeking to criticise China look to other points of historical reference. World War Two provides these in the shape of Nazi policy. In February 2014, Benigno Aquino, the President of the Philippines, compared China's claim to islands in the South China Sea to the Nazi annexation of territories in the run up to World War Two.

Japan and the USA

After the war, Japan and the USA speedily came to a mutually-positive relationship, tensions notwithstanding. Nevertheless, in Japan, more specific criticism was directed postwar at the USA than at China. American policies in 1940–1 were held as provocative and threatening, and thus as in some way responsible for the outbreak of the Pacific War, and as justifying the Japanese attack on Pearl Harbor. This critique, which neglected Japanese expansionism in China and Indo-China, looked towards the argument that the American use of the atom bombs in 1945 was unjustified. The Japanese losses suffered at Nagasaki and Hiroshima, amounting to over 280,000 deaths, either at once or, eventually, through radiation poisoning, were presented not only as war crimes, but also as, in some way, extenuating earlier Japanese conduct. Thus, there was a parallel to the German treatment of the bombing they had experienced. Moreover, there was a failure to provide a context. For example, in the original displays at the Hiroshima Peace Museum, there was no real explanation of why the American use of the atomic bombs was thought to be necessary.

History is contentious in Japan in part because of political partisanship. More than politics, however, is involved. There is also the ability to think critically about the past. In 2007, the cult of Japanese victimhood was challenged when Kyūma Fumio, the Defence Minister, said that the atomic bombings 'couldn't be helped' and 'ended the war', which indeed was the case. In the face of the resulting furore, however, he resigned within the week. The public responses were striking. Nagasaki rejected the government in the elections the following month, while Kyūma's replacement as Defence Minister, Koike Yuriko, had links with the groups who proposed nationalist textbooks.

In turn, there was criticism within the USA over wartime policy towards Japan, although largely only by revisionist scholars. The political resonance was very limited. There was academic debate over the American policy which led to the standoff with Japan in 1940–1, but, more particularly, over the dropping of the atom bombs on 6 and 9 August 1945. The immunity postwar given by the USA to the Japanese involved in Unit 731 in biological warfare, in return for providing its scientific data, became a matter of controversy in the 1980s,[20] while the American decision to launch the costly attack on the island of Iwo Jima in 1945 became one in the 2000s.[21]

There was also the claim that American policy (and also that of Australia and Britain) displayed an extreme degree of racism towards the Japanese, and that this could be seen in the merciless fighting in the Pacific, as well as in the use of the atom bombs against urban populations. The issue is particularly instructive for military historians as it provides an opportunity to discuss methodology. The 'War and Society' approach so dominant in much of the literature since the 1960s led, and leads, to an emphasis on American racism and indoctrination.[22] This emphasis is given a domestic dimension in the USA by reference to the wartime internment of Japanese-American civilians, an issue that became more prominent from the 1990s, leading to officially supported memorialisation as well as apologies.[23]

Yet, in considering all of these issues, it is also possible, in addition to this valuable approach, to push issues of practicality to the fore. It has been argued that the mutual blood-shedding during the fighting was a product of the dynamics of the battlefield, rather than a consequence of outside social influences, notably racism; and that an appreciation of these dynamics depends on an understanding of the process and context of surrender on the battlefield. In particular, the reluctance of the Japanese to surrender, and their willingness to employ ruses – pretending to surrender and then attacking their would-be captors – helped mould American responses. Indeed, Japanese attitudes, including the belief in Japan that anyone who surrendered would be treated brutally by the Allies, and Japanese conduct, and not American racism, were largely responsible for the way in which the war in the Pacific was fought.[24] Moreover, in so far as charges of racism are concerned, it is appropriate to note heavy German military and civilian casualties as a result of American action: there was no comparable racist contrast in this case.

Of all the combatants, the Japanese were the least willing to surrender, and many of those who were captured were wounded. The Army Field Service Order of 1941 that forbade being captured was in accordance with strong currents in Japanese public culture that developed in earnest from the early 1930s, and with the government's emphasis on the war-winning character of willpower. Although there were signs of lower Japanese morale as defeats accumulated – for example in Burma in 1945 – the willingness of the Japanese to fight on made the destruction of their forces a key Allied objective.[25]

This objective fed into the character of Allied warmaking, in order to further the securing of what was seen as a uniquely difficult unconditional surrender, as well as into the Japanese leadership's attempt to leave no space for such a solution. The Japanese military expected civilians to share their commitment to honourable suicide, rather than surrender, and on Saipan in 1944 killed civilians, including women and children, who did not do so or who were not killed by family members. The nature of the conflict, including the American use of heavy firepower and bombing, as well as of flamethrowers to clear cave positions, scarcely aided discrimination between soldiers and civilians, but the character of the resistance did not offer a ready alternative.[26]

Moreover, recent efforts to stress the common humanity of the combatants, a theme in both literature and film, for example Clint Eastwood's *Letters from Iwo Jima* (2006),[27] and a background, explicit or implicit, to criticism of American warmaking, are potentially misleading. They neglect the extent to which Japanese expansionism was the cause of the war in the Pacific, and that this expansionism was accompanied and followed by brutality and atrocities. These atrocities began from an early stage. Thus, having sunk the heavily outgunned USS *Edsall* on 1 March 1942, the Japanese picked up about 40 survivors who were taken to the Japanese Military Headquarters at Kendari in the Celebes (Sulawesi), and then slaughtered.[28] Such atrocities were all-too-common.

The use of the atomic bombs has proved far more contentious. On 19 May 1943, Churchill told a joint session of the US Congress:

It is agreed between us that we should at the earliest moment bring our joint air power to bear upon the military targets in the homelands of Japan .... It is the duty of those charged with the direction of the war to overcome at the earliest moment the military, geographical, and political difficulties and begin the process, so necessary and desirable, of laying the cities and other munition centers of Japan in ashes. For in ashes they must surely lie before peace comes back to the world.

However, this indicates part of the problem: a city is not necessarily a munition centre: Hiroshima was a major military and industrial city, but Nagasaki was not.

Controversy over the strategic bombing campaign against Japan precedes chronologically that over the use of the atomic bombs against Hiroshima on 6 August 1945 and against Nagasaki three days later. However, this, the sole use of nuclear bombs, has proved politically totemic, in both Japan and the USA. The use of the atomic bombs, for example, led to a bitter dispute over the exhibition in Washington planned for 1995 by the Smithsonian Institution's National Air and Space Museum. Designed to centre on the *Enola Gay*, the plane that dropped 'Little Boy', an atomic bomb, on Hiroshima a half-century earlier, as well as to show the impact of the bomb on Hiroshima, the proposed exhibition was popularly berated as unpatriotic. In practice, the critical script that accompanied the plane reflected a major strand of revisionist scholarship that has sought to probe the cultural and social dimensions of the decision to drop the bomb. In the event, due to popular pressure, especially by conservatives, not least extensive coverage in the *Washington Post*, a belated and curtailed display was, instead, offered.

Although that controversy had more to do with contemporary 'culture wars' in the USA than with World War Two, the Smithsonian continued to be a source of contention after 1995. The *Enola Gay* was displayed in the Steven F. Udvar-Hazy Center, the annexe of the National Air and Space Museum that opened at Washington Dulles International Airport in 2003. The opening day saw a protest that focused on the plane, with the complaint that the accompanying information did not discuss the effects of the bomb. The protesters included atomic-bomb survivors from Japan, and a container of red paint, symbolising blood, was thrown at the plane, denting it. The complaint of the protesters accorded with the views of some historians, but the Museum Director, John Dailey, an ex-general, defended the Smithsonian's policy: 'we're going to present the aircraft primarily in terms of its technical capabilities and leave the interpretation as to how it was used to the visitor'.

This approach lessened the emotional charge, but was criticised on the grounds of failing to provide adequate contextualisation, which is a complaint also directed against Japanese treatment of the sufferings at Hiroshima and Nagasaki, as well as by Japanese visitors concerned by the commemoration at Pearl Harbor; a commemoration that in fact has changed greatly over the years.[29]

The academic debate over the use of the atom bombs remains a vexed one, not least with frequent claims that they were not necessary to ensure Japanese surrender but were used in order to intimidate the Soviet Union into being more accommodating in Europe, and to restrict its gains in the Far East by ensuring a rapid Japanese surrender, one moreover that would not require Soviet assistance in an invasion of Japan itself.[30] An identical claim about the impact on the Soviets was to be made about the devastating Dresden air raid.

At the popular level, similar charges were made about the use of the atom bombs. Thus, the director of Philip Glass's opera *Dr Atomic* gave interviews in London in 2009 repeating all the familiar accusations. Memorialisation plays a different role in the particular context of 'Japanese' America, for example the Japanese Garden in Balboa Park in San Diego which has a strongly 'apologist' feel, not least with memorials to the dead of Hiroshima.

Anti-Americanism has been involved in some criticism of the dropping of the atom bombs, which, so far, have only been used by the USA. There is also a critique of their use as an aspect of opposition to modernism: the use of atom bombs ushered in a form of warfare in which unprecedented power could be wielded by very few units; and, alongside the terrible destruction, this appeared greatly disconcerting, indeed apocalyptic, to many observers. More Japanese had been killed in the conventional bombing earlier in 1945 – the firebombing of Tokyo on 9–10 March 1945 killing more than 100,000 on one night, but that campaign required more planes and raids.[31] Although there was no comparison in scale, the Japanese had also begun air attacks on Asian cities, both in China from 1937 and in their war of expansion from 1941, notably against Rangoon on 23 December 1941. These cities were poorly, if at all, protected.

Given the fighting determination and ferocity the Japanese had already displayed in defence, it is understandable in the context of the time that the atomic bombs should have been used to try to ensure a speedy Japanese surrender.[32] In the face of the total warfare of conflict between the Allies and Japan, the atom bombs offered a short-circuiting by modern warfare, and one that was the logical consequence of strategic bombing doctrine. The heavy Japanese and American losses on Iwo Jima, Okinawa and Luzon suggested that an invasion of Japan, in the face of a suicidal determination to fight on, would be very costly. The Japanese XIV Area Army in Luzon lacked fuel, ammunition and air support, but the Americans suffered more than 140,000 casualties in their operations on the island. The Japanese Homeland Army was poorly trained and equipped, and lacked mobility and air support, but, on the defensive faced by an Allied invasion, it would have the capacity to cause heavy casualties.[33]

Moreover, on 23 June 1945, the Japanese Diet passed a volunteer military service law establishing the People's Volunteer Combat Corps. Building on the People's Volunteer Units, established by the Cabinet on 23 March 1945 and designed to help the military in tasks such as road repair and air defence, the new Corps was to be raised from men aged from 15 to 60 and women aged from 17 to 40 and was to provide local defence. The lack of weapons, however, ensured training with bamboo spears and staves.

General Douglas MacArthur remarked to a British general in April 1945 that his troops had not yet met the Japanese army properly, and that when they did they were going to take heavy casualties. Indeed, much of the Japanese army was not involved in the Pacific War, being deployed in China. President Truman wrote of his decision to use the atom bomb, 'My object is to save as many American lives as possible'.[34] The same thinking was encapsulated in the Vietnam War American slogan of 'expend bombs, not bodies'. Ensuring an end to the war also prevented large-scale military (and civilian) fatalities elsewhere, for example arising from Operation Zipper, the British amphibious invasion of western Malaya, which had been planned for 9 September 1945.

Had a compromise peace been negotiated, as the Japanese military hoped to achieve through wrecking an American invasion of the southern island of Kyushu, the planned destination for the initial American attack, then critics would have focused on the fact or terms of such a compromise. This point is also relevant to discussion of the possibility of a negotiated peace with the German generals. Barton Bernstein has also pointed out the analytical problem, namely 'that there had long been a gap between the nation's military weakness and its vulnerability to air attacks and an invasion, and the acceptance of defeat by key Japanese leaders'.[35]

This gap, which was apparent from November 1944, needs to be borne in mind when considering the counterfactuals of not using the bomb, and also the debate on revisionist views on relative guilt. At the Potsdam Conference, the Allied leaders had issued the Potsdam Declaration on 26 July 1945, demanding unconditional surrender, as well as the occupation of Japan, Japan's loss of its overseas possessions, and the establishment of democracy in the country. It was unclear, however, how best to obtain this surrender. The threatened alternative from the Allied leaders at Potsdam was 'prompt and utter destruction', but, on 27 July, the Japanese government decided to ignore the declaration.

In the event, the dropping of the atom bombs shockingly demonstrated, even more than the firebombing of Tokyo, that Japanese forces could not protect the homeland. This weakness was underlined by the Soviet success in speedily overrunning the key puppet state of Manchuria, or Manchukuo. The invasion, launched on 8 August, removed any chance that the Soviets would act as mediators for a peace on more generous terms than those otherwise to be obtained from the USA, although it was the use of the bombs that led Japan to surrender.[36]

It is also pertinent to emphasise the German and Japanese attempts to develop nuclear armaments.[37] Their failure highlights the intellectual ability, organisational sophistication and resources available for the American's Manhattan Project. The Axis nuclear projects underline the extent to which the understanding of civilians as legitimate targets for mass-slaughter was a widespread one.[38]

In the passage quoted above, Truman, writing of his decision to use the atom bomb, continued, 'but I also have a human feeling for the women and children of Japan'. Had the war continued, civilian casualties would indeed have been immense. Aside from the direct and indirect consequences of an invasion, the continuation of the conventional bombing campaign would have been very costly, both directly and indirectly. For instance, had the war lasted to 1946, then the destruction of the Japanese rail system by bombing would have led to famine, as it would have been impossible to move food supplies. Counterintuitively, therefore, the use of atom bombs, however lethal and lasting, can be seen as a devastating but limited strike to achieve the total war goal of unconditional surrender without having to resort to a fight to the finish.

Meanwhile, as a reminder of the role of the present in the reconsideration of the past, the treatment of the War in the Pacific in the USA was reinvigorated for the American public by the experience of the terrorist attacks of 2001. Although Pearl Harbor, a surprise attack in peacetime, was very different to the September 11 attacks, each served as a reference to and for the other.

At the same time, Pearl Harbor did not serve to excite American criticism of modern Japanese policy. The same point was true as a whole of Japan's conduct in World War Two. A significant instance occurred in early 2014. The Japanese kamikaze pilots mounted suicide attacks on Allied (principally American but also British) warships, about 4,000 being killed in the process in an unsuccessful attempt to prevent the growing pressure on the Japanese Home Islands at the close of the war. The pilots' base in Minamikyushu became the site of the Chiran Peace Museum for Kamikaze Pilots, and officials in the city proposed in 2014 to have the letters written by the pilots included in the UNESCO Memory of the World programme, the list of important world history documents.

The Chinese state news agency, Xinhua, ran an editorial calling for the rejection of the request, using the headline: 'Kamikaze letters bid for world memory disgraces Japan itself'. The article added:

> How could the letters evoke peace? Kamikaze attackers were an insane creature of Japan's past militarism and the pilots were fanatic spiritual followers of the horrible policy and parts of Japan's war machines.
>
> It is hoped that UNESCO could turn down the application of the kamikaze letters, as if it succeeds there would be someone who will file Adolf Hitler's *Mein Kampf* as the world memory and the notorious Yasukuni Shrine as world heritage.[39]

In contrast, there was no formal American response. The role of present politics was clear in these contrasting attitudes.

The end of empires

To end this chapter with the controversies over the use of the atom bombs may appear logical, but also overlooks the greater salience of the war in continental Asia for the countries there, and, in particular, the extent to which postwar narratives of the war did not always align with the debates within the leading principals: the USA, Japan and China. Instead, the role of the war in weakening, if not ending, empires was a key aspect of narratives within former colonies. The prestige and power of these empires had been shattered by defeat. This was notably the case with the humiliating British loss of Malaya, Singapore and Burma in 1941–2 in campaigns in which British forces were completely and rapidly out-fought. In September 1944, Admiral Sir Geoffrey Layton, Commander-in-Chief Ceylon (now Sri Lanka), argued for:

> the vital importance of our recapturing those parts of the Empire as far as possible ourselves. I would specially mention the recapture of Burma and its culmination in the recovery of Singapore by force of arms and not by waiting for it to be surrendered as part of any peace treaty ... the immense effect this will have on our prestige in the Far East in postwar years. This and only this in my opinion will restore us to our former level in the eyes of the native population in these parts.

Admiral Louis Mountbatten, Supreme Commander of South-East Asia Command, strongly agreed,[40] as did Churchill. In the event, there was to be no such outcome. Britain regained much of its Asian Empire on the coattails of the American use of the atom bombs, and then helped the French and Dutch to regain their colonies, a process that involved fighting with local nationalists and, ironically, some use of support by Japanese forces that had surrendered. Yet, the British Empire also came to a rapid end, and both where British forces did drive out the Japanese (Burma) and where they retained control throughout the war (India).[41]

In part, this collapse of the European empires reflects the extent to which the imperial powers were only ever in partial control of the fate of their colonies; and this partial control looks towards the subsequent narratives of the newly-independent colonies. India provides an important instance, not least because it was a key participant in the war (and not only against Japan), even though as a colony, and not as an independent state. Indeed, India provided the largest volunteer force in history, including about 500,000 troops who served overseas. Moreover, the Royal Indian Navy increased from eight minor warships to 117 combat vessels and 30,000 men. During the war, there was a major shift in military culture, with a determined attempt by the British to promote Indians, as well as recruitment from races such as South Indians, hitherto seen as lacking in martial quality. There were problems with the quality of parts of the army, including issues of combat motivation, but its general loyalty was good and morale rose with success in 1944.[42]

The relationships between the major Indian war effort[43] and the views of both the Congress Party and of those in the Indian National Army who looked to Japan for aid in expelling the British by force were obscured by Congress's postwar dominance of the national myth, one that linked the war to independence in 1947 and that focused on Congress's Quit India campaign of 1942, a campaign of civil disobedience directed against the British and one that in part arose from anger at the Viceroy's commitment of India to war against the Axis in 1939 without consulting nationalist leaders.

Yet again, the political resonances of the war are one of the most interesting aspects of the conflict.[44] Although an individual stance, the attitude of Radhabinad Pal, the Indian judge at the Tokyo war crimes trials, was also indicative, as he insisted that all the Japanese accused were not guilty of any crime; in effect excusing Japanese aggression and conduct towards civilians. There has also been discussion in India, albeit less comfortably than over Congress's position, of Subhas Chandra Bose and the Indian National Army, with their anti-British nationalism emphasised and their role as a Japanese client force[45] underrated. Bose is regarded in his home province of Bengal as a great nationalist leader, which he had been before World War Two, and Kolkata (Calcutta) airport is named after him, but his status elsewhere in India is far more ambivalent. Indeed, he provides a fascinating case of how memory varies, even within a single country. Bose visited the Andaman Islands while they were under Japanese occupation: at the same time the Japanese authorities there were treating the local population with considerable brutality.

Unlike in the case of Germany, which had lost its empire with World War One, there was already a Japanese empire prior to World War Two, but it collapsed with Japan's defeat. From 1945, in both North and South Korea, the impact of Japanese rule from 1910 was depicted as unrelentingly brutal. There was an emphasis on atrocities, not least enforced prostitution for Japanese troops, and, conversely, the erasure from the record of extensive Korean collaboration with Japan. The same process was seen with Taiwan. South Korean and North Korean politicians have both referred to the history of Japanese occupation when playing the nationalist card against Japan. This has helped make it difficult for the USA to ensure co-operation between South Korea and Japan in containing both North Korea and China, a problem that angered American policymakers in 2013–14.

For Thailand, an ally of Japan in 1942–4, which was then able to reconcile itself to the Allies, the erasure was that of a co-operation with Japan which yielded wartime territorial gains from Malaya and Burma, as well as of the conflict with France in early 1941, which had also yielded territory from the French colonies of Laos and Cambodia. Relations with Thailand also exposed differences between the Allies, differences which were not restricted to American hostility to British imperialism. There were tensions between Britain, which treated Thailand as an enemy from which territory could be gained in the Kra Isthmus, and the USA which saw Thailand as occupied by Japan. Successful American pressure ensured lenient peace terms for Thailand.

The memory politics seen in the Asian states were more generally true of the process by which World War Two played a key role in the discussion and deployment of national identities in East and South-East Asia,[46] although, as discussed later, by no means necessarily the leading role. The role of the war in the development, discussion and deployment of national identities within the international and imperial structures of the European colonial world is a lasting consequence of the struggle, and one still influential today.

The end result

Indeed, this result helps address a point about the limited lasting legacy of war that echoes a wider, but mistaken, sense of the futility of conflict. In a review of a volume in Jonathan Sumption's account of the Anglo–French Hundred Years' War (1337–1453), Christopher Hart observed:

> Looking down the long, blood-smeared telescope of history at this terrible series of war, punctuated only by calamitous harvests, peasants' revolts and further outbreaks of bubonic plague, the question of who was right and who was wrong seems almost laughable. The combatants – English, Welsh, French, Portuguese, Berber, Turk – all had God on their side. Yet all we can do now is survey the wrecked battlefields, the sacked towns, the desolated valleys of the Loire and the Gironde, the massacred women and children of Limoges, and wonder that it achieved little.[47]

The accuracy of this presentation of the Hundred Years' War, and even for the period covered in the volume of Sumption's work, 1369–99, is dubious, not least as the war was highly important both to the development of English and French nationhood and to the growth of parliamentary governance in England.

Yet, Hart's comment is of importance for the subject of this book, as it reflects a modern tendency to stress the futility of war and, by implication, the moral equivalence of all combatants, an approach towards World War One widely (and mistakenly) taken at the time of the centenary of its start.[48] Moreover, Hart's point requires discussion in this chapter, as it is likely to be the use of the atomic bombs that commands particular attention in terms of the lasting memory of the fighting, or, at least, for Japan and the West; although not for China nor for Russia. This attention will be the case whether such weaponry is used anew or not, as, in the former case, 1945 will be treated as worthy of consideration, because it saw their first employment and, in the latter case, their sole employment.

So, consider for a moment a review, like that by Hart, written six centuries hence of World War Two. The reviewer, pointing out that the combatants all claimed good cause, notes the resulting devastation, doubtless focusing on the atom bombs. Merit, if at all awarded, becomes that of having caused fewest civilian casualties, which could leave the British and Chinese on the moral high ground in Asia, as opposed to the Americans and, even more, Japanese, while the moral high ground in Europe might, ironically, but maybe typically, be claimed for the French, or the Swiss and the Swedes.

As already indicated, however, and the theme will be taken further in the next chapter, there is a significance to the fighting in Asia, as there also was in the Hundred Years' War, namely their formative role for the development of nations. This point even pertains in Europe where World War Two superficially brought less change. It is true that the nation state remained the dominant model in Europe, and indeed one confirmed by the enforced large-scale population expulsions, that territorial boundaries changed relatively little, and that a potent empire, that of the Soviet Union, dominated Eastern Europe from the last stage of the war until 1989. Yet, in destroying Nazi ideology and German imperialism, World War Two was formative for the development of Europe's states, and also helped in the advancing of a different concept of European co-operation, even unity, one shot through with multiple problems but scarcely the problems posed by the Third Reich.

Thus, the question of, to quote Hart, 'who was right and who was wrong' is scarcely 'laughable', although, for World War Two in both Europe and Asia, it is sometimes easier to see 'wrong' than 'right'. To note two, very different, cases, German power, like its Japanese counterpart, was wrong, but the 'right' posed by the Soviet advance or by the re-introduction of colonial rule, for example in French Indo-China and the Dutch East Indies, was, and is, very much open to qualification, and both were resisted by local political movements. The latter, indeed, helped ensure that the re-introduction of colonial rule proved only temporary in Asia.

To link the use of violence to the issue of right and wrong flies in the face of much modern thought, notably both anti-war arguments and moral relativism, but, however superficially plausible, neither is ultimately pertinent for the war in Asia, no more than for its European counterpart. The use of force to destroy tyranny was both necessary and a noble aim that justified the sacrifice and the killing. The loss was shared, but not the rectitude nor the reason of the struggle.

CHAPTER SEVEN

Conclusions

World War Two, as re-fought by apologists and commentators, filmmakers and novelists, journalists and historians, can appear ridiculous, even prurient, compared to the grievous suffering and enormous loss of those directly involved in the war. Yet, this contention is important, indeed crucial, to the way in which this suffering and loss are understood and remembered, and more so as those directly involved die, and their lives can only be remembered by others and through the efforts of others. This understanding, in turn, reflects both wartime and subsequent political circumstances. Thus, in Britain, where the war was conducted by a coalition government, it was diffused (and defused) as a wider social memory with an emphasis on national cohesion. In contrast, in the Soviet Union, there was a more political focus on the role of the Communist state under Stalin in winning the 'Great Patriotic War'. That legacy was complicated from the 1990s by the divergence between a revived nationalism and a defunct Communism, but the nationalist account of the war won out.

Contention over World War Two is frequently bitter as well as directly linked to central issues of national identity and political affiliation. In November 2013, the Hungarian legacy from the war was contested in central Budapest as a new statue was unveiled. The subject was an unimpressive bust of Miklós Horthy (1868–1957), Regent of Hungary from 1920 till 1944, and an increasingly equivocal ally of Germany until he was overthrown in October 1944 by Hungarian Fascists supported by German special forces. In Budapest, the statue was endorsed by the far-right Jobbik party, but condemned by the Left. The governing Centre-Right Fidesz party adopted a more equivocal stance, in part because of its ambivalent stance towards both Hungarian populism today and the interwar legacy. Political calculation also played a role, as Fidesz sought support across the Right.

Horthy's policy toward Hungary's Jews causes particular controversy, with the argument that he bore responsibility for the mass deportations to slaughter in Auschwitz in 1944. Some 425,000 were deported, with the active support of Hungarian officials. Again, the historical issue relates to present legitimation, notably in a European Union concerned about Fidesz's authoritarian and populist tendencies. A Fidesz government itself instituted Holocaust Memorial Day in 2001, founded the Budapest Holocaust Memorial Centre in 2002, and established a commission to commemorate the 70th anniversary of the 1944 deportations. In 2013, Tibor Navracsics, the Fidesz Deputy Prime Minister, declared that the Hungarian state had, in 1944, turned on its own Jewish citizens. Thus, he did not seek to shift the blame to the Germans as many had done. On the other hand, there have been accusations of whitewashing wartime collaboration, while the government's treatment of Hungary's Roma (Gypsies) has been a matter of great controversy and has led critics to make reference to the war: the Roma were brutally persecuted by the Germans in an attempted genocide.

If war, therefore, is in part a matter of politics by other means, this is even more the case with the recollection of war. Much of this book addresses this issue within the context of the particular politics of individual states, but there is also the issue of more general moral considerations, indeed politics. The morality of the conflict is one that has engaged many commentators, but, in turn, that can produce a contest of different moralities. In Chapter 5, there was reference to the views of M. R. D. Foot and Nicholson Baker on the British bombing of Germany, yet there are other, very different, views, not only of the bombing but also of the struggle as a whole. For example, Mickael Burleigh's *Moral Combat. A History of World War II* (2010) criticised Baker for establishing a moral equivalence of death by attacking Allied bombing, while M. R. D. Foot's comment on babies (see p. 136) can be contrasted by the engagement offered by Andrew Roberts in his *The Storm of War. A New History of the Second World War* (2009): 'Even two-thirds of a century later, it is still impossible not to feel fury against Hitler and the Nazis for forcing baby Rita Gains to grow up without her father'.

A key element in the memorialisation of the war is what can be termed, in writing about the Holocaust, 'diminishment'; in short, not the denial of the Holocaust, for which you have to be bad, mad or both, but its attempted diminishment by discussing it alongside other outrages. This approach does violence to the particular horrors of the Holocaust; and similar points can, and should, be made about attempts to rewrite other aspects of World War Two. Most prominently, the fact that the Allies, particularly, but not only, the Soviets, were responsible for terrible episodes, and that Soviet conduct is a permanent stain on that past empire, not least because this conduct captured its essential instrumentality and brutality towards people, does not lessen the evil of the Axis cause. Moreover, attempts to relativise the two sides by stressing the common horror of war, the experience of combat, the miseries of occupation, and the strains of the Home Front, miss the point about Axis intentions. These attempts also miss the central role of the Axis in causing the war, in both Asia and Europe, and in sustaining it, with heavy casualties, even when Germany and Japan were clearly losing and had obviously lost.

An instructive example from the time about the deficiencies of this focus on common horror was provided by George Lansbury, the pacifist former leader of the Labour Party, an honourable but mistaken figure, who told the House of Commons on 3 September 1939, as the British declaration of war on Germany was debated:

The cause that I and a handful of friends represent is this morning apparently going down to ruin, but I think we ought to take heart of courage from the fact that after 2,000 years of war and strife, at least, even those who enter upon this colossal struggle have to admit that in the end force has not settled, and cannot and will not settle anything. I hope that out of this terrible calamity there will arise a real spirit, a spirit that will compel people to give up reliance on force, and that perhaps this time humanity will learn the lesson and refuse in the future to put its trust in poison gas, in the massacre of little children and universal slaughter.

Yet, there was to be a potent difference between the two sides, and Lansbury ironically captured this with his phrase 'put its trust in poison gas, in the massacre of little children and universal slaughter'. Those of course were Nazi remedies and goals, and not those of Britain. The Nazi regime might try to sustain German public commitment to the war in 1944–5 by holding out the prospect of mass slaughter at the hands of the Soviets, but the latter was neither their intention nor what occurred. In contrast, the Germans could, and did, follow genocide as a policy. In reply to Lansbury, Churchill, on 3 September 1939, told the Commons:

This is not a question of fighting for Danzig [Gdansk] or fighting for Poland. We are fighting to save the whole world from the pestilence of Nazi tyranny and in defence of all that is most sacred to man. This is no war for domination or imperial aggrandisement or material gain, no war to shut any country out of its sunlight and means of progress. It is a war, viewed in its inherent quality, to establish on impregnable rocks, the rights of the individual, and it is a war to establish and revive the stature of man.

That was scarcely true of Britain's eventual ally, Stalin, but, looked at objectively, and with an understanding of context, it is clear that Lansbury was wrong. War did end the Nazi and Imperial Japanese regimes. Pacifism did not, and could not have done so. Moreover, to take a current perspective, and to suggest that Nazi Germany could have fallen as Communist rule in Europe and the Soviet Union was to do in 1989–91, in other words through the efforts of domestic opposition and without war, is to misunderstand completely the nature of Nazi Germany, not only of the regime but also, more contentiously yet accurately, of the widespread support that it enjoyed and, indeed, was able to retain in 1943–5 despite repeated defeats.

Furthermore, Allied failure in the war would have had terrible consequences, and to all the combatants, the Germans and Japanese as well as the
Allies. Allowing for the frequently flawed use of counterfactual arguments,
it is appropriate to consider these possible outcomes, both because these
arguments were employed at the time, and as they also throw light on the
likely consequences of inaction or failure. However dire the consequences
for Eastern Europe of the Soviet system that prevailed from the war for
another 45 years, the situation would have been far worse had Germany
continued as a Nazi state and aggressive empire. A similar point can be
made as far as the Japanese war is considered, albeit with the caveat that
North Korea is still ruled by a vicious dictatorship. The situation, however,
is very different in South Korea.

The continuing resonance of these issues, notably, but not only, in
Western culture, does not simply reflect their significance for national
identities, a point shared by a range of combatants. There is also the
extent to which key aspects of the war are deployed in order to establish
and demonstrate moral standards. The role of the Holocaust, and thus of
Holocaust denial, in establishing a pathological 'other' that can provide
universal values for the EU is particularly notable. In 2007, Germany
utilised its presidency of the EU to ensure the passage of race-hate laws for
the entire union.

The likely future direction of these discussions is worthy of consideration, for the war ended nearly 70 years ago, and will soon be receding
into a situation, without living witness, to match World War One. In
particular, it is unclear how far World War Two will remain significant as
a basic source of national identities and a key standard for discussion of
international relations and international law. In many respects, it does so
because there is a lack of comparable national narratives for many states.
On the global scale, the key other element is decolonisation, whether in the
New World in 1775–1830 or in the Old World in 1945–75. Decolonisation
acts as the origin moment of modern states, going back in the case of the
USA to 1776. The resonance of these episodes remains strong, not least
because in many states in which the formative experience has occurred over
the last 70 years, it is linked to current political groupings, for example the
Congress Party in India and the African National Congress in South Africa.

This legacy was also for a while true of World War Two, notably with
the Gaullists in France, with the Communist state in the Soviet Union, with
the Tito system in Yugoslavia, with the Communist Party in China, and
with the role of the Left in the Resistance in Italy. However, these links have
been weakened by time and disrupted by circumstance. Moreover, their
future traction, in, say, 50 years, will probably be weak.

The decolonisation narrative, however, is not possible for most of
the combatants in World War Two, with the significant complicating
exception of the states of Eastern Europe and the Soviet Union brought
under the Communist sway in the 1940s and freed from it in 1989–91.

Instead, the war offers narratives for winners and losers. For the former, it serves as a source and expression of an exemplary national identity, with an existential threat rising to a peak in a crisis that showed the mettle of national character, and thus acts as a rallying point for present and future. This approach flattens the rest of the historical landscape, or treats it with reference solely to the crisis.

In doing so, the war offers an incorporating approach that is more widely diffused than one that is useful largely, or solely, to one political movement. That has certainly been the approach in Britain and the USA, and has also been significant in Russia once (non-Communist) nationalism became a more prominent part of the political landscape after the fall of the Soviet Union. In France, although they also served as implicit criticisms of President Mitterrand and of the National Front, the apologies for the crimes of Vichy offered under President Chirac served to help move the war from the partisan to the national scale. In China, the national dimension has been emphasised in the use of the war as a nationalist tool against Japan. At the same time, the war serves to maintain the role of the Communist Party in China as part of an account in which the Party has played the key role in protecting China from multiple external threats and internal challenges.

A focus on Europe, indeed, can be intensely misleading. The majority, indeed a growing majority, of the world's population live outside the West, and, while greatly affected by the conflict, were so in accordance with a different narrative to that of Europe. China and India, the world's two most populous states, were in many respects transformed by the conflict; although, in each case, this transformation was also an instance of the accentualisation of prewar trends: the rise of Communism and the decline of British imperial power respectively. As part of the British Empire, India produced the largest volunteer army in history, but there is a marked degree of ambivalence in modern India about the war, in part because participation is seen as at the behest of the imperial power. Although figures are difficult to establish with certainty, China suffered the largest number of casualties of any of the combatants or the largest number after the Soviet Union.

There is also ambivalence in modern views in the world's fourth most populous state, Indonesia. There, the war replaced Dutch rule by that of Japan in 1942, and helped build up demands for independence, demands that were to come to a successful fruition in 1949. Indeed, a demographically-loaded account of World War Two would put the accent on Japan's war, and not Germany's, and, moreover, for Japan's war, on the conquests in East and South-East Asia, and not those in the Pacific. An emphasis on Japan's war cannot but help link the conflict to the postwar political changes: decolonisation in India and Indonesia, and the triumph of Communism in China, all completed within five years. The parallel is with the close linkage between the war and the onset of Communist rule in Eastern Europe.

In the case of India, Indonesia and China, it is not surprising that a causal link is drawn between the war and the subsequent developments, and, thus, that the war is understood in large part in terms of these developments. This situation is a key element of the politics of the war, and helps explain why they cannot be studied in isolation from what came later.

It is likely that this elision of conflict and context, the latter understood in terms of subsequent developments, will become more insistent. Given the value attached to the outcome of the end of Western imperial control, and the degree to which the war in Asia is attributed to Japan, the net result in the long term may well be an acceptance of the heavily-inaccurate Japanese account propagated in the 1940s, namely that the war was a rejection of Western imperialism. This is still an account offered by some Japanese commentators as part of the debate over the causes of the war in Asia.

Yet, this approach will be challenged by the powerful animosity between Japanese and Chinese historical accounts. Precisely because China was not a Western colony in 1937, the war there can be presented in terms of an imperialist assault mounted by Japan, itself a reasonable charge which captures much of the dynamic and intentions of Japanese aggression. As a reminder of complexity, it is necessary to add a longer-lasting Japanese animosity towards China, the great power just over the horizon and one towards which the Japanese had a long-standing inferiority complex. This perception of Japanese aggression, and the linked anger over Japanese conduct, are likely to remain the case even if China ceases to be Communist. While it remains Communist, the 1940s will continue to play a crucial role in the foundation account of modern China, an account that very much locates the war with Japan as a crucial episode.

There is no parallel position for any major state in the West. The war was responsible for the formation of the Fourth Republic in France and, out of the Occupation by Britain, France and the USA, of West Germany. However, in each case, the political situation was subsequently to be transformed fundamentally, with consequences for the relevant historical foundation myth of the state. The Fourth Republic was replaced by the Fifth in 1958, although de Gaulle's key role as the first, and formative, President of the latter ensured that the war continued to play an important role in the politics of French nationalism. This role, however, has changed with the decline of the historical account of Gaullism as the central theme of the French Right, and, indeed, with the move on the Right from an historical account of French politics. Instead, a more managerial prospectus has been offered by the conventional Right, while the National Front does not focus on the details of the war and, instead, seeks to propagate its more mythical version of an essential French identity. West Germany itself was transformed into Germany following the fall of the Iron Curtain in 1989, and this transformation required a different narrative of recent German history.

More profoundly, the constitutional basis of European states changed greatly with the creation of the European Economic Community (EEC) in 1957 and its subsequent development. The historical myth deployed by the European Union (EU) was ambiguous about aspects of the war, in part because of its potentially divisive character: the EEC, the basis of the EU, included West Germany and Italy from the outset, as two of the original six members, while the other four, France, Belgium, the Netherlands and Luxembourg, had all been occupied in 1940.

An acknowledgment and rejection of the Holocaust in place of an earlier elision[1] became a central theme in the European Union,[2] notably from the 1990s, and, even more, the 2000s, in part because it could be employed against the Far Right, and also testified to a repentance by the EU's leading power, Germany. However, on the other hand, attempts, especially by the new Eastern European members of the EU, to argue an equivalence between Communism and Nazism proved highly disruptive in the 2000s and 2010s. These attempts captured the extent to which the expansion of the European Union have made it difficult to project any historical account other than one that is, at once, vacuous in generalities, but illuminated by particular episodes held to be of specific importance.

Looking ahead, it is unclear how far it will be possible to retain the current (confused) situation in European public history. One challenge is posed by the large numbers in immigrant communities in Europe and the extent to which the war does not often have particular meaning for them, nor indeed a meaning comparable to that held by the host community. Thus, the 3,000,000 Turks in Germany are descendants of one of the few powers to remain neutral for most of the conflict, and Turkey had no experience of German aggression or occupation. Were the European Union to be expanded to include Turkey, then the situation would be still more problematic.

What can be anticipated in Europe and elsewhere, is a period in which existing collective memories and established accounts face increased obsolescence for part of the population, an obsolescence accompanied by periodic attempts to press the salience of the war. These attempts will be most pronounced in the case of the victors; and there will probably be a repetition, with the final survivors of World War Two, of the recent memorialisation focused on World War One. For the young across Europe, and in certain other states, there will be a continuing emphasis on the Holocaust in the educational process, although this emphasis will probably be vociferously resisted by some Muslims, as in France in 2013–14. There will also be more (misplaced) calls for comparative treatment of the Holocaust alongside other historical episodes, most prominently the Slave Trade from Africa to the New World. Aside from misguided public remarks on this topic, there is also academic discussion of it.[3]

Yet, looking ahead for 50 years, the situation appears less likely to be one of an adapted continuation of the present; and the same is likely to be even more true of the situation 50 years later. Indeed, it is instructive, in this context, to consider what of the world of 1845 is understood today. This point may not capture the ability of some historical moments, episodes and developments to maintain a powerful and long-lasting after-impact in memorialisation and even contention, for example the Crusades, which began in the 1090s. Nevertheless, this process is challenged by the impact of time and the loss of perspective and understanding that can come with time. For example, in his scathing review of the film *The Reader*, which deals with the Holocaust, Frederick Raphael commented on how it has proved possible, and very misleadingly so, to treat German killers, and their victims, in 'a common category of history's unfortunate little people'.[4]

Such erroneous elisions of truth and judgment may well become more common. They will serve a variety of goals, from rabid revisionism to the more insidious cause of conveniently reconsidering uncomfortable episodes, not least in an attempt to gain 'closure', to pursue reconciliation, and to create a universal account. Elisions thus serve to deal with individual and collective guilt, enabling not only a forgetfulness but also an active excusing of the inexcusable. Indeed, with time, the war will very probably become an episode, rather than a moral standpoint. In 1967, Richard Glover, a Canadian historian, could use a comparison of Mussolini joining Hitler against Britain in 1940 in order to present in a very poor light the American decision to declare war on Britain in 1812 while the latter was at war with Napoleon.[5] Such a comparison has scant impact in 2014.

In becoming an issue of, rather than for, commemoration, the politics of World War Two will therefore be not only how the war is memorialised, but even whether it is commemorated at all. The likely lessening of public provision in commemoration may well mean that the memorialisation is most pronounced at the level of individual communities whose historical memory is particularly focused on the struggle. Thus, far from being 'a topic less charged with both emotions and taboos',[6] or one characterised by a 'more normalised and less emotionally fraught relationship' to the past,[7] the war will probably be an aspect of the politics of loss, and one that sits alongside other such episodes.

The situation will be affected by contingencies, notably the possibility of other wars coming to the fore, but also by social and cultural trends, particularly a reaction against what is defined as bellicosity or nationalism. The changing treatment of World War One is instructive. In that case, the emphasis in 2014 was on casualties and suffering, and not on eventual success for the Western Allies.

At the same time, pushing forward another type of commemoration, World War Two will continue to be a great gift to the film industry, not least because of the scale and tragedy of the conflict, which remains unmatched. Yet, a probable switch in emphasis within that industry, from the USA to Asia, may well mean that different emphases are offered. In the case of China, the stress is likely to be on the conflict prior to 1939 as many of the heroic episodes, such as the defence of the Shanghai region against

Japanese attack in 1937, occurred then. The latter stages of the conflict were particularly unsuccessful.

Given the salience of visual images in our appreciation of World War Two, the development of export markets for Chinese and Indian war films of this period would be of great importance to their wider impact, although it is unclear how easy these films would find it to penetrate into Western markets. The numerous Soviet films on the war had no such impact.[8]

If film will be a key battlefield for the memory of the war, it will be so as an aspect of a general visual culture that will include computer games and other interactive media well attuned to use for wargaming. The resulting opportunities for partisanship are far greater than what might be provided in the field of historical scholarship, but the latter should be seen as distinctly secondary in the public understanding of the past and in the 'history wars' by which this understanding is contested. The idea of a 'trickle-down' from scholarship to the wider public is comforting to scholars, but largely erroneous.

Yet, it is still worth considering how the scholarship might develop. It is most probable that there will be a greater accent on the underrated aspects of the conflict, notably the war in China, which remains largely underplayed in the scholarship produced elsewhere, and inadequately covered in that produced within China. This emphasis will ensure that the account of the war with Japan remains very different in China and the USA. The former account may well come to have greater influence elsewhere, although the resonance of the American experience within the Anglosphere will remain very strong.

Turning to another issue, the extent to which failing powers look to World War Two for the validation of their role is clear in the case of Britain and, to a lesser but still readily-apparent case, Russia; and notably so as far as their martial memory and their sense of a special role are concerned. For Britain, being on the winning side in the war encouraged a long period of 'self-deception about Britain's world status',[9] one arguably sustained in the 1980s and 1990s by the consequences of the availability of North Sea oil, and in the 1990s and early to mid-2000s by the expansion of the financial services industry.

The war serves not only as an important and heroic episode in the historical myth of the victors, but also as a demonstration of a one-time role now tarnished by problems, if not relative decline. During the 1960s and 1970s, World War Two provided the USA with a counterpoint to the Vietnam War. 'Declinists' argue that a USA in difficulties looks for solace to World War Two. This certainly seems apparent as a reaction to dysfunctional difficulties in the American political system. In Russia, the Putin government has made much of the war as a proof of Russia's supposed status, not only as a great power, but also as a great power with a key mission validated by history.

In Britain, for the *Daily Mail* of 19 March 2009 to devote its front page to an attack on the government for failing to subsidise veterans so that they could visit the D-Day invasion beaches, was both an attack on the Labour government, one made explicit in the article, and a reminder of past national glory. The latter was particularly comforting given the fiscal and economic crisis of the period. At one level, therefore, an escapism was involved, but this escapism was particularly pointed due to its direct reference to past success.

At the same time, the divide between escapism and drawing lessons from the past is a tenuous one. Indeed, to make a political point of, or from, the past, it is necessary to simplify the latter; and this simplification generally entails a strong degree of escapism. So also does the very process of referring to the past for clear lessons, rather than underlining the controversial nature of the past and the problematic nature of its lessons, or, even, seeking the 'lessons' from a measured understanding of present issues.

If a role of the past is to provide apparently clear lessons, then World War Two will continue to resonate as long as it can be thus quarried. Of course, this quarrying will lead to a focus on what can be readily discussed in such terms. Thus, for Europeans, the Holocaust will be to the fore, followed, for the anglophone world, by Appeasement, but, for much of Eastern Europe, by the relationship between the war and the subsequent advance of Communist power. Pearl Harbor served in the USA as a basis for discussion of the 11 September 2001 terrorist attacks, and vice versa.

Where, however, such quarrying is less effective, then the war may well recede from attention or be diminished. Thus, in former Yugoslavia, the past for reference may become primarily that of the conflicts of the 1990s; and the 1940s may be understood largely in relation to them: there were indeed links in terms of animosities. Across Eastern Europe, the rejection of Communism may well come to dominate the historical record, not only the events of 1989–91, but also the Hungarian Rising of 1956 and the Solidarity Movement in 1980s Poland. The former was more heroic than wartime alliance with Germany, while both episodes looked towards the fall of Communism. At the same time, the willingness or otherwise of Western powers to support those in Eastern Europe against Soviet pressure led to references back to Appeasement as a frame of reference.[10]

Even in Israel, where there is an understandable stress on the Holocaust, it was not to the fore in the early years of independence,[11] and it is still the case that there is a stronger current of emphasis on the subsequent travails of the independent state itself. Thus, the Arab–Israeli Wars from 1948 provide the core narrative of the Israeli state, and not least due to the collective identity and experience represented by conscription. The Holocaust is incorporated into this narrative by being seen as a warning about the consequences of defeat. This reading is also offered to foreign, non-Israeli, audiences, as in the late 2000s and early 2010s with warnings about the alleged consequences if Iran developed the capacity to produce nuclear power.

Leaving aside the contentious question of the applicability of this argument, the argument again indicates the salience of World War Two in public discussion of the past. Unsurprisingly, the war does not have the same resonance in the Arab world, except as a cause of unwelcome international support for the foundation of Israel. This was also the theme of the Iranian President in his address to a United Nations' Conference at Geneva in 2009.

In part, World War Two saw an unsuccessful Islamic nationalism, notably in Iraq, Iran and Egypt, all of which were brought under Allied control in 1941–2, the first two by invasion and the last by the British use of force. Yet, this episode of Islamic nationalism does not resonate greatly in the modern Islamic world, as the governing regimes of today do not trace their identity to the 1940s. Furthermore, with the exception of the foundation of Israel, the decade does not have particular significance for Islamic fundamentalists. In addition, many of the key episodes of the conflict in the Islamic world involved fighting between Western powers. The Allies conquered Syria and Lebanon in 1941 and Morocco and Algeria in 1942, but from Vichy forces, and not from Arab nationalists. In Egypt, Libya and Tunisia, the conflict was between Allied and Axis forces and, again, did not involve Arab nationalists.

This point indicates the extent to which the applicability of the argument about the primacy of different issues in the Asian recollection of the war with Japan extends further. Indeed, as in that case, the key developments of the 1940s in the Middle East can be seen as those subsequent to the war, particularly Syria and Lebanon gaining independence from France, the establishment of Israel in 1948, and the First Arab–Israeli war, that of 1948–9. Each can be seen as a consequence of World War Two, but they also represented longer-term trends, such as rising nationalism in the Arab world, and prewar Arab–Jewish tension in Palestine, notably the Arab Rising of 1936–9.

Moreover, the local recollection of these events, understandably, is largely in terms of these long-term trends, rather than of the war itself. Drawing links between the long-term trends and the war frequently involves interjecting an unwelcome complexity and diluting the message that is being propagated. The mismatch is relatively apparent in North Africa. British veterans discuss the campaigns in great detail, and the memoirs from the 'battle of the generals' saw bitter contention over British command decisions in 1941–2. Yet, to the historians, commentators and public of the North African countries, these campaigns are of little relevance, indeed no more important than earlier and other campaigns in their history. This point will probably be echoed with the later local recollection of recent Western campaigning in Afghanistan and Iraq. Outside forces are likely to find their goals misunderstood and condemned, and their achievements ignored and denigrated.

For Egypt and Algeria, the key nationalist episodes occurred later, from the mid-1950s, with the struggles for independence and national sovereignty seen as being waged against the victors of World War Two; which necessarily complicates the understanding of the latter. The driving back of Axis forces from Egypt in 1942, the British conquest of Libya that year, the Anglo–American overthrow of Vichy forces in Morocco and Algeria in 1942, and the final defeat in Tunisia by the Allies of the Axis armies in North Africa in 1943, are not seen as liberation. The latter view was propagated in North Africa by the Gaullists and under the Fourth Republic, but it never struck much resonance; and opposition to French rule in Algeria began with the bloodily-suppressed Sétif uprising in May 1945. Talk of driving back Rommel and the Afrika Korps from the approaches to the Nile Valley in 1941–2 had a strong resonance in Britain, but the Egyptian response was far more complex, not least as the British presence was widely seen as unwelcome, while there were influential pro-German circles in Egypt. Both Nasser and, his successor, Sadat, used their role as nationalists during the war to boost their postwar popularity.

Moreover, even in Britain, the resonance of the Desert War of 1940–3 in North Africa, although strong while imperial themes played a major role in public consciousness, diminished markedly once this imperial role was lost. References to this experience at the time of the NATO air intervention in Libya in 2011 appeared misplaced and curious to many. Instead, ideas of imperial destiny seemed anachronistic, and the idea that Britain should have devoted so much effort during World War Two to holding Egypt less readily apparent. The revenge of the present and subsequent on the past was shown with the impact of the Suez Crisis of 1956 on the recollection of the war in the Middle East. Widespread opposition then to Anglo–French intervention against Egypt, and the failure of this intervention, ensured that Britain's wartime role in North Africa fewer than 20 years earlier appeared less appropriate, and indeed part of an unwelcome pattern of intervention. However, to make that point involves drawing clear-cut connections between episodes that, in practice, require modification, as well as entails suggesting a unity of views that is misleading.

This lack of unity is readily apparent for many of the former combatants. The discussion in Chapter 5 of the recollection of the war, and specifically of Vichy, in France, underlines a difference within states in basic assumptions that is also seen in Eastern Europe. Thus, the politics of the war, as in these states, can be a politics of division, a politics that sustains and represents this division.

In other states, such as Britain, Russia, and the USA, this politics seems to be more the case of supporting a relatively unitary public memory. These latter public memories, however, in practice, overlay different accounts within these states. At the most obvious, there were groups very clearly not included in this unitary public memory, such as interned Japanese-Americans and Japanese-Canadians or the millions detained in the Soviet *gulags*. Again, the equivalence here is misleading, as the treatment of people in the *gulags* was far harsher than that of the Japanese-Americans, and the process in the Soviet Union entailed a deeply compromised legality. Yet, even if these groups were excluded, there were still significant differences in the experience of the war within these states.

With time, the constant series of news stories about World War Two will abate in some respects. First, the death of survivors will be a factor, not least in ending the issue of war criminals escaping justice. When, in 2009, a Berlin court issued an arrest warrant for John Demjanjuk, a resident of Ohio who was said to be 'Ivan the Terrible', a murderous concentration camp guard, he was 88. *The Times* on 25 Marsh 2009 could devote considerable space to how the film *The Great Escape* misrepresented the experience of those involved in the escape from a German prisoner of war camp that was thus presented, an item that recurred in 2014. However, such a story, relying as it did on those involved, will not be possible a half-century later. The same is true of the powerful account of Shlomo Venezia, a Jew from Thessaloniki who survived being a member of the Auschwitz *Sonderkommando*. His account has now been published in English and French.[12] The interviewees able to discuss the murderous activities of the German *Einsatzgruppen* (and thus to provide evidence for Patrick Desbois's attempt in *The Holocaust by Bullets* (2009) to emphasise their slaughter of Jews), are dying off. Moreover, veterans will no longer be present for the unveiling of memorials, such as the US Navy Normandy D-Day Monument, dedicated on Utah Beach on 27 September 2008.

While veterans die off, so also will those whose frame of reference is the war. It was instructive to see the sender of the following letter in *The Times* on 19 May 2009:

> If the decision by the Court of Appeals that the European Convention on Human Rights applies even on the battlefield, would commanders in 1940 have found it impossible to send Fighter Command aircraft – outnumbered, outgunned and often underperformed by their Luftwaffe equivalents – into the Battle of Britain? If this had been the case, I wonder what human rights legislation would be in force now?

The sender was Group Captain John Platt (Retd).

More broadly, alongside the potency of traumatic events, such as World War Two and the Holocaust,[13] in the history of memory, a whole host of other issues will supervene in order to provide other subjects of commemoration and contention. In many respects, the Cold War did not serve this purpose in Europe as, with some exceptions, notably in Hungary in 1956, it lacked the drama of World War Two. More generally, there is the issue whether Communist rule provided a comparison with that of the Germans. Such a comparison was argued in Eastern Europe after the end of the Cold War, and indeed not without reason for the Stalin years, but this case had limited impact in the West and, in particular, in the world of Hollywood that plays such a role in sustaining images. Instead, the Nazis remained the key figures in villainy, as in two of the popular Indiana Jones films.

Looking ahead, however, it is likely that other issues will supervene, in part because the resonance of evil is more effective when the source is not seen as occurring in the distant past. If Hitler is to be treated as a form of secular Devil, then it is worth noting that belief in the Devil was effective in large part because he was seen as a living presence with agents such as witches active in local communities.

To keep the past relevant will be a major challenge as far as World War Two is concerned. First, for many of the young, the war does indeed seem very distant. Secondly, the move into a new century and millennium in 2000 was an important psychological moment, as it left the twentieth century, not as the current one, but as one that was part of an historical sequence. The impact of this shift will be least for those who lived through the war, which is therefore history to them in a very distinctive sense. However, they are a declining minority and their frames of reference are no longer those of subsequent generations.

Moreover, for much of the world, World War Two is an ambiguous frame of reference. This is true not so much of the states defeated in that conflict, but, rather, of those produced by decolonisation. The war is an ambiguous legacy in these societies, as the extensive and crucial service of their men in the militaries of the imperial powers, Botswana, for example, sending over a fifth of its adult men abroad to support the British army,[14] is often seen as an unwelcome or embarrassing consequence of being a colony, or as something that is best not discussed, or is subordinated to more exemplary narratives of decolonisation. It is scarcely surprising that the argument that the evils of Britain's Empire were vindicated by its existence as a resource for Britain and the cause of good in the war does not command much support other than in the former Dominions, which are held to have consented to the struggle and proud to have taken part. This is true of Australia, Canada and New Zealand, but far less so of South Africa.

The key stories in many former colonies became narratives of decolonisation. Moreover, post-independence conflicts proved central issues. Thus, the politics of World War Two in modern Nigeria or Bangladesh are distinctly secondary to, or are shaped with reference to, what came later. This point needs to be borne in mind when considering the long-term legacy of the war. It is especially pertinent for Africa and South Asia, which did play a major role in the war, and for Latin America which did not.

For many states, in these regions and elsewhere, it is the unintended consequences of the war that are notable or ones that are as part of a longer process; for example, by 1949, the Communist triumph in China and the establishment of the state of Israel in 1948. Thus, in French Africa the overthrow of Vichy provided a marked encouragement for the use, both by the new French government and by anti-colonial leaders, of a language of republicanism focused on liberty, equality and fraternity. This usage looked towards the political transformation of the empire, and, ultimately, its end: most of French Africa gained independence in 1958–62. De Gaulle himself wished to preserve the French empire by both strengthening it and expanding it at the expense of Italian-ruled Libya,[15] the latter a goal he shared with Churchill.

Long-term trends were also accelerated in Latin America, notably the decline of European influence and the increase of that of the USA, especially of American military, diplomatic and economic influence, if not, in some cases, a degree of control. There was also an acceleration of economic modernisation, a degree of state-building, and changes in the political position within individual states. Yet, these trends were also played through local circumstances, such that, while several dictators fell, others continued to hold power.

Particular agendas could still be pursued, notably in Peru's rapid (and lasting) defeat of Ecuador in a frontier war in 1941. This defeat settled the fate of an important section of Amazonia on the eastern side of the Andes.[16] This war indicated the extent to which the 1940s saw the pursuit of established territorial agendas, most of which overlapped with World War Two.

Returning to the question of the supposedly unitary views in the major wartime combatants, and their resultant wartime politics, contrasting views about the war within Britain and the USA in the early stages of the conflict were significant. However, the potential extent of these differences was greatly lessened by the changing pattern of alliances. In particular, Hitler's dramatic breaching of the German–Soviet alignment undercut left-wing criticism of the war in Britain, while his declaration of war on the USA lessened American isolationism as well as criticism of Roosevelt's efforts to weaken Germany, as opposed to Japan. Neither of these developments were inevitable, and in each case there was an incipient, or more than incipient, process of division over policy in the Allied country.

Hitler did not appreciate such points, as he treated peoples as units (as well as commodities), and also subordinated the details of policy to his vision of appropriate action, indeed of historical destiny. As a result, the lessening of real or potential political division within Britain and the USA owed much to Axis policies. Those of Germany were particularly important in the case of Britain, while those of both Germany and Japan were instrumental in the case of the USA. In particular, the ending of isolationist pressures in the USA owed much to German and Japanese policy and actions, and thus the major American rift over foreign policy was brought to an end. This development was significant, as isolationism was not only a policy option but also an expression of a political vision of the USA and of its relationship to the wider world.

Isolationism was to re-surface after the war, notably in response to the issue of commitment to Europe in order to limit the advance of Communism, but isolationist sentiments had been weakened by the circumstances of American entry into the war, and the subsequent history of the conflict did not lead to any significant revival of them. Thus, the USA did not repeat after World War Two the trajectory seen from 1917: that from entry into war to postwar isolationism. Instead, there was a determination in the USA, during and after World War Two, to learn what were presented as the lessons of the earlier conflict, and, in the formation of the United Nations, the USA played a very different role to its stance over the League of Nations. Much of American foreign and military policy from 1945 to the present day can be traced to American involvement in World War Two. The consequences for the nature of the American state and of American public culture have been profound.

An instrumental account of the value, use and recollection of the war does not downplay its significance as a collective memory, or rather, increasingly recovered memory. The war plays a key role in individual, family and community narratives and related explanations. Whether instrumental or not, however, there is the issue of how far the war will continue to serve its current purpose, and, if not, what purpose it will serve. There is no sight of any comparable struggle occurring that can challenge this experience, at least on the global scale. At the same time, all periods are inter-war periods, and the likelihood that the differences and disputes of the twenty-first century will be confronted without large-scale conflict is minimal. Nevertheless, the resulting warfare will probably be of shorter duration and more specific in scale than that of 1937–45.

Conclusions about impact necessarily shade off therefore into speculation. The context is provided by the inexorable change of new generations, new experiences and new memories, and the resulting distancing of the past. That does not mean that World War Two will lose its relevance but, rather, suggests that this relevance will owe much to the expectations and circumstances engendered by this process of change. This process has already occurred with the greater salience of the Holocaust in the collective memory from the 1980s, and with the stronger focus on the war in Asia from the 2000s than was the case earlier.

The perspective of the individual observer on the contents of changing interpretation will inevitably vary; and necessarily so because World War Two was an umbrella war encompassing a range of conflicts. However, there is no doubt of the reality of change. While the details of the conflict have been, and are, more studied than those of any other major war, so that most of the facts appear clear, the interpretation remains sufficiently significant to ensure both debate and change, the two being closely linked. As such, World War Two provides the key instance and topic of public history, one that moulds identities even as it provides a focus for their expression.

NOTES

Preface

1   The decline of Britain and the weakness of Nationalist China were least apparent and there were contrary signs in each case.

Causes

1   J. Record, 'The Use and Abuse of History: Munich, Vietnam and Iraq', *Survival*, 49 (2007), pp. 163–80; *Washington Post*, 19 March 2013.

2   D. Chuter, 'Munich or the Blood of Others', in C. Buffet and B. Heuser (eds), *Haunted by History. Myths in International Relations* (Oxford, 1998), pp. 65–79.

3   Mikhail Saakashvili, former Prime Minister of Georgia, BBC Radio Four, 8.00 News, 6 March 2014; D. Johnson, 'Reality check for the West', *Standpoint*, 61 (April 2014), p. 5.

4   A. Hillgruber, 'England's place in Hitler's plans for world domination', *Journal of Contemporary History*, 9 (1974), pp. 5–24.

5   S. Marks, 'Mistakes and Myths: The Allies, Germany, and the Versailles Treaty, 1918–1921', *Journal of Modern History*, 85 (2013), pp. 632–59.

6   D. Ford, 'Britain's Strategic View of Japanese Naval Power, 1923–1942', in A. Patalano (ed.), *Maritime Strategy and National Security in Japan and Britain: From the First alliance to Post-9/11* (Folkestone, 2012).

7   R. Self, *Neville Chamberlain: A Biography* (Aldershot, 2006).

8   B. J. C. McKercher, *Transition of Power: Britain's Loss of Global Pre-eminence to the United States, 1930–1945* (Cambridge, 1999).

9   W. Cole, *Roosevelt and the Isolationists* (Omaha, NE, 1993).

10   C. G. Reynolds, *The Fast Carriers: The Forging of an Air Navy* (New York, 1968); T. Wildenberg, *Destined for Glory: Dive Bombing, Midway, and the Evolution of Carrier Airpower* (Annapolis, MD, 1998); M. R. Matheny, *Carrying the War to the Enemy: American Operational Art to 1945* (Norman, OK, 2011).

11   J. A. Gunsburg, *Divided and Conquered: The French High Command and the Defeat of the West, 1940* (Westport, CT, 1979); E. Kiesling, *Arming*

Against Hitler: France and the Limits of Military Planning (Lawrence, KS, 1996).

12   N. Jordan, *The Popular Front and Central Europe. The Dilemmas of French Impotence, 1918–1940* (Cambridge, 1992); P. N. Hehn, *A Low Dishonest Decade: The Great Powers, Eastern Europe, and the Economic Origins of World War II, 1930–1941* (London, 2006).

13   J. A. Maiolo, *Cry Havoc: The Arms Race and the Second World War, 1931–1941* (London, 2010).

14   R. Hamilton and H. Herwig (eds), *Decisions for War, 1914–1917* (Cambridge, 2004).

15   A. Gregory, *The Last Great War. British Society and the First World War* (Cambridge, 2008).

16   Eire was then part of Britain and was represented in the Westminster Parliament, rather than being a Dominion.

17   A. Lentin, *Lloyd George and the Lost Peace. From Versailles to Hitler, 1919–1940* (Basingstoke, 2001), p. 103.

18   M. Bassin, 'Race contra Space: The Conflict between German Geopolitik and National Socialism', *Political Geography Quarterly*, 6 (1987), pp. 115–34.

19   E. B. Reynolds (ed.), *Japan in the Fascist Era* (Basingstoke, 2004).

20   D. Gillard, *Appeasement in Crisis. From Munich to Prague, October 1938–March 1939* (Basingstoke, 2007).

21   K. Neilson, *Britain, Soviet Russia, and the Collapse of the Versailles Order, 1919–1939* (Cambridge, 2006); J. A. Maiolo, 'Anglo–Soviet Naval Armaments Diplomacy Before the Second World War', *English Historical Review*, 123 (2008), p. 352.

22   J. Lukacs, *June 1941: Hitler and Stalin* (New Haven, Connecticut, 2006).

23   G. K. Roberts, *The Unholy Alliance: Stalin's Pact with Hitler* (London, 1991); R. Moorhouse, *The Devils' Alliance: Hitler's Pact with Stalin, 1939–1941* (London, 2014).

24   D. B. Lungu, *Romania and the Great Powers, 1933–1940* (Durham, NC, 1989).

25   H. Ragsdale, *The Soviets, the Munich Crisis, and the Coming of World War II* (Cambridge, 2004), p. 185. This was particularly valuable for its inclusion of the Soviet dimension.

26   A. Richie, *Warsaw 1944: Hitler, Himmler and the Warsaw Uprising* (London, 2013).

27   T. Snyder, *Bloodlands: Europe Between Hitler and Stalin* (London, 2010); L. Briedis, *Vilnius: City of Strangers* (Vilnius, 2008).

28   R. J. Overy, *1939: Countdown to War* (London, 2009).

29   A. Tooze, *The Wages of Destruction: The Making and Breaking of the Nazi Economy* (London, 2006), pp. 665.

30   R. E. Frankel, *Bismarck's Shadow: The Cult of Leadership and the Transformation of the German Right, 1898–1945* (Oxford, 2005).

31 G. F. Sander, *The Hundred Day Winter War: Finland's Gallant Stand against the Soviet Army* (Lawrence, KS, 2013).

32 A. Coox, *Nomonhan: Japan against Russia 1939* (Stanford, CA, 1985).

33 Tooze, *Wages of Destruction.*

34 T. C. Imlay, *Facing the Second World War: Strategy, Politics, and Economics in Britain and France, 1938–40* (Oxford, 2003); D. Edgerton, *Britain's War Machine: Weapons, Resources, and Experts in the Second World War* (Oxford, 2011).

35 A. Claasen, 'Blood and Iron, and "der Geist des Atlantiks": Assessing Hitler's Decision to Invade Norway', *Journal of Strategic Studies*, 20 (1997), pp. 71–96.

36 J. A. Gunsburg, 'La Grande Illusion: Belgian and Dutch Strategy Facing Germany, 1919–May 1940 (Part I)', *Journal of Military History*, 78 (2014), pp. 101–58, esp. 141–54.

37 R. A. Doughty, 'Myth of the Blitzkrieg', in L. J. Matthews (ed.), *Challenging the United States Symmetrically and Asymmetrically: Can America be Defeated?* (Carlisle, PA, 1998), pp. 57–79; J. S. Corum, 'Myths of Blitzkrieg: The Enduring Mythology of the 1940 Campaign', *Historically Speaking*, 6 (2005), pp. 11–13; W. Murray, 'May 1940: Contingency and Fragility of the German RMA', in M. Knox and W. Murray (eds), *The Dynamics of Military Revolution 1300–2050* (Cambridge, 2001), pp. 154–75.

38 D. Alexander, 'Repercussions of the Breda Variant', *French Historical Studies*, 8 (1974), pp. 459–88; M. S. Alexander, 'The Fall of France, 1940', *Journal of Strategic Studies*, 13 (1990), pp. 10–44; N. Jordan, 'Strategy and Scapegoatism: Reflections on the French National Catastrophe, 1940', in J. Blatt (ed.), *The French Defeat of 1940: Reassessments* (Providence, RI, 1998), pp. 13–38.

39 M. Vaisse (ed.), *Mai-Juin 1940: Défaite française, victoire allemande, sous l'oeil des historiens étrangers* (Paris, 2000); J. Jackson, *The Fall of France. The Nazi Invasion of 1940* (Oxford, 2003).

40 T. Jersak, 'Blitzkrieg revisited: a new look at Nazi war and extermination planning', *Historical Journal*, 43 (2000), pp. 569, 582.

41 M. Barone, 'Dems 2014 like French generals in 1940', *Conservative Chronicle*, 26 March 2014, p. 1.

42 W. L. Langer and S. E. Gleason, *The Challenge to Isolation: the World Crisis of 1937–1940 and American Foreign Policy* (New York, 1952); B. R. Farnham, *Roosevelt and the Munich Crisis: A Study of Political Decision-Making* (Princeton, NJ, 1997).

43 Churchill to Hoare, 18 September 1940, Churchill Papers.

44 Note by Clementine Churchill in margin of Churchill's draft war memoirs, Churchill Papers.

45 Churchill to de Gaulle, 7 October 1940, Churchill Papers.

46 G. B. Strang (ed.), *Collision of Empires. Italy's Invasion of Ethiopia and its International Impact* (Farnham, 2014).

47   R. Mallett, *The Italian Navy and Fascist Expansionism, 1935–1940* (London, 1998).

48   R. M. Salerno, *Vital Crossroads. Mediterranean Origins of the Second World War, 1935–1940* (Ithaca, NY, 2002), p. 149.

49   M. Knox, *Common Destiny: Dictatorship, Foreign Policy, and War in Fascist Italy and Nazi Germany* (Cambridge, 2000); R. Mallett, *Mussolini and the Origins of the Second World War, 1933–1940* (Basingstoke, 2003); G. B. Strang, *On the Fiery March: Mussolini Prepares for War* (Westport, CT, 2003).

50   G. Ciano, *Diario 1937–39* (Milan, 1980), p. 209.

51   Ciano, *Diario*, p. 140.

52   K.-M. Mallmann and M. Cüppers, *Nazi Palestine: The Plans for the Extermination of the Jews in Palestine* (New York, 2010).

53   Hsiao-ting Lin, *Tibet and Nationalist China's Frontier* (Vancouver, 2006).

54   R. C. Raack, *Stalin's Drive to the West: 1938–1945* (Stanford, CA, 1995); E. Mawdsley, 'Crossing the Rubicon: Soviet Plans for offensive war in 1940–1941', *International History Review*, 25 (2003).

55   O. Pinkus, *The War Aims and Strategies of Adolf Hitler* (London, 2005).

56   J. Herf, *The Jewish Enemy: Nazi Propaganda during World War II and the Holocaust* (Cambridge, MA., 2006); L. Waddington, *Hitler's Crusade. Bolshevism and the Myth of the International Jewish Conspiracy* (London, 2007).

57   M. Mazower, *Hitler's Empire: Nazi Rule in Occupied Europe* (London, 2008).

58   G. Gorodetsky, *Grand Delusion: Stalin and the German Invasion of Russia* (New Haven, CT, 1999); D. E. Murphy, *What Stalin Knew: The Enigma of Barbarossa* (New Haven, CT, 2005).

59   I. Lukes, 'The Tukhahevsky Affair and President Edvard Benes: Solutions and Open Questions', *Diplomacy and Statecraft*, 7 (1996), pp. 505–29.

60   D. M. Glantz, *Stumbling Colossus: The Red Army on the Eve of World War II* (Lawrence, KS, 1998).

61   R. M. Citino, *Death of the Wehrmacht: The German Campaigns of 1942* (Lawrence, KS, 2007). For German defensive doctrine, M. Strohn, *The German Army and the Defence of the Reich: Military Doctrine and the Conduct of the Defensive Battle 1918–1939* (Cambridge, 2011).

62   J. Black, *War. The Cultural Turn* (Cambridge, 2011).

63   P. A. Hanebrink, *In Defense of Christian Hungary: Religion, Nationalism and Anti-Semitism, 1890–1944* (Ithaca, NY, 2006).

64   M. Turda, 'In Pursuit of Great Hungary: Eugenic Ideas of Social and Biological Improvement, 1940–1941', *Journal of Modern History*, 85 (2013), pp. 588–91.

65   R. Ioanid, *The Holocaust in Romania* (Chicago, IL, 2000).

66   D. Deletant, *Hitler's Forgotten Ally: Ion Antonescu and his Regime, Romania 1940–1944* (Basingstoke, 2006).

67   J. H. Herzog, 'The Influence of the United States Navy in the Embargo of Oil to Japan, 1940–1941', *Pacific Historical Review*, 35 (1966), pp. 317–28.

68   J. Taylor, *The Generalissimo. Chiang Kai-shek and the Struggle for Modern China* (Cambridge, MA, 2009), p. 172.

69   A. Cox, 'The Effects of Attrition on National War Effort: the Japanese Experience in China, 1937–38', *Military Affairs*, 32, no. 2 (October 1968), pp. 57–62; E. Kinmonth, 'The Mouse that Roared: Saitō Takao, Conservative Critic of Japan's "Holy War" in China', *Journal of Japanese Studies*, 25 (1999), pp. 331–60.

70   M. R. Peattie, E. Drea and H. van de Ven (eds), *The Battle for China: Essays on the Military History of the Sino-Japanese War of 1937–1945* (Stanford, CA, 2010).

71   D. Kaiser, *No End Save Victory* (New York, 2014), p. 15.

72   W. Heinrichs, *Threshold of War: Franklin B. Roosevelt and American Entry into World War II* (Oxford, 1988); J. C. Schneider, *Should America Go To War? The Debate Over Foreign Policy in Chicago, 1939–1941* (Chapel Hill, NC, 1989).

73   D. F. Harrington, 'A Careless Hope: American Air Power and Japan, 1941', *Pacific Historical Review*, 43 (1979), pp. 217–38.

74   A. Iriye, *The Origins of the Second World War in Asia and the Pacific* (London, 1987); D. M. Goldstein and K. V. Dillon (eds), *The Pearl Harbor Papers: Inside the Japanese Plans* (McLean, VA, 1993).

75   E. Rosenberg, *A Date Which Will Live: Pearl Harbor in American Memory* (Durham, NC, 2003).

76   R. W. Tucker, *Woodrow Wilson and the Great War: Reconsidering America's Neutrality, 1914–1917* (Charlottesville, VI, 2007).

77   I. Kershaw, *Fateful Choices. Ten Decisions that Changed the World, 1940–1941* (London, 2007) pp. 382–430.

78   N. Lochery, *Brazil: The Fortunes of War* (New York, 2014).

79   J. Wise, *The Role of the Royal Navy in South America, 1920–1970* (London, 2014), pp. 112–13.

80   F. D. McCann, *The Brazilian-American Alliance, 1937–1945* (Princeton, NJ, 1973); M. L. Francis, *The Limits of Hegemony: United States Relations with Argentina and Chile during World War II* (Notre Dame, IN, 1977); R. A. Humphreys, *Latin America and the Second World War* (2 vols, London, 1981–2); S. I. Schwab, 'The Role of the Mexican Expeditionary Air Force in World War II: Late, Limited, but Symbolically Significant', *Journal of Military History*, 66 (2002), pp. 1115–40.

81   N. Wylvie, 'Problems of Neutrality: Swiss Diplomatic Documents, 1939–1945', *Diplomacy and Statecraft*, 11 (2000), pp. 260–71 and (ed.), *European Neutrals and Non-Belligerents during the Second World War* (Cambridge, 2002).

82   H. Bowen, *Spain During World War II* (Columbus, OH, 2006).

83   S. P. Halbrook, *The Swiss and the Nazis: How the Alpine Republic Survived in the Shadow of the Third Reich* (London, 2006).

84   W. Webster, 'Enemies, Allies and Transnational Histories: Germans, Irish, and Italians in Second World War Britain, *Twentieth Century British History*, 25 (2014), pp. 85–6.

85   B. Girvin and G. Roberts (eds), *Ireland and the Second World War: Politics, Society, Remembrance* (Dublin, 2000). For an overly favourable account, C. Wills, *That Neutral Island: A Cultural History of Ireland during the Second World War* (London, 2007).

86   See e.g. D. J. Alvarez, 'The Vatican and the War in the Far East, 1941–1943', *The Historian*, 40 (1978), pp. 508–23.

87   G. Krebs, 'Operation Super Sunrise? Japanese–United States Peace Feelers in Switzerland, 1945', *Journal of Military History*, 69 (2005), pp. 1081–120.

88   H. Stenius, M. Österberg and J. Östling (eds), *Nordic Narratives of the Second World War: National Historiographies Revisited* (Lund, 2011).

Alliance Politics and Grand Strategy

1   A. Roberts, *A History of the English-Speaking Peoples since 1900* (London, 2006); W. R. Mead, *God and Gold: Britain, America and the Making of the Modern World* (New York, 2008).

2   M. A. Stoler, *Allies in War: Britain and America against the Axis Powers, 1940–1945* (London, 2005); A. Roberts, *Masters and Commanders. How Roosevelt, Churchill, Marshall and Alanbrooke Won the War in the West* (London, 2008).

3   J. P. Duffy, *Target: America. Hitler's Plan to Attack the United States* (Westport, CTt, 2004).

4   J. Cole, 'Iraq in 1939: British Alliance or Nationalist Neutrality toward the Axis?', *Britain and the World*, 5 (2012), pp. 220–2.

5   Field Marshal Lord Alanbrooke, *War Diaries, 1939–1945* (London, 2001), pp. 245–7.

6   L. Paterson, *Hitler's Grey Wolves: U-boats in the Indian Ocean* (London, 2004).

7   R. Mitter, *China's War with Japan, 1937–1945. The Struggle for Survival* (London, 2013).

8   J. L. Cox, 'The Background to the Syrian Campaign, May–June 1941: A Study in Franco–German Wartime Relations', *History*, 72 (1987), pp. 432–52; J. J. Sadkovich, 'German Military Incompetence Through Italian Eyes', *War in History*, 1 (1994), pp. 39–62.

9   O. Vehviläinen, *Finland in the Second World War: Between Germany and Russia* (Basingstoke, 2002).

10   H. Rautkallio, *Finland and the Holocaust: The Rescue of Finland's Jews* (New York, 1987).

11   J. R. Adelman, 'Conclusions', in Adelman (ed.), *Hitler and His Allies in World War II* (Abingdon, 2007), p. 197; K. Urbach, 'Keeping Secrets: How Important was Intelligence for the Conduct of International Relations, 1914–1989', conference report, *German Historical Institute London, Bulletin*, 30 (2008), p. 155.

12   M. Mazower, *Hitler's Empire. Nazi Rule in Occupied Europe* (London, 2008), pp. 556–60.

13   J. J. Sadkovich, 'Understanding Defeat: Reappraising Italy's Role in World War II', *Journal of Contemporary History*, 24 (1989), pp. 27–61. For unsympathetic German treatment of Italian soldiers on the Eastern Front, N. Revelli, *Mussolini's Death March: Eyewitness Accounts of Italian Soldiers on the Eastern Front* (Lawrence, KS, 2013).

14   J. Greene and A. Massignani, *The Naval War in the Mediterranean, 1940–1943* (Rockville Centers, NY, 1999).

15   U. E. Sundberg and A. D. Harvey, 'The Siege of Tobruk. The Struggle to maintain the Coastal Supply Line, 1941', *RUSI Journal*, 154, 1 (February 2009), pp. 78–82.

16   K. Ungváry, *Battle for Budapest: One Hundred Days in World War II* (London, 2005), p. 315.

17   B. Kočović, *War and Revolution in Yugoslavia, 1941–1945. Occupation and Collaboration* (Stanford, CA, 2001); G. J. Kranjc, *To Walk with the Devil: Slovene Collaboration and Axis Occupation, 1941–1945* (Toronto, 2013).

18   D. P. Barrett and L. N. Shyu (eds), *Chinese Collaboration with Japan: The Limits of Accommodation* (Stanford, CA, 2001).

19   P. Preston, 'Franco and Hitler: the Myth of Hendaye', *Contemporary European History*, 1 (1992), pp. 1–16; R. Wigg, *Churchill and Spain: The Survival of the Franco Regime, 1940–1945* (Portland, OR, 2008).

20   I. Kershaw, 'Did Hitler Miss his Chance in 1940', in N. Gregor (ed.), *Nazism, War and Genocide* (Exeter, 2005), pp. 110–30.

21   A. Jackson, *The British Empire and the Second World War* (London, 2006).

22   A. Stewart, 'The British Government and the South African Neutrality Crisis, 1938–39', *English Historical Review*, 123 (2008), pp. 947–72.

23   C. P. Stacey, *Arms, Men and Government: The War Policies of Canada, 1939–1945* (Ottawa, 1970); D. Dilks, 'The Great Dominion'. *Winston Churchill in Canada, 1900–1954* (Toronto, 2005), pp. 235–7.

24   D. M. Horner, *High Command: Australia and Allied Strategy, 1939–1945* (London, 1982); K. Tsokhas, 'Dedominionization: The Anglo–Australian Experience, 1939–1945', *Historical Journal*, 37 (1994), pp. 861–83; C. Waters, 'Australia, the British Empire and the Second World War', *War and Society*, 19 (2001), pp. 93–107; J. Gooch, 'The Politics of Strategy: Great Britain, Australia, and the War against Japan, 1939–1945', *War in History*, 10 (2003), pp. 424–47.

25 B. P. Farrell, *The Defence and Fall of Singapore, 1940–1942* (Stroud, 2005), p. 406.

26 War Cabinet Minutes, 29 July 1942, NAA, p. 1404. See also, e.g., 30 June 1942, pp. 1378–9.

27 N. E. Sarantakes, 'One Last Crusade: The British Pacific Fleet and its Impact on the Anglo–American Alliance', *English Historical Review*, 121 (2006), p. 446.

28 A. Stewart, *Empire Lost. Britain, the Dominions and the Second World War* (London, 2008), p. 169.

29 For example, B. P. Farrell, *The Basis and Making of British Grand Strategy, 1940–1942: Was There a Plan?* (New York, 1998).

30 A. Danchev, 'Great Britain: The Indirect Strategy', in D. Reynolds et al. (eds), *Allies at War* (New York, 1994), pp. 1–26.

31 A. J. Prazmowska, *Britain and Poland, 1939–1943: The Betrayed Ally* (Cambridge, 1995); H. Kochanski, *The Eagle Unbowed: Poland and Poles in the Second World War* (Cambridge, MA, 2012).

32 E. D. R. Harrison, 'The British Special Operations Executive and Poland', *Historical Journal*, 43 (2000), pp. 1071–91, esp. pp. 1080, 1082, 1088.

33 I. Tombs, 'The British TUC between Germany and Russia: From the Outbreak of War to the World Trade Conference of February 1945', *European History Quarterly*, 28 (1998), pp. 219–43.

34 J. Haslam, 'Stalin's Fears of a Separate Peace, 1942', *Intelligence and National Security*, 8, 4 (1993), pp. 97–9.

35 For an overly sympathetic account, G. Roberts, *Stalin's Wars: From World War to Cold War, 1939–1953* (New Haven, CT, 2007).

36 The year American independence from Britain was declared.

37 D. Hein, 'Vulnerable: HMS *Prince of Wales* in 1941', *Journal of Military History*, 77 (2013), pp. 968–74.

38 M. A. Stoler, 'The "Pacific-First" alternative in American World War II strategy', *International History Review*, 2 (1980), pp. 432–52.

39 M. Howard, 'The Second World War in Perspective', *RUSI Journal*, 150 (2005), p. 58.

40 C. E. Kirkpatrick, *An Unknown Future and a Doubtful Present. Writing the Victory Plan of 1941* (Washington, 1992), p. 128.

41 M. A. Stoler, *Allies and Adversaries: the Joint Chiefs of Staff, the Grand Alliance, and U.S. Strategy in World War II* (Chapel Hill, NC, 2000).

42 S. Morewood, *The British Defence of Egypt, 1935–1940: Conflict and Crisis in the Eastern Mediterranean* (London, 2004).

43 R. M. Salerno, *Vital Crossroads. Mediterranean Origins of the Second World War, 1935–1940* (Ithaca, NY, 2002), p. 172.

44 T. Benbow, '"Menace" to "Ironclad": The British Operations against Dakar (1940) and Madagascar (1942)', *Journal of Military History*, 75 (2011), pp. 807–8.

45   N. Stone, *World War Two. A Short History* (London, 2013), p. 156.

46   S. Ball, *The Bitter Sea: The Struggle for Mastery in the Mediterranean, 1935–1949* (London, 2009).

47   D. Massam, *British Maritime Strategy and Amphibious Capability, 1900–40* (D. Phil. Oxford, 1995).

48   D. Stone, *Summits: The Meetings That Shaped World War II and the Postwar World* (Dulles, VI, 2006).

49   E. Mawdsley, *Thunder in the East. The Nazi–Soviet War, 1941–1945* (London, 2005), p. 401.

50   B. Wegner, 'The Ideology of Self-Destruction: Hitler and the Choreography of Defeat', *German Historical Institute London. Bulletin*, 26 (2004), pp. 18–33.

51   D. K. Yelton, '"Ein Volk Steht Auf": The German Volkssturm and Nazi Strategy, 1944–45', *Journal of Military History*, 64 (2000), pp. 1061–83.

52   M. E. Glantz, *FDR and the Soviet Union: The President's Battles over Foreign Policy* (Lawrence, KS, 2005).

53   F. J. Harbutt, *Yalta 1945. Europe and America at the Crossroads* (Cambridge, 2009).

54   N. Smith, *American Empire: Roosevelt's Geographer and the Prelude to Globalization* (Berkeley, CA, 2003), p. 360; W. R. Louis, *Imperialism at Bay: The United States and the Decolonisation of the British Empire, 1941–1945* (New York, 1978); A. J. Whitfield, *Hong Kong, Empire, and the Anglo–American Alliance at War, 1941–45* (Basingstoke, 2001).

55   F. Venn, *The Anglo–American Oil War. International Politics and the Struggle for Foreign Petroleum, 1912–1945* (London, 2009).

56   T. C. Mills, 'Anglo–American Economic Diplomacy During the Second World War and the Electrification of the Central Brazilian Railway', *Diplomacy and Statecraft*, 20 (2009), pp. 69–85.

57   C. D. O'Sullivan, *Sumner Welles, Postwar Planning, and the Quest for a New World Order, 1937–1943* (New York, 2009).

58   F. Prochaska, *The Eagle and The Crown. Americans and the British Monarchy* (New Haven, CT, 2008), p. 154.

59   V. de Grazia, *Irresistible Empire: America's Advance Through Twentieth-Century Europe* (Cambridge, MA, 2005).

60   B. Singer and J. Langdon, *Cultured Force. Makers and Defenders of the French Colonial Empire* (Madison, WI, 2004), p. 239.

61   M. Bilton, 'The Dirty War on our Doorstep', *Sunday Times Magazine*, 15 March 2009, pp. 20–8. More generally on the Free French exile see D. Kelly and M. Cornick (eds), *A History of the French in London. Liberty, Equality, Opportunity* (London, 2013).

62   J. E. Farquharson, 'Anglo–American Policy on German Reparations from Yalta to Potsdam', *English Historical Review*, 112 (1997), pp. 904–26; S. Casey, 'The Campaign to Sell a Harsh Peace for Germany to the American Public, 1944–1948', *History*, 90 (2005), pp. 62–92.

63   M. Beyen, 'Resisting Hyperbole: Professional historians in Belgium and
      the Netherlands and their relationship with wartime historical culture,
      1940–1945', *Storia della Storiografia*, 53 (2008), pp. 130–44.
64   V. Mastny, *The Cold War and Soviet Insecurity: the Stalin Years* (New
      York, 1996); V. Zubok and C. Pleshakov, *Inside the Kremlin's Cold War:
      from Stalin to Khrushchev* (Cambridge, MA, 1996); P. Kenez, *Hungary
      from the Nazis to the Soviets. The Establishment of the Communist Regime
      in Hungary, 1944–1948* (Cambridge, 2009).

Domestic Politics

1   J. Noakes (ed.), *The Civilian in War: The Home Front in Europe, Japan and
      the USA in World War II* (Exeter, 1992); E. R. Beck, *The European Home
      Fronts, 1939–1945* (Arlington Heights, IL, 1993).
2   H. Sitkoff, 'The Detroit Race Riot of 1943', *Michigan History*, 53 (1969),
      pp. 183–206.
3   D. R. Wells, *Baseball's Western Front: The Pacific Coast League During
      World War II* (Jefferson, NC, 2004).
4   S. Ritchie, *Industry and Air Power: the Expansion of British Aircraft
      Production, 1935–1941* (London, 1997).
5   For anger over price control in the Punjab, T. T. Yong, 'Mobilisation,
      Militarisation and "Mal-Contentment": Punjab and the Second World War',
      South Asia, 25 (2002), pp. 147–51.
6   K. Garside, 'An Intelligence Library in Germany', *Journal of
      Documentation*, 3 (1947), pp. 99–106.
7   B. R. Koerner, R.-D. Müller and H. Umbreit, *Germany and the Second
      World War. V. Organization and Mobilization of the German Sphere
      of Power. Part 2. Wartime Administration, Economy, and Manpower
      Resources, 1942–5* (Oxford, 2003).
8   S. H. Lindner, *Inside I. G. Farben: Hoechst During the Third Reich*
      (Cambridge, 2008).
9   N. Gregor, *Daimler-Benz in the Third Reich* (New Haven, CT, 1998).
10   R. J. Overy, 'Hitler's War and the German Economy: A Reinterpretation',
      in A. Marwick, C. Emsley and W. Simpson (eds), *Total War and Historical
      Change: Europe, 1914–1955* (Buckingham, 2001), p. 157; A. Tooze, *The
      Wages of Destruction: The Making and Breaking of the Nazi Economy*
      (London, 2006).
11   R. Gildea, O. Wieviorka and A. Warring (eds), *Surviving Hitler and
      Mussolini: Daily Life in Occupied Europe* (Oxford, 2006).
12   J. Lund, *Working for the New Order: European Business under German
      Domination, 1939–1945* (Copenhagen, 2006).
13   U. Herbert, *Hitler's Foreign Workers: Enforced Labor in Germany under
      the Third Reich* (Cambridge, 1997); J. Stephenson, 'Germans, Slavs and the

Burden of Work in Rural Southern Germany during the Second World War', in N. Gregor (ed.), *Nazism, War and Genocide* (Exeter, 2005).

14 R. J. Evans, *The Third Reich at War, 1939–1945* (London, 2008), p. 339.

15 N. Terry, 'How Soviet was Russian Society under Nazi Occupation?', in C. C. W. Szejnmann (ed.), *Rethinking History, Dictatorship and War* (London, 2009), p. 141.

16 M. Mouton, *From Nurturing the German Nation to Purifying the Volk: Weimar and Nazi Family Policy, 1918–1945* (Cambridge, 2007).

17 G. J. Horwitz, *Ghettostadt. Łodz and the Making of a Nazi City* (Cambridge, MA, 2008).

18 P. Thompson, *The Battle for Singapore* (London, 2005), p. 372.

19 K. C. Berkhoff, *Harvest of Despair: Life and Death in Ukraine under Nazi Rule* (Cambridge, MA, 2004); B. Shepherd, *Blood on the Snow. The German Army and Soviet Partisans* (Cambridge, MA, 2004); W. Lower, *Nazi Empire-Building and the Holocaust in Ukraine* (Chapel Hill, NC, 2005).

20 A. Hill, *The War behind the Eastern Front: The Soviet Partisan Movement in North-West Russia, 1941–1944* (London, 2005).

21 M. Mazower, 'Military violence and National Socialist values: the *Wehrmacht* in Greece, 1941–1944', *Past and Present*, 134 (1992), pp. 129–58; T. Anderson, 'A Hungarian *Vernichtungskrieg*? Hungarian troops and the Soviet Ukraine, 1942', *Militärgeschichtliche Mitteilungen*, 58 (1999), pp. 345–66; J. E. Gumz, '*Wehrmacht* perceptions of mass violence in Croatia, 1941–1942', *Historical Journal*, 44 (2001), pp. 1015–38, esp. 1036–7.

22 A. Gill, *An Honourable Defeat. The Fight against National Socialism in Germany, 1933–1945* (London, 1994).

23 S. Berger, *Representation of the Past: The Making, Unmaking and Remaking of National Histories in Western Europe after 1945* (Pontypridd, 2002), pp. 5–6.

24 H. Mommsen, *Germans Against Hitler. The Stauffenberg Plot and Resistance Under the Third Reich* (London, 2008).

25 N. Gregor, 'A *Schicksalsgemeinschaft*? Allied Bombing, Civilian Morale, and Social Dissolution in Nuremberg, 1942–1945', *Historical Journal*, 43 (2000), pp. 1051–70; J. Stephenson, *Hitler's Home Front: Württemberg Under the Nazis* (London, 2006).

26 E. Johnson and K.-H. Reuband, *What We Knew: Terror, Mass Murder, and Everyday Life in Nazi Germany: An Oral History* (New York, 2005).

27 N. Ferguson, *The War of the World. History's Age of Hatred* (London, 2006), pp. 539–43.

28 M. Pugh, 'The Liberal Party and the Popular Front', *English Historical Review*, 121 (2006), pp. 1349–50.

29 Lentin, *Lloyd George and the Lost Peace*, p. 128.

30 G. Campion, *The Good Fight: Battle of Britain Propaganda and The Few* (Basingstoke, 2009).

31 War Cabinet, Chiefs of Staff Committee, Weekly Résumé, no. 56, Churchill Papers.

32 J. Chapman, *The British at War: Cinema, State and Propaganda, 1939–1945* (1998).

33 H. Jones, *British Civilians in the Front Line: Air raids, productivity and wartime culture, 1939–1945* (Manchester, 2006).

34 *Annual Research Reports of the BBC, 1937–c.1950*, British Online Archives from Microform Academic Publishers, 2007. www.britishonlinearchives. co.uk

35 S. R. Grayzel, *At Home and Under Fire: Air Raids and the Culture in Britain from the Great War to the Blitz* (Cambridge, 2012); P. Jalland, *Death in War and Peace: A History of Loss and Grief in England, 1914–1970* (Oxford, 2010).

36 R. Toye, *The Roar of the Lion: The Untold Story of Churchill's World War Two Speeches* (Oxford, 2013).

37 G. Best, *Churchill and War* (London, 2005).

38 A. Danchev and D. Todman (eds), *War Diaries, 1939–1945, Field Marshal Lord Alanbrooke* (London, 2001), p. 240.

39 C. M. Bell, *Churchill and Seapower* (Oxford, 2013).

40 R. Callahan, *Churchill and His Generals* (Lawrence, KS, 2007).

41 A. J. Foster, 'The Politicians, Public Opinion and the Press: The Storm over British Military Intervention in Greece in December 1944', *Journal of Contemporary History*, 19 (1984), pp. 453–94; A. Thorpe, 'In a rather emotional state'? The Labour Party and British intervention in Greece, 1945–6', *English Historical Review*, 121 (2006), pp. 1075–105.

42 P. C. Logan, *Humphrey Jennings and British Documentary Film: A Re-Assessment* (Farnham, 2011).

43 P. Bairoch, 'International Industrialization Levels from 1750 to 1980', *Journal of European Economic History*, 11 (1982), p. 296; K. E. Eiler, *Mobilizing America: Robert P. Paterson and the War Effort, 1940–1945* (Ithaca, NY, 1997); P. A. C. Koistinen, *Arsenal of World War II: The Political Economy of American Warfare, 1940–1945* (Lawrence, KS, 2004).

44 M. Klein, *A Call to Arms: Mobilizing America for World War II* (New York, 2013).

45 M. J. Forsyth, 'The Military Provides Lincoln a Mandate', *Army History*, 53 (2001), pp. 11–17.

46 H. P. Willmott, *The Battle of Leyte Gulf: The Last Fleet Action* (Bloomington, IN, 2005).

47 Initial reactions to Churchill's 'Iron Curtain' speech were highly critical.

48 J. M. Blum, *V was for Victory: Politics and American Culture during World War II* (London, 1976).

49   R. A. Divine, *Foreign Policy and U.S. Presidential Elections, 1940–1948* (New York, 1974).

50   M. Warren, 'Focal Point of the Fleet: US Navy Photographic Activities in World War II', *Journal of Military History*, 69 (2005), pp. 1045–80.

51   J. J. Stephan, *Hawaii Under the Rising Sun: Japan's Plans for Conquest After Pearl Harbor* (Honolulu, HI, 2003).

52   L. M. Lees, *Yugoslav-Americans and National Security during World War II* (Urbana, IL, 2007).

53   War Cabinet Minutes, 4, 12 February 1941, NAA, A5954, 805/1, pp. 562, 572.

54   J. Plamper, *The Stalin Cult: A Study in the Alchemy of Power* (New Haven, CT, 2012).

55   R. Bidlock and N. Lomagin, *The Leningrad Blockade, 1941–1944: A New Documentary History from the Soviet Archives* (New Haven, CT, 2012).

56   K. C. Berkhoff, *Motherland in Danger: Soviet Propaganda during World War II* (Cambridge, MA, 2012).

57   M. Perrie, *The Cult of Ivan the Terrible in Stalin's Russia* (Basingstoke, 2001); D. Brandenberger, *National Bolshevism. Stalinist Mass Culture and the Formation of Modern Russian National Identity, 1931–1956* (Cambridge, MA, 2002); K. M. F. Platt and D. Brandenberger (eds), *Epic Revision: Russian History and Literature as Stalinist Propaganda* (Madison, WI, 2006).

58   A. J. Kay, *Exploitation, Resettlement, Mass Murder: Political and Economic Planning for German Occupation Policy in the Soviet Union, 1940–1941* (Oxford, 2006).

59   C. Merridale, *Ivan's War. The Red Army, 1939–1945* (London, 2005).

60   M. M. Harrison (ed.), *The Economics of World War II: Six Great Powers in International Comparison* (Cambridge, 1998).

61   S. Wilson, *The Manchurian Crisis and Japanese Society, 1931–1933* (London, 2002); W. A. Skya, *Japan's Holy War: The Ideology of Radical Shintō Ultranationalism* (Durham, NC, 2009); H. Bix, *Hirohito and the Making of Modern Japan* (New York, 2000).

62   S. Jun'Ichiro, 'The Quest for International Justice and Asianism in a "New Order in East Asia"; Fuminaro Konoe and His Vision of the World', in W. Murray and T. Ishizu (eds), *Conflicting Currents. Japan and the United States in the Pacific* (Santa Barbara, CA, 2010), pp. 58–60.

63   B. Kushner, *The Thought War: Japanese Imperial Propaganda* (Honolulu, HI, 2006).

64   T. Havens, *Valley of Darkness: The Japanese People and World War Two* (New York, 1978); B. A. Shillony, *Politics and Culture in Wartime Japan* (2nd edn, Oxford, 1991); S. Lone (ed.), *Daily Lives of Civilians in Wartime Asia* (Westport, CT, 2007).

65   K. P. Wervell, *Blankets of Fire: U.S. Bombers over Japan during World War*

II (Washington, DC, 1996); H. S. Wolk, *Cataclysm: General Hap Arnold and the Defeat of Japan* (Denton, TX, 2010).

66   P. Morgan, *The Fall of Mussolini: Italy, the Italians, and the Second World War* (Oxford, 2007).

67   E. Agarossi, *A Nation Collapses: the Italian Surrender of September 1943* (Cambridge, 2000).

68   C. Baldoli, A. Knapp and R. J. Overy (eds), *Bombing States and Peoples in Western Europe, 1940–1945* (London, 2011); Baldoli and Knapp, *Forgotten Blitzes. France and Italy under Allied Attack* (London, 2012).

69   J. Hinton, *Women, Social Leadership, and the Second World War: Continuities of Class* (Oxford, 2003); S. O. Rose, *Which People's War? National Identity and Citizenship in Wartime Britain, 1939–1945* (Oxford, 2003).

70   R. Mackay, '"No place in the corporation service": the BBC and conscientious objectors in the Second World War', *Media History*, 12 (2006); and 'An Abominable Precedent: the BBC's Ban on Pacifists in the Second World War', *Contemporary British History*, 20 (2006).

71   J. W. Baird, 'The Myth of Stalingrad', *Journal of Contemporary History*, 4 (1969), pp. 187–204.

72   D. Welch, *Propaganda and the German Cinema, 1933–45* (London, 2001).

73   T. W. Ryback, *Hitler's Private Library. The Books that Shaped his Life* (London, 2009), pp. 201–3, 206–11.

74   R. J. Evans, *The Third Reich in Power, 1933–1939* (London, 2005).

75   J. Echternkamp, 'At War, Abroad and at Home. The Essential Features of German Society in the Second World War', in Echternkamp (ed.), *Germany and the Second World War. IX. Part I, German Wartime Society 1939–1945* (Oxford, 2008), pp. 19–24.

76   M. Bucur, 'Edifices of the Past. War Memorials and Heroes in Twentieth-Century Romania', in M. Todorova (ed.), *Balkan Identities. Nation and Memory* (London, 2004), p. 172.

77   I. McLaine, *Ministry of Morale: Home Front morale and the Ministry of Information in World War II* (London, 1979); J. Gardiner, *Wartime: Britain, 1939–1945* (London, 2004).

78   T. Karube, *Maruyama Masao and the Fate of Liberalism in Twentieth-Century Japan* (Tokyo, 2008).

79   E. Katz, 'Memory at the Front: The Struggle over Revolutionary Commemoration in Occupied France, 1940–44', *Journal of European Studies*, 35 (2005), pp. 153–68.

80   J. Adler, 'The Jews and Vichy: Reflections on French Historiography', *Historical Journal*, 44 (2001), pp. 1065–82; P. Mazgaj, *Imagining Fascism: The Cultural Politics of the French Young Right, 1930–1945* (Newark, DE, 2007).

Explanations of Victory

1   The key work is R. J. Overy, *Why the Allies Won* (London, 1995).

2   G. L. Weinberg, 'Some Myths of World War II', *Journal of Military History*, 75 (2011), pp. 701–18.

3   P. Sabin, 'Why the Allies Won the Air War, 1939–45', in C. C. W. Szejnmann (ed.), *Rethinking History, Dictatorship and War* (London, 2009), p. 159.

4   D. Edgerton, *Britain's War Machine: Weapons, Resources, and Experts in the Second World War* (Oxford, 2011); M. Klein, *A Call to Arms: Mobilizing America for World War II* (New York, 2013).

5   See, for example, D. P. Marston, *Phoenix from the Ashes: The Indian Army in the Burma Campaign* (Westport, CT, 2004) and T. Moreman, *The Jungle, the Japanese and the British Commonwealth Armies at War, 1941–1945: Fighting Methods, Doctrine and Training for Jungle Warfare* (London, 2005).

6   H. Shukman (ed.), *Stalin and the Soviet-Finnish War, 1939–1940* (London, 2001).

7   B. Bond and M. Taylor (eds), *The Battle of France and Flanders. Sixty Years On* (Barnsley, 2001), especially S. Badsey, 'British High Command and the reporting of the Campaign', pp. 139–60.

8   W. J. Astore, 'Loving the German War Machine: America's Infatuation with *Blitzkrieg*, Warfighters and Militarism', in M. S. Neiberg (ed.), *Arms and the Man: Military History Essays in Honor of Dennis Showalter* (Leiden, 2011), pp. 14–17, 29.

9   J. E. Harrold (ed.), *Turning the Tide: The Battles of Coral Sea and Midway* (Plymouth, 2013).

10 J. H. Lambert and N. Polmar, *Defenseless: Command Failure at Pearl Harbor* (St Paul, MN, 2003).

11 'History Makes History (and Money)', [no author], *Advertisers Weekly*, 7 April 1967, pp. 32–4.

12 Director of the Imperial War Museum to the editor, Barrie Pitt, 26 April 1966, LH, Liddell Hart papers, 3/183.

13 Patrick Cavendish to Liddell Hart, 13 October, reply 19 October, Norman Marshall to Liddell Hart, 24 October 1966, LH, Liddell Hart papers, 3/183.

14 Liddell Hart to Barrie Pitt, 14 May 1967, LH, Liddell Hart papers, 3/183.

15 Stafford-Northcote, 28 June 1967, LH, Liddell Hart papers, 3/183.

16 B. Fischer, *Albania at War, 1939–1945* (West Lafayette, IN, 1999), pp. 186–7.

17 D. M. Glantz, *Zhukov's Greatest Disaster: The Red Army's Epic Disaster in Operation Mars* (Lawrence, KS, 1999).

18 A. Warren, *Singapore 1942* (London, 2002), p. xii. For conclusions, pp. 291–3. For command issues, see also W. F. Buckingham, *Arnhem 1944, A Reappraisal* (Stroud, 2002).

19   D. M. Glantz, *Soviet Operational and Tactical Combat in Manchuria, 1945: 'August Storm'* (London, 2003).

20   H. Strachan, *The Direction of War. Contemporary Strategy in Historical Perspective* (Cambridge, 2013).

21   K.-H. Frieser, 'Kursk – Turning Point of the War?', *RUSI Journal*, 148, no. 5 (October 2003), p. 80.

22   J. Holland (ed.), *An Englishman at War. The Wartime Diaries of Stanley Christopherson* (London, 2014), p. 510.

23   S. H. Newton (ed.), *Kursk. The German View. Eyewitness Reports of Operation Citadel by the German Commanders* (Cambridge, MA, 2002), esp. pp. 405–6, 441.

24   D. Reynolds, '1940: fulcrum of the twentieth century', *International Affairs*, 66 (1990), pp. 325–50.

25   W. Murray, 'May 1940: Contingency and Fragility of the German RMA', in M. Knox and W. Murray (eds), *The Dynamics of Military Revolution 1300–2050* (Cambridge, 2001), p. 173; J. Jackson, *The Fall of France. The Nazi Invasion of 1940* (Oxford, 2003).

26   J. S. Corum, 'Myths of *Blitzkrieg*: The Enduring Mythology of the 1940 Campaign', *Historically Speaking*, 6 (2005), pp. 11–13.

27   J. P. Levy, 'Was There Something Unique to the Japanese That Lost Them the Battle of Midway?', *Naval War College Review*, 67 (2014), pp. 123–4.

28   J. S. Corum, *Wolfram von Richthofen: Master of the German Air War* (Lawrence, KS, 2008).

29   A. D. Harvey, 'The Battle of Britain in 1940 and "Big Week" in 1944: A Comparative Perspective', *Air Power History*, 59, no. 1 (spring 2012), p. 35.

30   For the latter, see R. Higham (ed.), *The Writing of Official Military History* (Westport, CT, 1999); J. Grey (ed.), *The Last Word? Essays on Official History in the United States and British Commonwealth* (Westport, CT, 2003); T. Cook, *Clio's Warriors: Canadian Historians and the Writing of the World Wars* (Vancouver, 2006).

31   D. Stahel, *Operation Barbarossa and Germany's Defeat in the East* (Cambridge, 2009).

32   D. M. Glantz, *Barbarossa: Hitler's Invasion of Russia, 1941* (Stroud, 2001); Glantz (ed.), *The Initial Phase of the War on the Eastern Front, 22 June – August 1941* (London, 1993).

33   For a critical view of counterfactuals and World War Two as a whole, R. J. Evans, *Altered Pasts. Counterfactuals in History* (London, 2014), pp. 70–80, 95–129.

34   For counterfactuals see M. Burleigh, 'Nazi Europe: What If Nazi Germany Had Defeated the Soviet Union?', in N. Ferguson (ed.), *Virtual History* (London, 1997), pp. 321–47; S. S. Montefiore, 'Stalin Flees Moscow in 1941', in A. Roberts (ed.), *What Might Have Been* (London, 2004), pp. 134–53; H. H. Herwig, 'Hitler Wins in the East but Germany Still Loses World War II', in P. E. Tetlock, R. N. Lebow and G. Parker (eds), *Unmaking*

the West: 'What-If' Scenarios That Rewrite World History (Ann Arbor, MI, 2006), p. 33.

35   S. T. Barry, *Battalion Commanders at War: US Army Tactical Leadership in the Mediterranean Theater, 1942–1943* (Lawrence, KS, 2013).

36   LH. Alanbrooke papers 6/2/37.

37   J. Buckley, *Monty's Men* (New Haven, CT, 2013), esp. pp. 15–17.

38   A. N. Caravaggio, '"Winning" the Pacific War. The Masterful Strategy of Commander Minoru Genda', *Naval War College Review*, 67 (2014), pp. 85–118.

39   For a crisp summary, D. A. Yerxa, '*Armageddon*: An Interview with Sir Max Hastings', *Historically Speaking*, 6 (2005), p. 15.

40   NA, PREM (Prime Minister's Office) 3/328/5 (Operations in Northern Norway, May–June 1940), pp. 23–6.

41   R. M. Citino, *The German Way of War* (Lawrence, KS, 2005).

42   A. Beevor, *D-Day: The Battle for Normandy* (London, 2009).

43   Ideology is also an issue for democracies.

44   M. R. Matheny, *Carrying the War to the Enemy: American Operational Art to 1945* (Norman, OK, 2011).

45   M. Edelstein, 'The Size of the U.S. Armed Forces during World War II: Feasibility and War Planning', *Research in Economic History*, 29 (2001), pp. 47–97; R. D. Marcuss and R. E. Kane, 'U.S. National Income and Product Statistics: Born of the Great Depression and World War II', *Survey of Current Business*, 87 (2007), pp. 32–46.

46   S. I. Schwartz (ed.), *Atomic Audit: The Costs and Consequences of U.S. Nuclear Weapons since 1940* (Washington, DC, 1998), p. 58; R. Rhodes, *The Making of the Atomic Bomb* (New York, 1988).

47   P. A. Ndiaye, *Nylon and Bombs: DuPont and the March of Modern America* (Baltimore, MD, 2007).

48   M. Walker, *German National Socialism and the Quest for Nuclear Power, 1939–1945* (New York, 1989).

49   J. Holland (ed.), *An Englishman at War*, p. 4.

50   T. D. Biddle, 'Dresden 1945: Reality, History, and Memory', *Journal of Military History*, 72 (2008), p. 449.

Recollection: The War in Europe

1   A. J. Kochavi, 'The Moscow Declaration, the Kharkov Trial, and the Question of a Policy on Major War Criminals in the Second World War', *History*, 76 (1991), pp. 401–17.

2   F. Hirsch, 'The Soviets at Nuremberg: International Law, Propaganda, and the Making of the Postwar Order', *American Historical Review*, 113 (2007), p. 726.

3   P. Heberer and J. Matthäus (eds), *Atrocities on Trial: Historical Perspectives on the Politics of Prosecuting War Crimes* (Lincoln, NE, 2008).

4   D. Bloxham, *Genocide on Trial. War Crimes Trials and the Formation of Holocaust History and Memory* (Oxford, 2001), pp. 156–81, 226.

5   D. Bloxham, '"The Trial that Never Was": Why there was no Second International Trial of Major War Criminals at Nuremberg', *History*, 87 (2002), pp. 41–60.

6   For criticism, N. Bethell, *The Last Secret* (London, 1977) and N. Tolstoy, *The Minister and the Massacres* (London, 1986). For an effective defence, R. Knight, 'Harold Macmillan and the Cossacks: was there a Klagenfurt Conspiracy?', *Intelligence and National Security*, 1 (1986), pp. 234–54.

7   A. J. Kochavi, *Confronting Captivity: Britain and the United States and their POWs in Nazi Germany* (Chapel Hill, NC, 2005).

8   M. J. Kurtz, *America and the Return of Nazi Contraband: The Recovery of Europe's Cultural Treasures* (Cambridge, 2006).

9   B. Frommer, *National Cleansing: Retribution against Nazi Collaborators in Postwar Czechoslovakia* (New York, 2005).

10   M. Black, 'Death in Berlin, 1933–1961', *Bulletin of the German Historical Institute, Washington*, 42 (2008), pp. 87–9.

11   W. J. Risch, *The Ukrainian West: Culture and the Fate of Empire in Soviet Lviv* (Cambridge, MA, 2011).

12   A. Warren, *World War II. A Military History* (Stroud, 2008), p. 341.

13   M. D. Brown, 'Forcible Population Transfers – A flawed legacy or an unavoidable necessity in protracted ethnic conflicts? The Case of the Sudeten Germans', *RUSI Journal*, 148 (2003), pp. 81–7.

14   G. Thum, *Uprooted: How Breslau became Wroclaw during the Century of Expulsions* (Princeton, NJ, 2011).

15   J. King, *Budweisers into Czechs and Germans: A Local History of Bohemian Politics, 1848–1948* (Princeton, NJ, 2002); C. Bryant, *Prague in Black: Nazi Rule and Czech Nationalism* (Cambridge, MA, 2007); Frommer, *National Cleansing*.

16   R. N. Lebow, W. Kansteiner and C. Fogu (eds), *The Politics of Memory in Postwar Europe* (Durham, NC, 2006).

17   N. A. Sørenson, 'Narrating the Second World War in Denmark since 1945', *Contemporary European History*, 14 (2005), pp. 295–315, and 'The Second World War and Continuity and Change in Danish History', in C. B. Christensen and A. Warring (eds), *Finland og Danmark: Krig og besaettelse, 1939–45* (Roskilde, 2007), pp. 143–54.

18   B. Singer, *Maxime Weygand: A Biography of the French General in Two World Wars* (Jefferson, NC, 2008), pp. 118–72.

19   M. Zanasi, 'Globalizing *Hanjian*: The Suzhou Trials and the Post-World War II Discourse on Collaboration', *American Historical Review*, 113 (2008), p. 740.

20   D. Reid, 'Resistance and Its Discontents: Affairs, Archives, Avowals and the Aubracs', *Journal of Modern History*, 77 (2005), pp. 97–137.

21   M. S. Alexander, *The Republic in Danger: General Maurice Gamelin, and the Politics of French Defence* (Cambridge, 1992).

22   For an instance of the continuing tendency to emphasise the role of the Resistance, M. Cobb, *The Resistance: The French Fight Against the Nazis* (London, 2009).

23   R. Vinen, *The Unfree French: Life under the Occupation* (New Haven, CT, 2006).

24   B. Singer, *Maxime Weygand: A Biography of the French General in Two World Wars* (Jefferson, NC, 2008).

25   S. R. Suleiman, *Crises of Memory and the Second World War* (Cambridge, MA, 2006).

26   C. Flood, 'The Politics of Counter-Memory on the French Extreme Right', *Journal of European Studies*, 35 (2005), pp. 221–36.

27   O. Wieviorka, *Divided Memory: French Recollections of World War II from the Liberation to the Present* (Stanford, CA, 2012).

28   B. Vergez-Chaignon, *Les Vichysto-Résistants de 1940 à nos jours* (Paris, 2008).

29   G. Mann, *Native Sons: West African Veterans and France in the Twentieth Century* (Durham, NC, 2006).

30   R. Scheck, '"They Are Just Savages": German Massacres of Black Soldiers from the French Army in 1940', *Journal of Modern History*, 77 (2005), pp. 325–44 and *Hitler's African Victims: The German Army Massacres of Black French Soldiers in 1940* (Cambridge, 2006). Scheck's work has not received the attention it deserves, not least from military historians.

31   G. Pritchard, *Niemandsland: A History of Unoccupied Germany, 1944–1945* (Cambridge, 2012).

32   K. H. Jarausch, *After Hitler: Recivilizing Germans, 1945–1995* (Oxford, 2006).

33   For the use of Nazi intelligence 'assets', R. Breitman, N. J. W. Goda, T. Nafati and R. Wolfe (eds), *U.S. Intelligence and the Nazis* (Cambridge, 2005). The East German *Stasi* also made large-scale use of Nazis as informants as well as using Nazi concentration camps, notably Sachsenhausen.

34   R. Bessel and D. Schumann (eds), *Life after Death: Approaches to a Cultural and Social History of Europe during the 1940s and 1950s* (Cambridge, 2003).

35   G. D. Cohen, *In War's Wake: Europe's Displaced Persons in the Postwar Order* (Oxford, 2012).

36   J. Herf, *Divided Memory: The Nazi Past in the Two Germanies* (Cambridge, MA, 1997).

37   J. K. Olick, *In the House of the Hangman: The Agonies of German Defeat, 1943–1949* (Chicago, IL, 2005); A. Grossmann, *Jews, Germans, and Allies* (Princeton, NJ, 2007).

38   C. R. Browning, *Ordinary Men: Reserve Police Battalion 101 and the Final Solution in Poland* (New York, 1992); D. Goldhagen, *Hitler's Willing Executioners* (London, 1996); G. Eley (ed.), *The 'Goldhagen Effect': History, Memory, Nazism. Facing the German Past* (Ann Arbor, MI, 2000).

39   R. G. Moeller, *War Stories: The Search for a Usable Past in the Federal Republic of Germany* (Berkeley, CA, 2001).

40   S. J. Wiesen, *West German Industry and the Challenge of the Nazi Past, 1945–55* (Chapel Hill, NC, 2001).

41   C. Morina, *Legacies of Stalingrad: Remembering the Eastern Front in Germany since 1945* (Cambridge, 2011).

42   For a comparison with attitudes in Japan, I. Buruma, *The Wages of Guilt: Memories of War in Germany and Japan* (New York, 1994).

43   P. Gassert and A. E. Steinweis (eds), *Coping with the Nazi Past: West German Debates on Nazism and Generational Conflict, 1955–1975* (Oxford, 2006); A. Schildt, 'The Long Shadows of the Second World War: The Impact of Experiences and Memories of War on West German Society', *German Historical Institute, London, Bulletin*, 29 (2007), pp. 29–31.

44   N. Stoltzfus and H. Friedlander (eds), *Nazi Crimes and the Law* (New York, 2008).

45   Turned into a film in 1981. See also M. L. Hadley, *Count Not the Dead: the Popular Image of the German Submarine* (Montreal, 1995).

46   R. Smelser and E. J. Davies, *The Myth of the Eastern Front: The Nazi–Soviet War in American Popular Culture* (Cambridge, 2008).

47   G. Reitlinger, *The SS: alibi of a nation* (London, 1962); W. Wette, *The Wehrmacht: History, Myth, Reality* (Cambridge, MA, 2006).

48   A. B. Rossino, *Hitler Strikes Poland: Blitzkrieg, Ideology, and Atrocity* (Lawrence, KS, 2003).

49   T. Schulte, *The German Army and Nazi Policies in Occupied Russia* (Oxford, 1989); H. Heer, 'The Difficulty of Ending a War: Reactions to the Exhibition "War of Extermination: Crimes of the Wehrmacht, 1941 to 1944"', *History Workshop Journal*, 46 (1998), pp. 187–203.

50   G. P. Megargee, *War of Annihilation: Combat and Genocide on the Eastern Front, 1941* (Lanham, MA, 2006).

51   N. Goda, 'Black Marks: Hitler's Bribery of His Senior Officers During World War II', *Journal of Modern History*, 72 (2000), pp. 413–52; R. A. Hart, *Guderian: Panzer Pioneer or Myth Maker?* (Washington, 2006).

52   D. O. Pendas, *The Frankfurt Auschwitz Trial, 1963–1965: Genocide, History, and the Limits of the Law* (Cambridge, 2006).

53   W. Kansteiner, *In Pursuit of German Memory: History, Television and Politics after Auschwitz* (Athens, OH, 2006).

54   E. B. Bukey, *Hitler's Austria: Popular Sentiment in the Nazi Era, 1938–45* (Chapel Hill, NC, 2000).

55   A. M. de Zayas, *A Terrible Revenge: The Ethnic Cleansing of the East European Germans* (2nd edn, Basingstoke, 2005); B. Niven, *Germans as*

Victims: Remembering the Past in Contemporary Germany (Basingstoke, 2006).

56 A. Demshuk, *The Lost German East: Forced Migration and the Politics of Memory, 1945–1970* (Cambridge, 2012).

57 T. D. Curp, *A Clean Sweep? The Politics of Ethnic Cleansing in Western Poland, 1945–1960* (Rochester, NY, 2006).

58 D. Barnouw, *The War in the Empty Air: Victims, Perpetrators, and Postwar Germans* (Bloomington, IN, 2005).

59 Rapes by Soviet soldiers were highlighted in the press reviews of A. Beevor's *Downfall*, on the Soviet conquest of Berlin. For rapes by American soldiers, J. R. Lilly, *Taken by Force: Rape and American GIs in Europe during World War II* (New York, 2007).

60 E. Mawdsley, *Thunder in the East. The Nazi–Soviet War, 1941–1945* (London, 2005), p. 406, correcting Earl Ziemke's *Stalingrad to Berlin* (Washington, 1968), p. 425 and 'later debates among West German historians'.

61 K. Schmider, 'The Last of the First: Veterans of the *Jagdwaffe* Tell their Story', *Journal of Military History*, 73 (2009), pp. 231–49. See, in particular, pp. 233–4. On Dönitz, H. H. Herwig, 'Germany and the Battle of the Atlantic', in R. Chickering, S. Förster and B. Greiner (eds), *A World at Total War. Global Conflict and the Politics of Destruction, 1937–1945* (Cambridge, 2005), pp. 81–5.

62 G. Ueberschur, 'Hitler's Decision to Attack the Soviet Union in Recent German Historiography', in J. L. Wieczynski (ed.), *Operation Barbarossa* (Salt Lake City, UT, 1993), p. 293.

63 N. Stargardt, 'Victims of Bombing and Retaliation', *Bulletin of the German Historical Institute of London*, 26, no. 2 (November 2004), pp. 57–70; J. Friedrich, *The Fire. The Bombing of Germany, 1940–1945* (New York, 2007).

64 F. Taylor, *Dresden: Tuesday, 13 February 1945* (London, 2004).

65 P. Addison and J. A. Crang (eds), *Firestorm: The Bombing of Dresden, 1945* (Chicago, IL, 2006).

66 H. Probert, *Bomber Harris* (London, 2001), p. 319.

67 E. Corwin, 'The Bombing of Dresden as Portrayed in German Accounts, East and West', *UCLA Historical Journal*, 8 (1987), pp. 71–96.

68 R. J. Evans, *Telling Lies About Hitler* (London, 2002), pp. 160–6.

69 H. P. Willmott, *The Great Crusade* (2nd edn, Washington, 2008), p. 299.

70 A. Tooze, *The Wages of Destruction: The Making and Breaking of the Nazi Economy* (London, 2006).

71 A. C. Mierzejewski, *The Collapse of the German War Economy, 1939–1945: Allied Air Power and the German National Railway* (Chapel Hill, NC, 1988).

72 N. Gregor, 'A *Schicksalsgemeinschaft?* Allied Bombing, Civilian Morale, and Social Dissolution in Nuremberg, 1942–1945', *Historical Journal*, 43 (2000), pp. 1068–70.

73 R. J. Overy, *The Bombing War. Europe 1939–1945* (London, 2013), pp. 59–205. An important work, not least for its discussion of the bombing of Soviet targets. For an attempt by a knowledgeable airpower specialist to extenuate the air attacks that, nevertheless, finds senior German commanders guilty of war crimes and of loyally supporting Hitler's fundamentally irrational programme of conquest, J. S. Corum, *Wolfram von Richthofen. Master of the German Air War* (Lawrence, KS, 2008), pp. 21–6.

74 G. C. Cocks, *The State of Health: Illness in Nazi Germany* (Oxford, 2012).

75 For an instructive review, see that by William Rubinstein, *History Today* (July 2008). See also the interview of Baker by David Aaronovitch in *The Times*, 7 June 2008.

76 M. R. D. Foot, 'Introduction', to Foot and Dear (eds), *The Oxford Companion to World War Two* (2nd edn, Oxford, 2001), p. xvii.

77 http://www.telegraph.co.uk/news/worldnews/europe/france/5378587/Allies-bombing-on-D-Day-close-to-war-crime-claims-historian.html (accessed 18 July 2014).

78 For an effective critique by a popular historian of the morality of German policy and warmaking, M. Hastings, *Armageddon. The Battle for Germany, 1944–45* (London, 2004), pp. 105, 199–200, 341.

79 K. Urbach, 'Between Saviour and Villain: 100 Years of Bismarck biographies', *Historical Journal*, 41 (1998), pp. 1150–2.

80 M. Fahlbusch, *German Scholars and Ethnic Cleansing, 1920–1945* (New York, 2005).

81 J. S. Eder, 'From Mass Murder to Exhibition: Museum Representations to Transatlantic Comparison', *Bulletin of the German Historical Institute*, 50 (Spring 2012), p. 160.

82 For the wider context, G. D. Rosenfeld and P. Jaskot (eds), *Beyond Berlin: Twelve German Cities Confront the Nazi Past* (Ann Arbor, Michigan, 2008).

83 N. Gregor, *Haunted City. Nuremberg and the Nazi Past* (New Haven, CT, 2008), p. 378.

84 G. H. Hartmann (ed.), *Bitburg in Moral and Political Perspective* (Bloomington, IN, 1986).

85 G. Schwan, 'Bridging the Oder', *Bulletin of the German Historical Institute, Washington*, 40 (2007), p. 46.

86 *Independent*, 31 May 2006, p. 22.

87 O. Chadwick, *Britain and the Vatican during the Second World War* (Cambridge, 1986).

88 Although for a linkage, in the case of the influential historian Martin Broszat, between membership in the Hitler Youth generation and of the Nazi Party, with a reluctance to accept widespread complicity in the Holocaust, see O. Bartov, 'Eastern Europe as the Site of Genocide', *Journal of Modern History*, 80 (2008), pp. 586–7.

89　L. Wildenthal, 'Human Rights Activism in Occupied and Early West Germany: The Case of the German League for Human Rights', *Journal of Modern History*, 80 (2008), pp. 554–5.

90　K. H. Jarausch, *After Hitler: Recivilizing Germans, 1945–1995* (New York, 2006); J. J. Sheehan, *Where Have All the Soldiers Gone? The Transformation of Modern Europe* (Boston, MA, 2008).

91　R. Knight, 'Denazification and Integration in the Austrian Province of Carinthia', *Journal of Modern History*, 79 (207), pp. 572–612.

92　H. Heer, W. Manoschek, A. Pollak and R. Wodak, *The Discursive Construction of History: Remembering the Wehrmacht's War of Annihilation* (Basingstoke, 2008); (for Berlin) U. Staiger, H. Steiner and A. Webber (eds), *Memory Culture and the Contemporary City. Building Sites* (Basingstoke, 2009); B. Niven and C. Paver (eds), *Memorialization in Germany since 1945* (Basingstoke, 2010); J. Arnold, *The Allied Air War and Urban Memory. The Legacy of Strategic Bombing in Germany* (Cambridge, 2011).

93　His seven-volume biography of Mussolini appeared from 1965 to 1992.

94　P. Ballinger, *History in Exile: Memory and Identity at the Borders of the Balkans* (Princeton, NJ, 2003).

95　D. Rodogno, *Fascism's European Empire: Italian Occupation during the Second World War* (Cambridge, 2006); S. Lecoeur, *Mussolini's Greek Island. Fascism and the Italian Occupation of Syros in World War II* (London, 2009). The novel and film *Captain Corelli's Mandolin* attracted Western popular attention to the Italian occupation.

96　M. Sarfatti, *The Jews in Mussolini's Italy: From Equality to Persecution* (Madison, W. I, 2006); N. Caracciolo, (trans F. R. Koffler and R. Koffler) *Uncertain Refuge: Italy and the Jews during the Holocaust* (Urbana, IL, 1995).

97　U. Blacker, A. Etkind and J. Fedor (eds), *Memory and Theory in Eastern Europe* (London, 2013).

98　S. K. Pavlowitch, *Hitler's New Disorder. The Second World War in Yugoslavia* (London, 2008), p. 282.

99　L. A. Kirschenbaum, *The Legacy of the Siege of Leningrad, 1941–1995: Myth, Memories, and Monuments* (Cambridge, 2006).

100　K. Slepyan, *Stalin's Guerrillas: Soviet Partisans in World War II* (Lawrence, KS, 2006).

101　N. Tumarkin, *The Living and the Dead: The Rise and Fall of the Cult of World War II in Russia* (New York, 1994).

102　M. Bucur, 'Edifices of the Past. War Memorials and Heroes in Twentieth-Century Romania', in M. Todorova (ed.), *Balkan Identities. Nation and Memory* (London, 2004).

103　I. Kershaw, *Hitler, the Germans, and the Final Solution* (New Haven, CT, 2008), p. 23.

104　L. Rees, *World War Two Behind Closed Doors. Stalin, the Nazis and the West* (London, 2008), p. 411.

105　R. Markwick, 'The Great Patriotic War in Soviet and Post-Soviet Collective

Memory', in D. Stone (ed.), *The Oxford Handbook of Postwar European History* (Oxford, 2012), pp. 692–3.

106   R. Ioanid, *The Holocaust in Romania* (Chicago, IL, 2000).

107   P. A. Hanebrink, *In Defense of Christian Hungary: Religion, Nationalism, and Antisemitism, 1890–1944* (Ithaca, NY, 2006).

108   D. Gaunt, P. A. Levine and L. Palosuo (eds), *Collaboration and Resistance During the Holocaust: Belarus, Estonia, Latvia, Lithuania* (Berne, 2004).

109   V. O. Lumans, *Latvia in World War II* (New York, 2006).

110   P. K. Grimsted, *Trophies of War and Empire. The Archival Heritage of Ukraine, World War II, and the International Politics of Restitution* (Cambridge, MA, 2001), pp. 196–209.

111   O. Bartov, *Erased: Vanished Traces of Jewish Galicia in Present-Day Ukraine* (Princeton, NJ, 2007). More generally, T. Snyder, *Bloodlands. Europe between Hitler and Stalin* (London, 2010), and R. Pyrah, 'From "Borderland" via "Bloodlands" to Heartland? Recent Western Historiography of Ukraine', *English Historical Review*, 129 (2014), pp. 139–56.

112   M. C. Steinlauf, *Bondage to the Dead: Poland and the Memory of the Holocaust* (Syracuse, NY, 1997).

113   J. T. Gross, *Neighbors: The Destruction of the Jewish Community in Jedwabne, Poland* (Princeton, NJ, 2001), and *Fear: Anti-Semitism in Poland after Auschwitz. An Essay in Historical Interpretation* (Princeton, NJ, 2006); A. Polonsky and J. B. Michlik (eds), *The Neighbors Respond: The Controversy over the Jedwabne Massacre in Poland* (Princeton, NJ, 2003).

114   P. M. H. Bell, 'Censorship, Propaganda and Public Opinion: The Case of the Katyn Graves, 1943', *Transactions of the Royal Historical Society*, 5th series, 39 (1989), p. 71.

115   D. E. Murphy, *What Stalin Knew: The Enigma of Barbarossa* (New Haven, CT, 2005).

116   R. R. Reese, 'Lessons of the Winter War: A Study in the Military Effectiveness of the Red Army, 1939–1940', *Journal of Military History*, 72 (2008), pp. 825–52. For a narrative account benefiting from access to the archives, C. Bellamy, *Absolute War: Soviet Russia in the Second World War* (London, 2007).

117   A. Hill, 'British Lend-Lease Aid and the Soviet War Effort, June 1941–June 1942', *Journal of Military History*, 71 (2007), p. 776.

118   Pavlowitch, *Hitler's New Disorder*, p. viii.

119   E. Redžić, *Bosnia and Herzegovina in the Second World War* (London, 2005).

120   M. A. Hoare, *Genocide and Resistance in Hitler's Bosnia: The Partisans and the Chetniks, 1941–1943* (Oxford, 2006).

121   C. Carmichael, 'Watch on the Drina: Genocide, War and Nationalist Ideology', *History*, 98 (2013), p. 605; G. Goldstein, *1941: The Year That Keeps Returning* (London, 2013).

122 D. Potočnik and J. Razpotnik, 'The Second World War and Socialistic Yugoslavia in Slovenian Textbooks', in C. Koulouri (ed.), *Clio in the Balkans. The Politics of History Education* (Thessaloniki, 2002), pp. 228–31.

123 M. Najbar-Agičić, 'The Yugoslav History in Croatian Textbooks', in Koulouri (ed.), *Clio*, pp. 239–43.

124 D. Stojanovic, 'Yugoslavia in a Broken Mirror. The Serbian Textbooks', in Koulouri (ed.), *Clio.*, pp. 249–60.

125 T. Snyder, *The Reconstruction of Nations: Poland, Ukraine, Lithuania, Belarus, 1569–1999* (New Haven, CT, 2003).

126 B. Moore, *Victims and Survivors: Nazi Persecution of the Jews in the Netherlands, 1940–1945* (London, 1997).

127 C. Fasseur, *Wilhelmina. Krijgshaftig in een vormeloze jas* (Amsterdam, 2001).

128 I have much benefited from the advice of Karl de Leeuw on this section.

129 A. Jackson, *The British Empire and the Second World War* (London, 2006).

130 J. Chapman, *War and Film* (London, 2008), p. 213.

131 S. P. Mackenzie, '"War in the Air": Churchill, the Air Ministry and the BBC Response to "Victory at Sea"', *Contemporary British History*, 20 (2006).

132 A. J. Cumming, 'The Air Marshal versus the Admiral: Air Marshal Sir Hugh Dowding and Admiral of the Fleet Sir Charles Morton Forbes in the Pantheon', *History*, 94 (2009), pp. 203–28.

133 A. J. Cumming, 'We'll Get By with a Little Help from Our Friends: The Battle of Britain and the Pilot in Anglo–American Relations, 1940–45', *European Journal of American Culture*, 26 (2007), pp. 11–26.

134 *Daily Telegraph*, 24, 26 August 2006, 30 October 2007.

135 See section 'The Making of a British Legend', in P. Addison and J. Crang (eds), *The Burning Blue: A New History of the Battle of Britain* (London, 2000).

136 For example, G. Corrigan, *Blood, Sweat and Arrogance and the Myths of Churchill's War* (London, 2006).

137 V. Rothwell, *War Aims in the Second World War: The War Aims of the Major Belligerents, 1939–45* (Edinburgh, 2005).

138 R. J. Overy, 'Identity, Politics and Technology in the RAF's History', *RUSI Journal*, 153, 6 (December 2008), p. 77.

139 A. C. Grayling, *Among the Dead Cities: Was the Allied Bombing of Civilians in World War Two a Necessity or a Crime?* (London, 2006).

140 *The Times*, 5, 8 December. 2003.

141 A. J. Cumming, *The Royal Navy and the Battle of Britain* (Annapolis, 2010).

142 B. Pertwee, *Dad's Army: The Making of a Television Legend* (Newton Abbot, 1989).

143 A. Parr (ed.), *The Big Show: New Zealanders, D-Day and the War in Europe* (Auckland, 2006); M. Hutching (ed.), *Against the Rising Sun: New Zealanders Remember the Pacific War* (Auckland, New Zealand, 2006).

144   For example, J. Thompson, *Dunkirk. Retreat to Victory* (London, 2008), p. xiv.

145   D. Johnson, 'We can make a difference', *Standpoint*, 12 (May 2009), p. 5.

146   M. Burleigh, *The Third Reich. A New History* (2000; London, 2001 edn), pp. 23, 811.

147   For example, T. Bower, 'My clash with death-camp Hanna', *Sunday Times*, 15 February 2009, and F. Raphael, 'Bad beyond imagination', *Standpoint*, 10 (March 2009), pp. 54–7.

148   F. Weissman, *Fantasies of Witnessing: Postwar Efforts to Experience the Holocaust* (Ithaca, NY, 2004).

149   D. Wheeler, 'Godard's List: Why Spielberg and Auschwitz are Number One', *Media History*, 15 (2009), p. 200.

150   T. Bower, *Nazi Gold: The Full Story of the Fifty-Year Swiss-Nazi Conspiracy to Steal Billions from Europe's Jews and Holocaust Survivors* (London, 1997); G. Kreis (ed.), *Switzerland and the Second World War* (London, 2000).

151   F. J. Coppa, *The Papacy, the Jews, and the Holocaust* (Washington, 2006).

152   M. Phayer, *Pius XII, the Holocaust, and the Cold War* (Bloomington, IN, 2008).

153   For a concise journalistic defence, S. Caldwell, 'This papal visit is a good time to reprieve Pius XII', *Spectator*, 16 May 2009, p. 20. For the plan to invade the Vatican, D. Kurzman, *A Special Mission* (Cambridge, MA, 2007).

154   *Last Days of the Reich. The Diary of Count Folke Bernadotte* (Barnsley, 2009), p. 101. Originally published as *The Fall of the Curtain: Last Days of the Third Reich* (London, 1945).

155   G. Kleinfeld and L. Tambs, *Hitler's Spanish Legion: The Blue Division in Russia* (Carbondale, IL, 1979).

156   W. H. Bowen, *Spain during World War II* (Columbia, Missouri, 2006); S. G. Payne, *Franco and Hitler: Spain, Germany, and World War II* (New Haven, CT, 2008).

157   S. Terkel, *The Good War: An Oral History of World War II* (New York, 1984); M. C. C. Adams, *The Best War Ever: America and World War II* (Baltimore, MD, 1994); M. Torgovnick, *The War Complex: World War II in Our Time* (Chicago, IL, 2005).

158   See, for example, M. A. Stoler, *Allies in War: Britain and America against the Axis Powers, 1940–1945* (London, 2005).

159   B. F. Pauley, *Hitler, Stalin, and Mussolini* (3rd edn, Wheeling, IL, 2009), p. xiii.

160   W. I. Hitchcock, *The Bitter Road to Freedom. A New History of the Liberation of Europe* (New York, 2008), pp. 368–70. For the pressures of Liberation in Belgium, P. Schrijvers, *Liberators. The Allies and Belgian Society, 1944–1945* (Cambridge, 2009).

161   M. Glantz, 'An Officer and a Diplomat? The Ambiguous Position of Philip

R. Faymonville and United States-Soviet Relations, 1941–1943', *Journal of Military History*, 72 (2008), pp. 176–7.

162 H. Luce, foreword to 1961 edition of J. F. Kennedy, *Why England Slept* (New York, 1940), pp. ix–xii.

163 K. Fermaglich, *American Dreams and Nazi Nightmares: Early Holocaust Consciousness and Liberal America, 1957–1965* (Waltham, MA, 2006).

164 Hitchcock, *Bitter Road to Freedom*, p. 370.

165 M. Spiering and M. Wintle (eds), *European Identity and the Second World War* (Basingstoke, 2011).

166 S. Moyn, 'Intellectuals and Nazism', in D. Stone (ed.), *The Oxford Handbook of Postwar European History* (Oxford, 2012), p. 690.

Recollection: The War in Asia

1 D. Gatu, *Village China at War: The Impact of Resistance to Japan, 1937–1945* (Vancouver, 2007).

2 J. Taylor, *The Generalissimo. Chiang Kai-shek and the Struggle for Modern China* (Cambridge, MA, 2009).

3 L. Huaiyin, *Reinventing Modern China: Imagination and Authentication in Chinese Historical Writing* (Honolulu, HI, 2013).

4 R. Mitter, 'Writing War: Autobiography, Modernity and Wartime Narrative in Nationalist China, 1937–1946', *Transactions of the Royal Historical Society*, 18 (2008), p. 210.

5 A. Waldron, 'China's New Remembering of World War II: The Case of Zhang Zizhong', *Modern Asian Studies*, 30 (1996), pp. 945–78; R. Mitter, 'Old Ghosts, New Memories: Changing China's History in the Era of Post-Mao Politics', *Journal of Contemporary History*, 38 (2003), pp. 117–31; P. Coble, 'China's "New Remembering" of the Anti-Japanese War of Resistance 1937–1945', *China Quarterly*, 190 (2007), pp. 394–410.

6 R. Mitter, *China's War with Japan 1937–1945: The Struggle for Survival* (London, 2013), p. 384.

7 Mitter, *China's War with Japan*, pp. 384–6.

8 C. Rose, *Sino–Japanese Relations: Facing the Past, Looking to the Future?* (London, 2004).

9 T. Berger, *War, Guilt, and World Politics after World War II* (Cambridge, 2012).

10 F. Seraphim, *War Memory and Social Politics in Japan, 1945–2005* (Cambridge, MA, 2006).

11 Y. Daqing, 'Convergence or Divergence? Recent Historical Writings on the Rape of Nanjing', *American Historical Review*, 104 (1999), pp. 842–65; J. Fogel (ed.), *The Nanjing Massacre in History and Historiography* (Berkeley, CA, 2000); P. Li (ed.), *Japanese War Crimes: The Search for Justice*

(New Brunswick, NJ, 2003); S. Richter and W. Höpken, *Vergangenheit im Gesellschaftskonflikt: ein Historikerstreit in Japan* (Cologne, 2003); R. B. Jeans, 'Victims or Victimizers? Museums, Textbooks, and the War Debate in contemporary Japan', *Journal of Military History*, 69 (2005), pp. 149–95.

12   J. H. Boyle, *China and Japan at War, 1937–1941: The Politics of Collaboration* (Stanford, CA, 1972); G. Bunker, *The Peace Conspiracy: Wang Ching-wei and the China War, 1937–1941* (Cambridge, MA, 1972); L. Lincoln, *The Japanese Army in North China, 1937–1941: Problems of Political and Economic Control* (Oxford, 1975); T. Brock, *Collaboration: Japanese Agents and Chinese Elites in Wartime China* (Cambridge, MA, 2005).

13   I have benefited from discussing this issue with Yasuo Naito.

14   M. G. Sheftall, *Blossoms in the Wind: Human Legacies of the Kamikaze* (New York, 2005).

15   Y. Totani, *The Tokyo War Crimes Trials: The Pursuit of Justice in the Wake of World War II* (Cambridge, MA, 2008); N. Boister and R. Cryer, *The Tokyo International Military Tribunal: A Reappraisal* (Oxford, 2008).

16   G. Hicks, *The Comfort Women: Japan's Brutal Regime of Enforced Prostitution in the Second World War* (New York, 1994); Y. Tanaka, *Japan's Comfort Women: Sexual Slavery and Prostitution during World War II and the US Occupation* (London, 2002).

17   U. S. Baclagon, *The Philippine Resistance Movement against Japan* (Manila, 1966).

18   M. W. Charney, *A History of Modern Burma* (Cambridge, 2009), p. 55.

19   W. Gruhl, *Imperial Japan's World War Two, 1931–1945* (New Brunswick, NJ, 2007).

20   P. Williams and D. Wallace, *Unit 731: Japan's Secret Biological Warfare in World War II* (London, 1989).

21   R. S. Burrell, *The Ghosts of Iwo Jima* (College Station, TX, 2006).

22   J. W. Dower, *War without Mercy: Race and Power in the Pacific War* (London, 1986); C. M. Cameron, *American Samurai: Myth, Imagination and the Conduct of Battle in the First Marine Division* (Cambridge, 1994); J. Weingartner, 'War Against Subhumans; Comparisons Between the German War Against the Soviet Union and the American War Against Japan, 1941–45', *Historian*, 58 (1996), pp. 557–73.

23   M. Sturken, 'Absent Images of Memory: Remembering and Reenacting the Japanese Internment', in T. Fujitani (ed.), *Perilous Memories: The Asia–Pacific War(s)* (Durham, NC, 2001), pp. 33–49.

24   E. Bergerud, 'No Quarter: The Pacific Battlefield', *Historically Speaking*, 3 (2002), pp. 8–10.

25   D. Ford, 'British Intelligence on Japanese Army Morale during the Pacific War: Logical Analysis or Racial Stereotyping?', *Journal of Military History*, 69 (2005), pp. 439–74.

26   H. T. Cook, 'Turning Women into Weapons: Japan's Women, the Battle of

Saipan, and the "Nature of the Pacific War"', in N. A. Dombrowski (ed.), *Women and War in the Twentieth Century: Enlisted With or Without Consent* (London, 2004), p. 254; M. Hughes, '"Collateral Damage" and the Battle for Saipan, 1944', *RUSI Journal*, 153 no. 6 (December 2008), pp. 78–81.

27   K. Kakehashi, *So Sad to Fall in Battle: An Account of War Based on General Tadamichi Kuribayashi's Letters from Iwo Jima* (New York, 2007).

28   D. M. Kehn, *A Blue Sea of Blood: Deciphering the Mysterious Fate of the USS Edsall* (Minneapolis, MN, 2008).

29   R. P. Newman, *Enola Gay and the Court of History* (New York, 2004); M. Gallicchio (ed.), *The Unpredictability of the Past: Memories of the Asia–Pacific War in U.S.–East Asian Relations* (Durham, NC, 2007).

30   G. Alperovitz, *Atomic Diplomacy: Hiroshima and Potsdam* (London, 1994) and *The Decision to Use the Atomic Bomb* (London, 1996); T. Hasegawa, *Racing the Enemy: Stalin, Truman, and the Surrender of Japan* (Cambridge, MA, 2005).

31   K. P. Werrell, *Blankets of Fire: U.S. Bombers over Japan during World War II* (Washington DC, 1996).

32   T. B. Allen and N. Polmar, *Code-Name Downfall: The Secret Plan to Invade Japan – and Why Truman Dropped the Bomb* (New York, 1995); R. J. Maddox (ed.), *Hiroshima in History: The Myths of Revisionism* (Columbia, MO, 2007); W. D. Miscamble, *The Most Controversial Decision: Truman, the Atomic Bombs, and the Defeat of Japan* (Cambridge, 2011).

33   G. Feifer, *Tennozan: The Battle of Okinawa and the Atomic Bomb* (New York, 1992); J. R. Skates, *The Invasion of Japan: Alternative to the Bomb* (Columbia, SC, 1994), esp. pp. 254–7; D. M. Giangreco, *Hell to Pay: Operation DOWNFALL and the Invasion of Japan, 1945–1947* (Annapolis, MD, 2009).

34   Major-General William Penney, Director of Intelligence, HQ Supreme Allied Commander S. E. Asia, to Major-General John Sinclair, Director of Military Intelligence at the War Office, 2 May 1945, LH, Penney papers 5/1; D. McCullough, *Truman* (New York, 1992), p. 458.

35   B. J. Bernstein, 'Compelling Japan's Surrender Without the A-bomb, Soviet Entry, or Invasion: Reconsidering the US Bombing Survey's Early-Surrender Conclusions', *Journal of Strategic Studies*, 18 (1995), p. 137.

36   H. Feis, *The Atomic Bomb and the End of World War II* (Princeton, NJ, 1966); R. B. Frank, *Downfall: The End of the Imperial Japanese Empire* (New York, 1999).

37   M. Walker, *German National Socialism and the Quest for Nuclear Power, 1939–1945* (New York, 1989); P. Henshall, *The Nuclear Axis: Germany, Japan, and the Atomic Bomb Race, 1939–1945* (Phoenix, AZ, 2001).

38   A. J. Rotter, *Hiroshima: the World's Bomb* (Oxford, 2008).

39   *The Times*, 7 February 2014.

40   Layton to First Sea Lord, 13 September., Mountbatten to Layton, 15 September 1944, BL. Ad⁴. 74796.

41   R. A. Spector, *In the Ruins of Empire: The Japanese Surrender and the Battle for Postwar Asia* (New York, 2007).

42   K. Roy, 'Military Loyalty in the Colonial Context: A Case Study of the Indian Army during World War II', *Journal of Military History*, 73 (2009), pp. 497–529.

43   A. Jeffreys and P. Rose (eds), *The Indian Army, 1939–47: Experience and Development* (London, 2012).

44   C. Bayly and T. Harper, *Forgotten Armies. Britain's Asian Empire and the War with Japan* (London, 2004).

45   C. Sundaram, 'A Paper Tiger: the Indian National Army in Battle, 1944–5', *War and Society*, 13 (1995), pp. 35–59.

46   G. W. Gong (ed.), *Memory and History in East and Southeast Asia: Issues of Identity in International Relations* (Washington DC, 2001); S. M. Jager and R. Mitter (eds), *Ruptured Histories: War, Memory, and the Post-Cold War in Asia* (Cambridge, MA, 2007).

47   C. Hart, review of J. Sumpton, *Divided Houses: The Hundred Years War III* in *Sunday Times*, Culture section, 29 March 2009, p. 43.

48   J. Black, *The Great War and the Making of the Modern World* (London, 2011).

Conclusions

1   P. Fritzsche, 'The Holocaust and the Knowledge of Murder', *Journal of Modern History*, 80 (2008), p. 613.

2   T. Judt, *Postwar: A History of Europe since 1945* (London, 2005), p. 803.

3   S. Drescher, 'The Atlantic Slave Trade and the Holocaust: A Comparative Analysis', in A. S. Rosenbaum (ed.), *Is the Holocaust Unique? Perspectives on Comparative Genocide* (3rd edn, Boulder, CO, 2009).

4   F. Raphael, 'Bad beyond imagination', *Standpoint*, 10 (March 2009), p. 57.

5   R. Glover, 'The French Fleet, 1807–1814: Britain's Problem; and Madison's Opportunity', *Journal of Modern History*, 39 (1967), pp. 249–51.

6   G. L. Weinberg, 'Unexplored Questions about the German Military During World War II', *Journal of Military History*, 62 (1998), p. 379.

7   G. D. Rosenfeld, 'A Looming Crash or a Soft Landing? Forecasting the Future of the Memory "Industry"', *Journal of Modern History*, 81 (2009), p. 144.

8   D. J. Youngblood, *Russian War Films: On the Cinema Front, 1914–2005* (Lawrence, KS, 2006).

9   B. Harrison, *Seeking a Role. The United Kingdom, 1951–1970* (Oxford, 2009), p. 540.

10   D. Johnson, 'Reality check for the West', *Standpoint*, 61 (April 2014), p. 5.

11   T. Segev, *The Seventh Million: The Israelis and the Holocaust* (New York, 1993).

12 S. Venezia, *Inside the Gas Chambers. Eight Months in the Sonderkommando of Auschwitz* (Cambridge, 2009).

13 H. Rousso, 'History of Memory, Policies of the Past: What For?', in K. H. Jarausch and T. Lindenberger (eds), *Conflicted Memories: Europeanizing Contemporary Histories* (Oxford, 2007), p. 29.

14 D. A. Schmitt, *The Bechuanaland Pioneers and Gunners* (Westport, CT, 2005).

15 R. Ginio, *French Colonialism Unmasked: The Vichy Years in French West Africa* (Lincoln, NE, 2006).

16 T. M. Leonard and J. F. Bratzel (eds), *Latin America during World War II* (Lanham, MD, 2006).

SELECTED FURTHER READING

The emphasis here is on recent works. Earlier scholarship can be approached through these valuable studies.

Adelman, J. R. (ed.) *Hitler and His Allies in World War II* (2007).
Ballinger, P. *History in Exile: Memory and Identity at the Borders of the Balkans* (2003).
Barnouw, D. *The War in the Empty Air: Victims, Perpetrators, and Postwar Germans* (2005).
Bayly, C. and Harper, T. *Forgotten Armies: The Fall of British Asia, 1941–45* (2006).
Bess, M. *Choices Under Fire: Moral Dimensions of World War II* (2006).
Blatt, J. (ed.) *The French Defeat of 1940: Reassessments* (1998).
Bosworth, R. J. B. *Explaining Auschwitz and Hiroshima: History Writing and the Second World War* (1993).
Bowen, H. *Spain During World War II* (2006).
Bryant, C. *Prague in Black. Nazi Rule and Czech Nationalism* (2007).
Buruma, I. *The Wages of Guilt: Memories of War in Germany and Japan* (1994).
Cole, W. *Roosevelt and the Isolationists* (1993).
Davies, P. *Dangerous Liaisons: Collaboration and World War Two* (2005).
Deletant, D. *Hitler's Forgotten Ally: Ion Antonescu and his Regime, Romania 1940–1944* (2006).
Evans, R. J. *In Hitler's Shadow: West German Historians and the Attempt to Escape from the Nazi Past* (1989).
Farrell, B. P. *The Defence and Fall of Singapore, 1940–1942* (2005).
Fujitani, T. (ed.) *Perilous Memories: The Asia-Pacific War(s)* (2001).
Glantz, M. E. *FDR and the Soviet Union: The President's Battles over Foreign Policy* (2005).
Gong, G. W. (ed.), *Memory and History in East and Southeast Asia: Issues of Identity in International Relations* (2001)
Hanebrink, P. A. *In Defense of Christian Hungary: Religion, Nationalism and Anti-Semitism, 1890–1944* (2006).
Herf, J. *Divided Memory: The Nazi Past in the Two Germanys* (1997).
Iriye, A. *The Origins of the Second World War in Asia and the Pacific* (1987).
Jackson, A. *The British Empire and the Second World War* (2006).
Jager, S. M. and Mitter, R. (eds) *Ruptured Histories: War, Memory, and the Post-Cold War in Asia* (2007).

Kansteiner, W. *In Pursuit of German Memory: History, Television, and Politics after Auschwitz* (2006).

Kershaw, I. *Fateful Choices. Ten Decisions that Changed the World, 1940–1941* (2007).

Knox, M. *Common Destiny: Dictatorship, Foreign Policy, and War in Fascist Italy and Nazi Germany* (2000).

Lentin, A. *Lloyd George and the Lost Peace. From Versailles to Hitler, 1919–1940* (2001).

McCann, F. D. *The Brazilian–American Alliance, 1937–1945* (1973).

Maier, C. S. *The Unmasterable Past: History, the Holocaust, and German National Identity* (1988).

Mawdsley, E. *Thunder in the East. The Nazi–Soviet War, 1941–1945* (2005).

—*World War II. A New History* (2009).

Mazower, M. *Hitler's Empire. Nazi Rule on Occupied Europe* (2008).

Moeller, R. G. *War Stories: The Search for a Usable Past in the Federal Republic of Germany* (2001).

Morgan, P. *The Fall of Mussolini: Italy, the Italians, and the Second World War* (2007).

Neilson, K. *Britain, Soviet Russia and the Collapse of the Versailles Order, 1919–1939* (2006).

O'Hara, V. P., Dickson, W. D. and Worth, R. (eds) *On Seas Contested: The Seven Great Navies of the Second World War* (2010).

Overy, R. J. *Why the Allies Won* (1995)

—*1939: Countdown to War* (2009)

—*The Bombing War. Europe 1939–1945* (2013).

Ragsdale, H. *The Soviets, the Munich Crisis, and the Coming of World War II* (2004).

Roberts, A. *Masters and Commanders. How Roosevelt, Churchill, Marshall and Alanbrooke Won the War in the West* (2008).

Rosenberg, E. *A Date Which Will Live: Pearl Harbor in American Memory* (2003).

Sarfatti, M. *The Jews in Mussolini's Italy* (2006).

Schneider, J. C. *Should America Go to War? The Debate Over Foreign Policy in Chicago, 1939–1941* (1989).

Stewart, A. *Empire Lost. Britain, the Dominions and the Second World War* (2008).

Stoler, M. A. *Allies in War: Britain and America against the Axis Powers, 1940–1945* (2005).

Stone, D. *Summits: The Meetings That Shaped World War II and the Postwar World* (2006).

Suleiman, S. R. *Crises of Memory and the Second World War* (2006).

Taylor, F. *Dresden: Tuesday, 13 February 1945* (2004).

Vehviläinen, O. *Finland in the Second World War: Between Germany and Russia* (2002).

Wigg, R. *Churchill and Spain: The Survival of the Franco Regime, 1940–1945* (2008).

Wylvie, N. (ed.) *European Neutrals and Non-Belligerents during the Second World War* (2002).

INDEX